Praise for The Liberation of Ivy Bottini . . .

"My friend Ivy Bottini dared to come out as her true self when that was far more difficult than it is today. Her story will inspire each reader to be honest and authentic—and what could be more important than that?" — Gloria Steinem

"Ivy Bottini, colorful, charismatic and a brilliant organizer, was there from the beginning of the second wave of feminism. She was the dynamic president of New York NOW (the premier chapter of the National Organization for Women). She was the driving force behind many of NOW's most dramatic and successful actions. She was a martyr to the homophobia of the early women's movement. Relocating to Los Angeles, Bottini reinvented herself, this time as a magnetic and effective leader for lesbian and gay causes. *The Liberation of Ivy Bottini* brings to life an important story of two crucial movements of the twentieth century and the huge, complex personality of a woman at the forefront of both movements." — Lillian Faderman

The Liberation of Ivy Bottini

The Liberation of *ivy bottini*

A Memoir of Love and Activism

as told to **Judith V. Branzburg**

BInk

Bink Books

Bedazzled Ink Publishing Company • Fairfield, California

978-1-945805-93-6 paperback

Cover Design
by

*Sappling
Studio*

Bink Books
a division of
Bedazzled Ink Publishing Company
Fairfield, California
http://www.bedazzledink.com

To my Mom, Ivy Irene Gaffney, for the chances she never had. To my Dad, Archibald Arthur Gaffney, for teaching me how to box and for his dream of living on a houseboat.

To my children, Laura and Lisa. I love you dearly. Thank you for your patience with me as I struggled to become my true self.

Ivy

To Ivy, for a lifetime of fighting to give chances to women and gay men that they might otherwise never have had.

Judith

Explanatory Note

The Liberation of Ivy Bottini: A Memoir of Love and Activism began over lunch at the 2014 Veteran Feminists of America Conference meeting in Los Angeles. Ivy, Jeanne Cordova, Lynn Ballen, and I were sitting in the hotel café when Ivy mentioned that the playwrights Al Schnupp and Ellyn Lerner had taped a number of interviews with her for a play they were planning to write on her life. Ivy had the transcribed transcripts to do with as she pleased. What she wanted, the then eighty-seven year old Ivy told us, was to use them to write a memoir, but she couldn't. Not only was she blind, she said, but she also wasn't a writer. But I was. Just retired from a career of writing, editing, and teaching composition and literature at Pasadena City College, inspired by the life of this woman I really barely knew at that point, I volunteered to try to put the transcripts in order and give a memoir a try. I was both naïve and fortunate.

Our odyssey began. Through the course of innumerable conversations, Ivy and I filled in holes, clarified events, and dug deeper into emotions. I verified dates of public events when I could and did research to provide historical and cultural contexts. Using these various materials, I created a narrative of Ivy's life and times, keeping as close to Ivy's voice as possible. To make sure the text accurately reflected Ivy's recollections, experiences and thoughts, my partner Amy and I read and reread drafts of the manuscript to Ivy for her corrections and amendments. The result is a memoir as Ivy recalled it and I shaped it. At times, conversations and incidents are recreated and not necessarily exact. Any errors in memory are in the nature of memory.

Judith V. Branzburg

"The Unsinkable Feminist Spirit of Ivy Bottini"

ABOUT SEVENTY-FIVE PEOPLE, mostly women in their sixties, seventies, and eighties with a few older men sprinkled in, had gathered in one of the meeting rooms in the West Hollywood Public Library on March 17, 2016. Many were old timers from my National Organization for Women (NOW) days but a generous portion were colleagues and friends from my more recent years of activism. Hollywood NOW and California State NOW were honoring me for what they called "The Unsinkable Feminist Spirit of Ivy Bottini." It had been a good award week for me. Just a few days earlier, on March 14, lesbian activist and Los Angeles County Supervisor Sheila Kuehl had presented me with the 2016 Woman of the Year award from her Third District. More testimonials were scheduled. I guess that since I was eighty-nine years old, people figured if they were inclined to honor me at all, they had better do it before I croaked.

Don't get me wrong. I have always, always cherished the many honors and accolades I have received over my fifty plus years of activism. I have been named a trailblazing activist, a pioneer in the feminist movement, a groundbreaker in gay and lesbian rights, a leader in the fight against AIDS, even an outstanding performer. I have ridden in parades, had trees planted in my name, and been featured in documentaries and anthologies about the rise of second wave feminism and the gay and lesbian rights movement. All have been greatly appreciated.

I've also been called unnatural, a freak, a bitch, a lezzy, a ball breaker, a bull dagger, a man-hater, and a traitor to my kind and country. Sometimes even by friends.

But this award from Hollywood NOW stands out, and not just because of all the accompanying tributes to me and my activism. I expected that. After all, it was an award ceremony for me. I knew what this night was about. At least I had thought I did. I listened to the heartfelt comments, and when called up and presented with a trophy and framed tribute of recognition for my work, I took advantage of the theme of the event and of my captive audience to describe one of my favorite protests, hanging the sign "Women of the World Unite" on the base of the Statue of Liberty in New York Harbor for all the world to see in 1970. The story went over well. I thanked everyone and my cane and I shuffled back to my seat.

But, instead of releasing us all for post-ceremony chatter and snacks, the Vice-President of Hollywood NOW, and friend, Karen Eyres, invited me to the front of the room again. Again I hobbled up. She then proceeded to read from another framed declaration. I was a bit confused. I wasn't expecting any more proclamations. But it wasn't long before I, and others in the room, realized that this was something else altogether.

"On behalf of Hollywood NOW and California NOW," Karen read, "we would like to formally apologize for your treatment by the National Organization for Women (NOW) during the late 1960s and 1970s. As one of the founders of the first chapters of NOW, as well as serving as the President of the New York chapter and designing the NOW logo that we still use, you brought a singular dedication to and passion for the fight for equal rights for women. The way NOW treated you, as well as all lesbian women, is a stain on our mission and living history." There was more, but that is the main gist.

I was stunned, as were many others in the room. I caught a few murmurs of "Well, what do you know!" and "It's about time" and even "Why now?" My thoughts, too. As I sat clutching my proclamations, I thought about what had brought NOW, me, and American society to this point. Where had my love for women led me? How had I become an almost ninety year old whose last fifty years have been consumed by feminist, lesbian, and civic activism after almost half a life of conformity to the standards of middle class suburbia? Well, I'll tell you how I remember it. But I warn you, hang on because it's a long story, and it's going to be a bumpy ride.

Ivy at the Third District Woman of the Year ceremony, 2016. Ivy is seated, at left. Supervisor Kuehl is standing next to Ivy, at left.

Ivy speaking at the 2016 NOW "The Unsinkable Feminist Spirit of Ivy Bottini" event where the Hollywood and California NOW apologies were presented.

March 17, 2016

Dear Ms. Bottini,

On behalf of Hollywood NOW and California NOW, we would like to formally apologize for your treatment by the National Organization for Women (NOW) during the late 1960s and 1970s. As one of the founders of the first chapters of NOW, as well as serving as the President of the New York chapter and designing the NOW logo that we still use, you brought a singular dedication to and passion for the fight for equal rights for women. The way NOW treated you, as well as all lesbian women, is a stain on our mission and living history.

No individual should ever be asked to closet themselves, and your refusal to do so as well as your continued activism inspires generations of lesbian and women activists to be true to who they are, no matter who or what is pressuring them to live in the proverbial closet. You are an integral force in empowering and bettering the lives of individuals from all walks of life through your commitment to women's programming, lesbian space, aging in place, sexual assault awareness and rape prevention, and sexual and reproductive rights initiatives.

Your continued work to end the statute of limitations on rape is emblematic of the need for continued awareness around women's liberation and the legacy of feminist activism you have created and continue to foster. As a result of the change you have worked to create, women and girls have a better and brighter future regardless of who they are, how they identify or whatever may occur in their lives.

Thanks to people like you, the world is a better place for people from all walks of life.

Sincerely,

Reina Martinez
President
Hollywood NOW

Jerilyn Stapleton
President
California NOW

The apology letter presented to Ivy at 2016 NOW event.

Ivy with her letter of apology from Hollywood and California Now.
Photo by James Mills 2017

NOW

YOU COULD SAY that feminism came into my life through Dolores Alexander. I met Dolores in 1964 at *Newsday,* the major Long Island evening news daily where I was working full time as a graphic artist. She was a tall, slender, striking brunette with the most graceful hands I had ever seen. When she laughed, which was often, her eyes crinkled up and sparkled. By the time I met and fell in love with her, I had been working at *Newsday* since 1955, was thirty-seven years old, married, and had two kids.

It hadn't been easy to get that job. Nine years earlier I had applied over and over again for six months, persisting because I had been captivated by the place after I had visited the paper's offices with a friend who worked in the advertising department. The newsroom with its sense that something new, interesting, and important could happen anytime was what hooked me. But when I was finally hired in 1955, I was assigned to do art for the "Women's Department," a multi-page section that just about all papers of the day carried. It was dedicated to bringing in middle class housewives as readers and training them in the mores of the day. Instead of me dealing with the news of the world, my work days were filled with designing illustrations and composing pages with information vital for the modern homemaker: engagement, marriage, and birth announcements; household hints running the gamut from how to remove stains from anything to recipes for the family and entertainment tips for those nights when your husband brings the boss or his colleagues home for dinner; health, beauty, and makeup guidance; fashion advice; and baby and child raising information. Starting in 1956, shortly after I joined the paper, "Dear Abby" became available to answer all the questions that had not already been answered. Ads on these pages often featured the newest labor saving devices and home appliances—refrigerators, toasters, mixers, vacuum cleaners, washing and sewing machines—all with their promise to make housework much easier and more efficient and fun.

As a wife and mother, I was as interested in labor saving devices and information about child raising as any other woman, but spending my days on that was not really what I was going for in a job. It was as boring as I found housework, and I had plenty of that. But, I put in my time, and after a few years, I moved up to the newsroom as a page designer. And I mean moved up. Maybe the columns on women's homemaking concerns helped bring in some readers and sell advertisements, but they, like women in general, weren't taken very seriously at the paper. They were the fluff. The real, important stories were about what men were doing in the world. I fell for it. It didn't occur to me or anyone I knew to question what this meant for women and their lives. It was just the way it was.

The newsroom with its constant adrenaline rush was all that I had anticipated. I would come in during the early afternoon, and my colleagues and I set to work to meet deadlines, fitting photos, illustrations, and advertisements into the empty spaces surrounding the ever-changing news. Sometimes we had free time during a shift waiting for the city room to get their late arriving news pages typeset. That's when my team and I would go a few blocks down the road to the newspaper watering hole where we would have a few martinis and hang out with reporters and other newspaper folks. Inevitably, just when we had gotten lubricated enough, we'd be called back to do our work. It was great fun, my dream job—wonderful camaraderie and the energy that comes from meeting the challenge of changing events. I had no idea then that those two elements would define much of the rest of my life, but that instead of filling the blanks around the news, I would be making it.

Dolores had also been hired to work on the women's pages when she arrived at the paper in 1964. Her main task was to cover the latest on those women's issues. But unlike most of the handful of other female reporters, she was permitted to write wide-ranging human interest stories about women. Those became her specialty. It was one of those stories that brought me to the National Organization for Women.

I kept my tremendous crush on Dolores hidden from her and everyone else. To expose same sex desires in the early sixties was just too dangerous, a threat to all I held dear: my marriage, children, job, friendships, and sense of belonging in the world. They could all go if word got out I was one of them, a lesbian. Nooo. I was not going to go there. Besides, Dolores was straight. At least that was the impression she gave. She dated a number of the male reporters, though she never seemed to date any one guy for long.

"I don't know what the problem is," she would lament when we went out on our own together, "but all these guys I date are unsatisfying. They don't really turn me on."

In my Dolores besotted mind, I'd think, "I know what the problem is. I could take care of you," but of course would not dare say that. I'm not even sure I knew what I meant. I'd murmur sympathetically, "Yeah, yeah. Guys can be a problem like that." I am pretty sure she never suspected my feelings for her, at least early on. After all, I gave all appearances of being straight, too. I mean, I was married with kids. What else would she think?

While Dolores and I often spent time hanging out at the bar together with my waiting group of page designers and the other reporters, sometimes just the two of us would go out to dinner somewhere close by after she had written up her stories. We even journeyed into Manhattan for a drink or a show now and again. On those occasions, I would get home even later than the usual nine or ten. I told myself that the kids, then around eight and ten, would be asleep anyway by the time I got home, so it was OK. As for Eddie, my husband, he would just have to accept it. What was I thinking?

Then one day in October of 1966, Dolores cancelled the late lunch date we had scheduled. "I can't have lunch with you because I've got to go into New York to interview some broad," she told me. That's how we talked back then, some broad. "She's announcing some women's group."

I was terribly disappointed. At that point I was so crushed out on Dolores and so eager to find moments of time that we could spend together that I was devastated by these kinds of cancellations. But what could I say.

"Fine," I replied.

Later in the afternoon, she called and demanded, "Come to the city room right now."

I went running into the city room. The usually unflappable Dolores, the cool character, was typing furiously at her desk, almost trembling with excitement. I stood waiting silently next to her desk. She was so consumed with what she was writing that she hardly noticed me.

Finally, after a few minutes, I asked, "What did you want?"

Without looking at me, she reached out, picked up a piece of paper and said, "Sign this," and went back to typing.

"What is it?"

"Never mind. Just sign it," she brusquely replied. I would have signed my home over. My first born. So, OK. I signed it.

Later when we did manage to meet for dinner, I asked again what I had signed.

She responded with a broad, satisfied smile, "You joined the National Organization for Women. NOW. They're going to pressure the government to promote women's rights and equality. That's what the press conference was about."

She went on to explain the unofficial back story she had gotten from one of the women at the press conference. A bunch of high powered women had attended the Conference of State Commissions on the Status of Women in June of that year, 1966. This meeting was billed as a check up on progress made since President Kennedy's original 1961 Presidential Commission on the Status of Women. Title VII of the Civil Rights Act of 1964 and the Equal Employment Opportunity Commission (EEOC), started in 1965, were the results of that first commission. They were supposed to have helped women secure their rights, particularly in the workforce. But the men who had power to enforce the laws and regulations they themselves had made had pretty much done nothing. When the women complained to the men at the 1966 meeting about this, none of them seemed to care. Adding insult to injury, when it came time for the conference report to be written, the male attendees insisted that they, rather than any of the women, were better qualified to write it, and they did. So, after the conference, about thirty of the women attendees gathered in Betty Friedan's hotel room to vent their frustration and to make a plan.

"Who is Betty Friedan?" I interrupted.

Dolores looked at me with a raised eyebrow. "She wrote the 1963 best seller, *The Feminine Mystique*. She claims that middle class housewives who are supposed to be happy living the American Dream with a house in the suburbs and 2.5 kids are actually terribly unhappy. Men especially don't like that, and they don't like that other women are agreeing with her."

I was intrigued. I worked full time, but I was also supposed to be satisfied with my life in the suburbs with my husband and kids. I wasn't. I had always thought my discontent came from secretly falling in love with women and not being able to do anything about it. For the first time I wondered if maybe there was more to it than that.

Dolores continued to explain that Pauli Murray, another person I had never heard of, a prominent black civil rights lawyer and conference attendee, told the gathered women that what they needed was their own version of the NAACP. That, the National Organization for the Advancement of Colored People, I had heard of. The Civil Rights movement with its sit-ins, boycotts, protests, and marches had been in the news a lot over the previous ten years. It wasn't my thing, but I knew about it and sympathized with the cause. At that point, nothing political was really my thing. According to Dolores, the other women in Friedan's hotel room liked the idea, so they began to write up a plan. As they talked and wrote, it seems Friedan doodled NOW on a napkin. The National Organization for Women was born.

More NOW

I ADMIT I didn't think that much about this organization again until a few weeks later, in November of 1966, when I heard through Dolores that a few of the leaders of NOW would be meeting uptown in NYC in one of the Barnard College conference rooms. Barnard was the women's college affiliated with Columbia University. I decided to go, but not because I was all that interested in the cause. Mostly it was because I had understood Dolores would be there. As I said, I leapt at any chance to be with her.

As it turned out, Dolores didn't go to this meeting, but I did. Sure, I had some interest in what Friedan and the others might have to say, but I knew I really wanted to go because, even if Dolores didn't show up, I hoped there would be some lesbians there. That was the whisper I heard in just about any discussion about anyone interested in this new women's liberation stuff, either they were lesbians or they were Communists out to destroy the country or both. I didn't care about the Communist part. Besides, from what Dolores told me, that didn't make any sense.

What intrigued me was the lesbian part. But to be clear, I had no intention of acting on my attraction to women. I just wanted some assurance that there were other women out there who loved women and that they managed to live somehow without going crazy. I wasn't sure how I would recognize one of them, but I wanted to give it a try. At the same time, I didn't want anyone to get even a hint that I was interested in women. I wanted to find lesbians, but I didn't want to look like one. That just shows how closeted and confused I was. Still, I was convinced that unless I did something to disguise myself, my feelings for women would show on my body, my face, my gestures, the way I moved, somehow. So, to appear especially feminine that night, I bought a new outfit: a navy blue shirt waist dress with a matching ruffle, a white polka dotted navy blue hat, and white gloves. For more cover, I brought my daughter Laura, thirteen years old at the time, with me. Crazy, I know.

I was a mess at that meeting. Before I had even left home, despite my getup and my daughter, I was still nervous that someone would recognize me as a lesbian. I became even more frazzled by getting lost on the drive from Long Island to uptown Manhattan where the meeting was being held at Barnard.

Once there, I became totally intimidated. Though none of the six or so women at my first NOW meeting seemed to be lesbians (I am not sure how I would have been able to tell anyway), they wowed me nonetheless. Most were from Manhattan, most married with children, most college graduates, all white (not that I would have really noted this at that time), and all somehow very intimidating to me. Their office-wear dresses and suits were well-cut, falling just the right amount below the knee. Their outfits struck me not so much as signs of wealth but of class and knowing the right clothes to wear, in contrast to me with my white gloves and polka dot hat. I was sure the seams on their nylons were straight and their heels just the right height. And even though I had a little makeup on—a gentle red lipstick, a bit of blush, and just a little eyeliner—I felt like I had more on than anyone else. They were, to me, on another level of sophistication.

Betty Friedan, in her dark suit with her shortish hair, sharp eyes, and prominent nose, was particularly impressive, but not only because I now knew who she was. Sitting across the table from me, she radiated a confidence and authority that no other woman I had ever encountered had. Doing most of the talking throughout the meeting, speaking in what I was to learn was her characteristically high volume, she had control of that room. I was not surprised that later she ruled NOW with an iron fist. Ti-Grace Atkinson also grabbed my attention at that meeting. I had never met anyone with a Ph.D. before, never mind a professional philosopher. I hadn't even known that such a profession existed. Ti-Grace was very tall and lanky with shoulder length, curly strawberry blond hair, and looked very proper in her black dress. What struck me most about her was that she had very white, almost translucent skin, so thin that all the blood vessels were visible. Even with that delicacy, I could feel the fighting energy pour from her. I was fascinated. I could hardly keep my eyes off of her.

Muriel Fox, also very beautiful with her short dark hair, clear skin, and kind of classic features, was there that day, too. She exuded a self-possessed graciousness. Muriel was probably the wealthiest of the NOW pioneers. Later, when I was invited to the downtown apartment she shared with her doctor husband, I understood what having money meant in a way I never had before. Hers was the first apartment I had seen in which the elevator opened directly into the living room rather than a hallway of apartment doors. I am pretty sure that elegant living room alone was larger than the suburban tract house I was living in at the time. What I took to be museum quality art on the walls and decorating the tables; a seating area with a heavy, flower patterned, upholstered couch and matching chairs; a grand piano; and stunning views of the city in that one room told me that I was in another world. I soon discovered that

Muriel worked under her maiden name in the public relations firm at which she was an executive, an unusual act of self-definition in those days. I was very impressed by this. Over the following years, she would use her public relations expertise to NOW's great advantage.

To tell the truth, I was so scared about the lesbian thing and so self-conscious in that room that I don't remember anything that was said. I certainly didn't say anything. Even though I had a college degree and a professional position at *Newsday*, I didn't see myself as being like these women. It was not just their titles like vice president of this or chair of that or professions like philosopher or writer, or even their wealth. Rather, it was everything about the way they presented themselves—their polish and self-assurance—that said they were successful and smart. I didn't have the strong sense that I deserved respect in the world that they projected. I had a kind of blue collar mind set. I saw myself as a wife and mother who just worked for a living. I wasn't one of them.

But I would become one. It just took quite a while.

Childhood

I WAS BORN in 1926 in the front bedroom of our two-story, four bedroom house on Edwards Street in Malverne, a small town in an un-developed area in Nassau County, Long Island, New York, and given the same name as my mother, Ivy Irene Gaffney. My father worked as a mosquito exterminator with the Nassau County mosquito extermination department and my mother was a housewife. I was their only child.

There may have been hints of the conflicts that would come to mark my years before feminism, but as a kid, I was blissfully unaware of them. I had a rather idyllic childhood. Certainly, I was a tomboy, but I wasn't a rebel. I never wanted to be a boy or resented that I had to wear dresses, skirts, and other girly clothes. My parents offered me dance lessons, but I told them I wasn't interested. That was fine with them. I didn't want to play with dolls, and that was all right, too. Instead, even though I was a short, chubby girl, I became the leader of a neighborhood gang of rough-housing boys. I was the king of the streets and fields and the boys were my subjects. We would ride our bikes and play hide and seek, tag, and dodge ball in the road. We hung baskets in driveways to play my favorite game, basketball, and built baseball diamonds in the nearby open spaces and empty fields. Under my rule, we armed ourselves with wooden swords to protect our local apple orchards from outsiders, in the meantime gobbling down apples ourselves.

In the summer, I would lead the charge for the slivers that fell off the trucks that lumbered into our neighborhood loaded with the large chunks of ice our families needed for our iceboxes. We'd smear the ice on our faces, necks, and exposed arms and legs to relieve the heat and humidity of Long Island. When the coal trucks would come by in the wintertime to pour coal down chutes into the basements of houses to fuel their furnaces, again, I would lead the pack down the street after them. This time, our goal would be to retrieve the lumps of coal that would inevitably fall out of the trucks and use them to draw our hopscotch courts on the sidewalk. The remainders of the lumps would be the stones we tossed in the game. And yes, the boys played hopscotch. If I wanted to play, we all played. This all seemed normal to me.

Perhaps I would have been more frustrated or conflicted if I hadn't had a dad who often treated me more like a son than a daughter. He gave me my first fielder's mitt and bought me my first fishing pole when I was in elementary school. When I was about thirteen, he gave me a copper BB gun and trained me to shoot at a nearby target range. I loved the single mindedness, the steadiness, and the deliberate focus necessary before the explosion that shooting involved. I became so good at it that when carnivals came to town every summer, I would rush over to the shooting booths, nestle the gun on my shoulder, take aim, pull the trigger, and poof, the candle would go out without even the smallest splash of wax. In a short time, I would walk away with large stuffed bears and bunnies. I didn't really care about this booty, but I liked to win. Once I got home, I would toss the animals into a corner of my room and go outside to play.

But boxing was the favorite of all the activities my father introduced me to. Turns out, my father had been a professional boxer before he got married, and, in 1932 when I was just six years old, he decided he would teach me how to box.

"You're a girl and you're going to need to know how to take care of yourself," he informed me as he fitted me with a miniature pair of boxing gloves.

Every night for the next few months, and then often during the next years, my father and I would get into the makeshift ring he would erect in our living room, and, with my mother ringing the rounds with a wooden spoon and a pot, he would get down on his knees so we could be more or less the same height and instruct me on how to punch, how to deflect punches, and how to move in the ring.

I loved it all—the hitting, the movement, the concentration, the strategy, and being in the ring with my dad. I also relished the challenge of boxing against others when I was allowed to fight the boys, and one other girl, in the backyard ring a local boxing instructor had set up for us neighborhood kids. Usually I won. Except against the other girl. We never talked about it, but by mutual agreement, we would fight to a draw. We seemed to understand intuitively that we were better off beating the boys and not hurting each other. Early sisterhood. I even enjoyed the professional boxing matches my father took me to in nearby Freeport when I was about twelve or thirteen. Along with the often drunk, raucously shouting men in the arena that smelled of cigarettes, cigars, and sweat, I would yell in sheer joy, "He's bleeding! He's bleeding." I absolutely loved it.

But something else also appealed to me about boxing. I often imagined that these fighters were underdogs battling their emotional as well as physical demons in the ring. That was me, too, in my ring fantasies, the underdog fighting against the odds. It was no surprise, then, that the 1976 film *Rocky*, which came out in the midst of the feminist movement, was my favorite movie of all times. By then, those kinds of battles had turned from fantasy to reality and had become mine, and I was going for the knockout.

IT WASN'T UNTIL high school that I learned that my parents had a child before me. My Aunt Myrtle, my mother's twin sister, unthinkingly spilled the beans while we were alone washing up after a family dinner. She mentioned how sad it was about my parents' lost baby. Then she glanced at me and stopped. I'm sure my jaw had dropped.

"I shouldn't have said anything," she murmured and went quiet. But I pushed until she told me, "About five years before you were born, there was a fire in their house. Your dad tried to save the baby—he was only about a year old—carrying him out of the burning house in his arms. But the baby died. That's all I'm going to say. No one talks about it and I shouldn't have told you. Don't tell anyone I told you and don't talk about it yourself."

I didn't.

THE ONLY TIME when I was growing up that it struck me that I wasn't like the other girls in my neighborhood was when I saw myself in a confirmation photo with the girls in my confirmation class. I was eleven years old. I had thought I looked pretty spiffy that day in the white satin dress decorated with big pink roses that my mother had made for me. The photo told me another story.

"I'm fat and ugly," I thought, for the first time contrasting my chubby body, fair Irish skin, big fat pink cheeks, and untamed curly hair with the slender, smoothly groomed girls in our neighborhood. I realized then, too, that I would never be the bubbly, cute Shirley Temple or the graceful Princess Elizabeth, both of whom were my age and my public icons. This double whammy of disappointment got me down for about a month. But then, once I got in the boxing ring again and continued running around in the streets with my friends, I realized that my body suited me just fine. It worked for the things I liked to do and that was good enough.

Ivy, age 5, and her parents, 1931.

Ivy (front right) and her first grade class, 1932. *Courtesy of ONE Archives at the USC Libraries*

Ivy at age 7, 1933.

Ivy's confirmation class, 1938.

Ivy and her mother. Ivy is wearing her confirmation dress, white dress with pink flowers, 1938. *Courtesy of ONE Archives at the USC Libraries*

End of Childhood

IN 1938, THE Democrats finally broke the stranglehold the Republicans had held in Nassau County for years. That meant that all the people, like my father, who had patronage jobs under the old regime were to be replaced by Democratic Party loyalists. I actually had and have no idea if my father really cared about either party. I just had been told that when my parents first moved to Long Island, the Republicans were in power, so my father registered Republican, showed up at party events, and displayed campaign posters for Republican candidates. He had played the winning side. But then, bam, it was over. He was fired from his job as mosquito exterminator. The Depression was just about at its worst. There were no jobs. There was no such thing as unemployment insurance. We had no savings. Instead of me chasing trucks for lumps of coal to play hopscotch with, my father was reduced to walking the local railroad tracks to pick up coal that dropped from the locomotives. Most traumatically, in what seemed no time at all, we lost our house on Edward Street to foreclosure.

We ended up moving in with my mother's oldest sister, Aunt Edna, and her husband Phil in Lynbrook, the next town over from Malverne. They lived in a dark and brooding two story, three bedroom Victorian house. My uncle owned a furniture store that did well all through the Depression—I guess people still needed furniture even if they only could pay for it a bit at a time—so they could afford to take us in. I knew from the start it wasn't going to be fun there even though we were served steak our first meal. This might seem like a good thing for a thirteen year old kid from a hamburger, hash, and chicken family, but I knew it was a "we're rich and you're a failure" taunt and a reminder of our lowly position in their house. It was impossible to escape that feeling all the time we lived there.

I MIGHT HAVE been unhappy, but my mother was miserable. In a way, when we lost the house, we lost her, too. The first sign of how serious the problem was came pretty much as soon as we moved in with her sister. One afternoon my mother went upstairs to the bedroom she and my father were using and stayed there. And stayed. I wasn't allowed to see her and no one would explain to me what was going on, even my dad. Weeks went by. I took to dragging a big green arm chair to the bottom of the stairs and sitting there for hours after school and on weekends. I tried to eavesdrop as relatives and doctors came and went but all conversations about my mother were so hushed that I couldn't really make out what anyone was saying. The only conclusion I could reach was that my mother was dying.

Finally, after a few months of this, my aunt told me that my mother wanted to talk to me. I went upstairs, certain I was going to find her lying in bed in a darkened room, skeletal, pale, and on the brink of death. Instead, there she was sitting on the double bed in a flowered house dress in the airy, sun-filled bedroom looking wan and worn but very much alive.

She smiled and gestured for me to sit next to her. Taking my hand in both of hers, she gazed soberly at me for a moment before speaking. "I wanted to die but gave up on the idea when Jesus came to me and sat right on the edge of the bed where you are sitting."

"Jesus?" I thought. "What is she talking about?"

"He told me it was my time to come with him," she continued, "but I told him, no, I had a little girl to take care of."

This didn't really make much sense to me but all that mattered was that she was alive and wasn't going to leave me. She came downstairs that day and took up her motherly duties again. But she became increasingly depressed, angry, and isolated. That's when she started to complain to me that her life was a failure. Her only defense when she felt her value as a human being was challenged, which could be any time, was that she had had jobs. "I was a telephone operator before I married your dad, you know." Or she would brag about her stint as a volunteer teacher in one of the cooking classes that the local gas company sponsored in order to sell gas stoves. Her favorite job was her short time as a cook at the German delicatessen in Malverne. She wasn't very interested in, or good at, cooking, but she got a kick out of the recipes she was taught at the deli. "I made the roast beef and I put beer on it. Isn't that strange? You put beer on it, Ivy," she would tell me. "Basted in beer," she would recall in wonder for years and years afterward.

It puzzled and disappointed me that my dad and I were not enough to make my mother feel good about herself, but I certainly came to understand it later.

AFTER A FEW months of living with my aunt and uncle, my father finally got a job driving a taxi at night. With the promise of money coming in once again, we rented a good sized one-story home in another part of Malverne, but my father overestimated what our income would be. It was still the Depression and people weren't splurging on cab rides. So we kept having to move to smaller and smaller places. That was bad enough, but what really got to me was that every few weeks my Aunt Edna and Uncle Phil would come by in their large, luxurious black Packard to leave off food. While my uncle waited in the car, my elegantly dressed aunt would march into our house with a few bags of groceries and tell my mother, "I thought you might need these." Out would come chicken, potatoes, carrots, and milk. I found this terribly humiliating.

I knew my childhood was over. Instead, of easy days leading my gang in crusades and adventures, I was an underdog up against the unseen forces of the real world. It was not an easy lesson to have to learn.

ONE DAY DURING this period, I came home from school to find my mom with her head in the oven and the gas turned on. I ran over to her and began to pull on her flower print house dress, crying and begging her to take her head out of the oven. Finally, she did, and we collapsed on the floor next to each other. Then she got up and started pulling food and pots and pans out of the cupboards to get dinner ready. I didn't know what to do, so I just went to my room.

This was a far cry from the mother I had known as a kid, the one who was always there, who rang the bell for our boxing matches, sewed me dresses and costumes, and made snacks for the neighborhood kids. She was no longer the one to whom any of us kids would hurry for her comfort, band aids, or whatever else was needed when we would get cut or hurt. That mom was long gone.

This was just the beginning of these oven episodes. Over the next six months or so, every once in a while I'd come home from eighth grade and my mom would have her head in the oven. Each time I would pull and yell at her until finally she would crawl backward, stand up, and start making dinner. About the fifth time that I came home and there she was with her head in the oven, I just stood there looking at her backside as it was sticking out into the kitchen. Finally, I said, "Mom, I'm going out to play," and I left. That was the last time my mother played that game.

SHORTLY AFTER THESE episodes, around the time I started high school, my parents' relationship began to truly disintegrate. My father had started drinking when he lost his county job and continued to drink once he started driving a taxi. After his late shift was over around midnight or one a.m., he and his buddies would go out and have a beer or two, or more. At three or four in the morning, he would arrive home drunk and weary.

Many nights my mother would be waiting up for him and demand he listen to her. She'd stand with her arms crossed in front of her chest next to the dining room table where my dad would sit with his head on his arms. Rocking back and forth from foot to foot, she would go through a litany of complaints for hours. I mean, hours. Mostly my dad never said a word but now and again he would respond with a promise that things would change, that we would move to California, and he would find a good job there. But for him, and us, it was only a fantasy. We never moved. And the yelling went on, sometimes until the morning when I would wake up to go to school, that is if I hadn't already been up making any efforts I could to calm things down. That's when my dad would finally go to bed.

These arguments came to a head one morning very early when I was up sitting between them trying to keep the peace. Without warning, my father stood up and started walking out of the room. My mom had to have the last word. I didn't catch what she said to him, but when he turned back to us with a crazed look in his eyes and strode toward my mother with his fists clenched, I was sure he was going to hit her. I had never seen him so angry. So, I stood up, stepped in front of him, and hauled off and socked him in the jaw with one of the punches he had taught me. He stopped, stunned, and rubbed his chin. I just stood there, too. A minute passed. Then we fell into each other's arms and hugged, both of us crying. After a moment, he let me go and left the room. I turned to my mother, said good night, and went to my room.

Even though that hug was a kind of reconciliation, the incident caused a divide neither my father nor I could cross. We would never hang out and have innocent fun together again. There were many losses from those years, but this was one of the worst.

Adolescence

THERE WAS ANOTHER problem on the horizon for me. My days as the leader of a boy gang were over not just because of my family's fall from prosperity. Around the time I began junior high school, the boys just didn't want to run around with me anymore. Or if they wanted to hang around, especially the older ones, they wanted to play games I wasn't interested in and had no instinct for. I knew I should start liking the guys the way many of the other girls had begun to, but I didn't. Try as I might, I just couldn't manufacture the feelings I knew I was supposed to have. As time went on and I picked up more of the rules about how to attract a boy, the idea of such behavior became even less enticing. I was instructed to be demure until one of them approached me and then figure out what he was interested in and talk to him about that. And never, never beat him in any games. That all went in one ear and out the other. I found such talk both irritating and irrelevant.

But, making things more confusing, much as I loved my dad and the guys in my gang, my body and emotions were drawing me toward other girls. Not that I would admit that to myself. If I had recognized sexual desire in any of the crushes I began to have on my gym teachers (yes, I know—stereotypical), or classmates, there was no way I would ever, ever acknowledge it. Even though I don't recall hearing about such feelings, even that such relationships between women existed in the world, I knew they were wrong—unwomanly, immoral, and unnatural. These ideas were just in the air. I also somehow knew that if I acknowledged these desires, any kind of relationship would be impossible. Perhaps that's why no one spoke of such feelings. Keeping silent meant that girls who were attracted to each other could at least continue to be friends.

I managed to get through junior high school and the chaos of my home life and emotions by buckling down to school work and playing on as many girls' school sports teams as I could. I also attached myself to Miss Majesky, the tall, slender, and regal physical education teacher. She took my heart when I was in tenth grade. I would hang around her office after basketball practice or phys ed classes as often as I could and babble on to her about the games and school work. In no time, I began walking her home from school. I know it sounds weird now but it was not all that strange then. At least not to me. I thought it all perfectly reasonable and innocent until a rival for her affections, Betsy Wells, arrived. She was a basketball player like me, and like me, she began to hang around Miss Majesky's office. Before I knew it, she had joined me in walking Miss Majesky home.

At first, I was angry and jealous, but the more I watched Betsy fawn over Miss Majesky, the more uneasy I got. I saw how unnatural and wrong such an emotional attraction to another female might look to others, how I might look. But there was nothing I could do to stop my feelings about Miss Majesky or the girls I had fleeting crushes on. They were just there, beyond my control. The only solution was to hide them, from myself if possible but at least from others. Just another addition to the turmoil and confusion of my life.

Peg Wilson

BY TENTH GRADE, I was close to drowning. Miss Majesky, sports, and school work weren't enough to counter the chaos of home. That's when Peg Wilson, my typing and shorthand teacher throughout junior and senior high, stepped in to help save me.

I had actually first encountered Peg when I was in seventh grade and enrolled in her courses, both required in the commercial curriculum I was taking, not imagining anything but a secretarial type job in my future. From the first moment I saw her on the first day of my seventh grade typing class, I was smitten. I loved the way her tightly curled, short black hair bounced around her pale face. I adored the sparkle in her dark eyes when she smiled, which was often. I needed some joy in my life and was convinced she would provide it.

We got off to a bit of a rocky start, though, I thought. In our very first shorthand class, explaining the supplies we would need for class, she held up a pen and said, "This is an Esterbrook pen. It's made specifically for shorthand, and we have a special price for students. You can buy this pen for $2.95."

"That's a lot of money. We can do better," I thought to myself. I turned to face the class and held up a pen I had brought with me. "Sixty-nine cents at Woolworth's. It's great."

She just looked at me then, but a couple of years later she told me, "When you did that pen routine, I knew I was really going to like you." I had already known that I was going to really like her.

Through the rest of my junior high school years, our relationship was bound to the classroom where I tried to get and keep her attention, working hard and always volunteering for class activities and staying after class to help her erase the blackboards and make sure the typewriters were covered and supplies put away. But when I was in tenth grade, she started inviting me over to her apartment after school. Her small apartment above a shoe repair store in Malverne village became my refuge.

Pretty soon, I couldn't wait for school to be out every day so I could rush home to change clothes or drop off some of my school things, and then run over to Peg Wilson's apartment. I had my own key and would let myself in pretty much every afternoon or early evening. We would prepare and have dinner together and then sit on the couch talking. Sometimes she'd put the player piano on and we'd sing or we'd listen to the news on the radio. On weekends, we often went shopping or to the movies. I didn't talk a lot about what was going on at home. Just being with Peg in a calm place where someone cared about me was enough. From the middle of my sophomore year in high school up until I went to college, I spent all the spare time I could with her, only going home when I had to.

I'm sure that at least part of Peg Wilson's attentions to me and my attraction to and dependence on her were motivated by my need for a sanctuary when things were such a mess at home. A therapist might have also said she was a mother, or even a father figure for me. If I had been more self-aware, or looking for an explanation, I might even have told myself that. But I never questioned my feelings for her. I didn't see myself as needy that way. If there was a sexual component on my part, or hers, I buried it deep. Still, almost instinctively, I kept the relationship hidden from all but my parents.

College

BEFORE I KNEW it, college was on the horizon. Yes, college. I was determined to go, much to my parents' surprise but not to mine. By that time, under the influence of Peg Wilson and a number of my other teachers, I had abandoned the commercial curriculum and enrolled in college prep. They had convinced me that in order to keep from being economically vulnerable the way my parents were, I had to go to college. It would give me choices. The problem was, I was conflicted about what course of study to follow. I had two camps of instructors fighting over my adolescent higher education soul, my physical education teachers and my art teacher, Miss Abel.

At first, it seemed that the gym teachers and coaches had won. I was about to apply to Penn State where many of them had gone, but I rejected it when my mother pleaded with me not to leave her and my father alone together. That was the excuse I gave myself anyway. In fact, there were two other reasons for my being relieved to take Penn State off the list. One was that I was a homebody. I had never gone very far from home and was not very eager to do so. The other was much harder to admit. On some semi-conscious level, I was frightened by the idea of ending up unmarried and living alone or with my best friend as so many of my gym teachers had. I knew that I wasn't really interested in bucking convention that way. I was not very brave.

Once Penn State was out, Miss Abel, my junior high and high school art teacher, jumped right in and urged me to apply to Pratt Institute in Brooklyn for their three year degree program. She was convinced, and convinced me, that I could make a career in art. Knowing my concerns about going away, she argued that I could live at home and commute. I knew it would be a daunting trek, but I also knew I loved art just about as much as I loved sports. I had been drawing forever, but it wasn't until Miss Abel took me under her wing, encouraging me and introducing me to the various tools and tricks of the trade, that I began to take my art and talent seriously, just as she did. If Miss Abel thought Pratt would work, I would trust her.

I got into Pratt, and my parents came through with just enough money to pay for the first year. I was never sure how they did this, but I was tremendously grateful. One year at a time.

MY COLLEGE CAREER got off to a rocky start. For one thing, I started and ended each day with that anxiety inducing commute. Then there was the fact that I had enrolled in courses I had no background in. I was planning to major in fine arts, but I had picked up the graphic arts brochure when registering, and, naive as I was, I thought everyone had to take all these courses no matter what their major. So, I ended up signing up for advertising, graphic design, and illustration. I struggled at first but soon discovered that I had made a fortunate mistake. I loved these courses and soon had a new major.

Then there was Judy Klink, one of my classmates. Now that I was in college and getting older, I knew I had to get interested in and start dating men, but instead, I became infatuated with Judy. Judy, of course, had no idea that I liked her as anything more than a friend. But I tried not to worry about it. I knew I couldn't control my feelings, but I could hide them. Besides, I still told myself, all would be OK in the end because the right attraction would kick in and I would marry and have kids. I had to hold on to that belief.

A Death in the Family

JUDY KLINK AND my courses were not the only things I had to worry about. In the middle of that first semester, my family lost the small bungalow where we had been living. My father's taxi driving was earning him even less than it had. Or at least that's what they told me. Sometimes I wonder if we had no money for the house because my parents spent it on my schooling. I'll never know. We wound up staying with my aunt and uncle again. Again temporarily, of course. But it wasn't all bad. At my aunt and uncle's, my mother's late-night harangues stopped, giving my father and me space to begin a reconciliation. We even had arranged to go fishing together a few weeks after Thanksgiving. That would have been our first outing together since the time I hit him.

I was half awake and half asleep in the early morning hours of the day of our excursion, anticipating my reunion with my dad when around five-thirty a.m. I heard someone walking up the stairs. I thought my father was coming a little early for my six a.m. wake up call, but as the footsteps passed by my door, I recognized them as my aunt's tread and realized she was going into my parents' room down the hall. That was strange. I was curious but not worried until I made out the words "accident" and "dead."

My heart dropped. I knew right away that my aunt was talking about my dad and that he was gone. Soon, after the sobbing from down the hall subsided, my aunt came in, sat on the side of my bed, and confirmed that he was dead. Earlier that morning, just as the bars were closing, a woman and a couple of sailors, all very drunk, had emerged from a local establishment and gotten into the woman's car. This woman took off, drove down the wrong side of the road, and crashed head on into my dad's parked taxi. Bim bam boom, my dad was gone. He was fifty-four years old. I was crushed. As far as I am concerned, my father was murdered.

At forty-five years old, my mother was husbandless, emotionally devastated, and destitute. There was no money coming in. Social Security had started about ten years earlier, in 1935, but my dad hadn't worked on the books enough to qualify for anything. Survivor's benefits, first distributed in 1939, were pretty paltry. The only money we got was from the lawsuit my mother brought against the driver of the other car, the mother of a girl I had gone all through school with as it turned out, but it was only eight thousand dollars. I remember standing in the doorway, seeing the attorney and my mother sitting on the couch in my aunt's living room, my mother stooped and crying, the settlement papers spread out on the coffee table in front of them. The attorney was talking to her in a low voice, almost whispering in her ear. I don't know what he said, but my mother was settling for less than she had asked for. My sense is that the attorney made a lot while she made very little. I just knew it was wrong and she was being cheated. But there was nothing I could do.

My mother insisted that I use the settlement money for college even though I didn't want to. How was she going to live if she gave it all to me? It was little enough to get her through the rest of her life. I refused the money and accepted that my college career was pretty much over. I would return to finish the year that had already been paid for, and that would be it.

Still, I threw myself into my school work. I left for school around eight o'clock in the morning every weekday, went to my classes, and got home at around six in the evening. Once home, I would eat dinner and then go to my room and work for hours on my drawing board on homework. No more Klink or anyone else. At least my grades were good. So I was surprised when one day during the spring semester, I was called into the Dean's office. I thought, "Oh, God, what'd I do? This could only mean more trouble." I couldn't have been more wrong.

After offering condolences on the death of my father, the Dean continued, "I know, too, that you weren't planning on coming back to school next year for financial reasons. But I've been looking over your transcript and am impressed that you still have kept your grades up. We don't want to lose you. So the Board of Directors has decided to give you a full scholarship for the rest of your time here."

I was stunned. I swear my heart stopped for a few seconds. Tears actually came to my eyes. I was going to be able to continue at school. After a few minutes of him talking and me barely able to listen, I managed to murmur an appropriate thank you. I couldn't quite believe that after all the bad that had happened, good could happen, too. But it could.

Recovery

MY STUDIES HELPED to distract me at Pratt, but as my sophomore year got into full swing, I knew I needed to get out more. It was just too depressing at my aunt and uncle's place for me. Besides, I was basically a social person. And I knew I needed to start showing more interest in men and camouflage any infatuations on women I might have had. Klink wasn't around—she hadn't returned to Pratt after our first year—but my heart was always being taken with mini-crushes on many of the women at school. The nearby naval station at Point Lookout in Long Beach offered me the perfect solution with its weekly dances and all the war-time servicemen stationed there looking for girls. Pretty much every week that fall, I would hop on the bus with a bunch of my female classmates and off we would go to dance.

These events offered another advantage besides the opportunity to display heterosexual interest. I loved to dance. Swing was my thing. I had learned a few steps watching my parents dance in the good old Edwards Street days when they would gather at friends' homes for drinks and dancing. But mostly I got my start in junior high school when at lunch time a teacher might put recordings by the big bands of the day—Glenn Miller, Benny Goodman, Artie Shaw—on a phonograph in the gym and a bunch of us kids would dance, or watch the dancing. That would be mostly the boys watching us girls dance together. That was fine with me.

In seventh grade, my favorite partner was Ruby. Ruby was one of the ten black kids—Negroes we called them then—who suddenly appeared in our classes in Malverne. No one seemed to have any idea why they had come or where they had come from, but one day there they were. I don't think I would be wrong in saying that this was probably the first exposure most of the kids in my pretty much all white neighborhood had to live black people. It certainly was mine. In fact, I had no inkling that there was an almost entirely black neighborhood, Lakeview, adjacent to my white community. I had heard the word Lakeview but had thought it was just a street on the other side of the bird sanctuary that ran the length of one side of my neighborhood. I had never gone into the bird sanctuary because all the girls in my area, including me, had been warned not to go there by ourselves. I did what I was told. I was a good kid.

None of these new students were in any of my academic classes, but Ruby was in my gym class. She loved sports and was fun. That was enough for me. We became friends and began to have lunch together and then to dance during these lunch time dances. She and her black girlfriends seemed to take special delight in teaching me dance moves I had never seen before. Even so, when Ruby and I danced, I took the lead. It simply felt natural. I have to say, we were pretty impressive together.

In my naiveté and obliviousness, it took me a number of months to notice that I was the only white kid who mixed with the black kids on the dance floor or elsewhere. I guess I missed the memo on racism. I don't remember ever seeing or hearing anything about race at home or around me, which is not to say it wasn't there. It's also not to say that the other white kids in my school were mean to the black kids or to me for hanging out with Ruby and her friends. The white kids simply didn't seem to care about the black kids at all. It was as though these new students were invisible. It was a kind of racism that took me a long time to recognize.

I finally did venture over to Lakeview, too. Ruby invited me to her house for lunch one Saturday, so I was allowed to go with her and traverse the usually forbidden bird sanctuary. We emerged into a many blocks area of small, neat, white houses. There was not a white face to be seen. I had had no idea that this place, or places like this, existed. Ruby's mother may have been surprised, too, that her daughter had thought to invite a short, stocky, white, freckle faced friend to their home, but Ruby had and there I was. Ruby's mom was very welcoming, greeting me with a warm smile and then serving us tomato soup and grilled cheese sandwiches as Ruby and I sat and giggled at the kitchen table.

The next school year all the black students were gone. That was the end of my friendship with Ruby. I found out years later that they had left my school because a new school had been built for them in Lakeview. They may have disappeared, but I never forgot the dance moves Ruby taught me and what it felt like to lead Ruby in the Lindy.

AT THESE WAR time dances, as soon as the music started, the guys would grab girls and soon everyone would be on the dance floor swinging and Lindy hopping well into the night. Including me. Unlike in junior high, I danced with men, and didn't lead. And I always refused invitations to slow dances. There was also no smooching on the dance floor with some guy, no making out in the corners or in the dark outside the dance hall, and no plans made for a later rendezvous for me. It was not as though guys didn't try. I remember one sailor in particular. All night, he kept insisting I dance with him and was constantly trying for a slow dance or to sneak a kiss, but I resisted all those efforts. Nonetheless, I was so gorgeous and he was so smitten that he followed my friends and me onto the bus when we were leaving at the end of the night. This was remarkably reckless on his part since the servicemen were not allowed to leave the base unless they had leave, and he didn't. He sat down next to me and kept leaning over, trying to kiss me. Finally, the Shore Patrol arrived and dragged him off the bus. Ah, men. They loved me but I could never love them back.

AT THE SAME time as I was dancing and presenting a heterosexual façade, I had a whole other outlet for my physical energy, one that offered a vastly different model than the heterosexual one of the dance floor. That was my women's basketball team, the Royal M's. I had started the Royal M's during my Pratt years because Pratt, like most other colleges and universities in those days, had few physical education options for women; rudimentary, if any, facilities; and no collegiate women's teams except maybe a few intramurals. In addition, few girls wanted to play hard. Being competitive was seen as way too masculine, even in the more acceptable upper-class sports like tennis or golf. And what man wants to date a competitive, masculine woman? Especially if you were good—whoa! That could drop you right to the bottom of the dating pool, if not out of it altogether. Keep in mind, these were the days when we girls were taught that if we wanted to get and keep a man, we had to let the guy win at any games we played with them, whether Monopoly or bridge or even causally shooting baskets in someone's back yard. Do or be better than a man and he might feel bad and not like us anymore. Best if he can show you how to do something.

Even sports played in all women gym classes were designed to not stress the delicate female. Take basketball. In those days, as today, men's teams had five players who could dribble endlessly all over the court. For women, six girl teams had three on offense and three on defense, each person limited to playing only on her designated half the court. We could also only dribble the ball three times before we were compelled to pass it or shoot if we were on the right side of the court. I just accepted these rules. I never thought to challenge them. If that's how women were supposed to play, that's how I would play. It didn't stop me from adoring the game and sports.

So I put the word out in my neighborhood that I was looking for women interested in forming a team, and immediately a dozen or so women responded. I was thrilled. We got permission to play in the gym at my old high school, Malverne High—thus The Royal M's, for Malverne—and formed a pick-up league with the few other women's teams in the area. Sometimes to get to games, we all piled into my dark blue four door 1936 Ford that used more oil than gas, packing our bodies on top of each other, on each other's laps, cheek to cheek, elbow to face, sometimes even legs out the window, like a clown car in the circus. I loved it. In fact, I loved everything about those games. I liked the warm, close feel of the air in the gym. I liked the sounds of running feet and the balls against the floor and the smell of new and old sweat. I liked the women yelling and grunting. I liked the strategy and play making when I coached, trying to figure out ways to get my team to play better. And I liked the camaraderie of women who enjoyed sports the way I did. I refereed for these games sometimes, too. I was not tall enough to be a great player, but I could run up and down the court and blow a whistle. After passing the umpire and refereeing tests, I earned $15 a game from the teams I refereed for. That was good money for me.

The women on my team became my best friends during college, especially Joan and Sharpie, on whom I had a deep crush, and Dor. There was just something about these women that attracted me, made me feel comfortable and at home, but I couldn't put my finger on it in those days. Maybe it was that they seemed less interested in men than most women, so I didn't have to fake an interest I didn't feel. And then there were the times a group of us would go to the back room of a club in Malverne after games where we would fill the juke box with nickels and dimes and dance with each other. I didn't slow dance, but some of the others, like Joan and Sharpie, would. No one made any comments about this or other relationships between the women. Even with my history of crushes on women, I just thought they were good friends. We were all just friends. I was still pretty naïve, and I couldn't really imagine any other kind of relationship.

Moving on

I LOVED THE Royal M's, but by the time I graduated from Pratt in 1947 in my early twenties, I was aware I had to do more about dating men than I was. I knew I would have to get married someday. That was a given. The problem was that while I wanted to like men, I kept falling in love with women. I even lost my first job out of Pratt because I spent so much time flirting with one of the women in the office, innocently, of course. After a few months of me spending more time hanging around her desk than designing ads for wallpaper, I was informed that I was not producing enough and was fired. I was determined not to let that happen again. I would have to be more careful.

My next job entailed designing bus cards for the New York ad agency Lackey and Lambdin. I made sure I had my work done before I spent much time with the women in the secretarial pool, the one place in this large firm where there were a lot of women. That's where I met Annette Neilson, who—you guessed it—I developed a serious, secret crush on. It was because of her that I joined in pooling money with five or six other women from work to rent a bungalow in Far Rockaway, a popular beach resort not far down on Long Island where inexpensive group rentals were common. I fantasized spending weekends swimming, fishing, and just hanging out with Annette and the other Lackey and Lambdin women I had become friendly with. But not surprisingly, men intruded.

With the end of World War II, everyone seemed eager to get back to normal, which meant marriage and families. Many of my girlfriends from school had already gotten married, and the women I was hanging out with were eager to do the same. So, we invited guys we knew down, as did the other women who were renting places for the summer, and would give and attend parties with these guys as well as those who had their own rentals at the beach.

As you might expect, I was ambivalent about dating any of these men, but I recognized the marriage opportunities, and normalcy, they represented. And I had another motivation. If I wanted to go out with Annette, and her boyfriend Bill, I had to find someone to date so I could double date with her. I began to stage manage my life. While I had always hidden my feelings for women, now I began to show fake affection for men. It didn't feel good. It was confusing and often shame-creating and depressing, not to mention exhausting. And sometimes it got out of hand, like the many times I got engaged to get married and then broke off the engagement. After two weeks of an engagement ring on my finger, I would start to panic and the ring would be gone. There was Raymond, for instance, who had lived on my block when I was a kid. Then there was Bob. And Gene, a handsome Air Force man. All served well as my necessary companions so I could double date with Annette. Except Gene. He was still in the service so was often away. I hadn't taken that into account. But, luckily for me as it turned out, there was Eddie Bottini.

I had known Eddie for years though I hadn't seen much of him. We had lived across the street from each other when I was living in Lynbrook the last few years of high school and my first years at Pratt. I don't recall ever noticing him particularly, but I later learned that for the two years after high school when he had been confined to bed with really serious asthma, he had watched me from his upstairs bedroom window as I walked to the train on my commute to Pratt. Later, when I was working in Manhattan and he had gotten healthy enough to have a job there, too, we would bump into each other on the train now and again. By this time, he was around six feet tall and lanky, weighing only about a hundred and forty pounds. He had short, dark brown, slightly wavy hair, and an angular face with high cheek bones, a long Italian nose, and a pointy chin, features that would allow me later to think of him as handsome. He was very much the quiet and shy type. We were pretty much little more than nodding companions.

Still, one of the times when Gene was away and I needed a date at the beach to go out with Annette and Bill, my mind turned to Eddie. He would be harmless and was presentable. So, I invited him down to Far Rockaway and dragged him out on this date. I had grown to be pretty manipulative by then.

Much to my surprise, I had a really nice time with Eddie. He had a reticence and courteousness that I really appreciated, especially in contrast to so many of the other guys I went out with who were always trying to cop a feel. So that was it for Gene Ryan. On his next furlough, I told him I was dating Eddie, broke the engagement, and never saw him again. I see now it was hard-hearted, but since for me there was little real feeling in these relationships, I had a difficult time imagining that there were deep feelings on the side of the guys either. I didn't mean to be cruel, but I probably was.

In the meantime, I was feeling increasing pressure to actually get married, not just engaged. Not only had many of my friends already walked down the aisle, but, at twenty-five I was getting on in the marriage pool. Social convention, though, was not the only consideration motivating me to think seriously about matrimony. I desperately wanted to get out of my Aunt Edna and Uncle Phil's house. The place depressed me. Mostly, they all just kind of existed, never changing their routines. My aunt and uncle rarely talked except to remind my mother she was a failure and how they had to save her. I hated that and watching my mother retreat into passivity in response. But in a way, I was no better.

If my aunt reprimanded me for violating one of the many rules of behavior and etiquette she and my uncle had established, like slouching on the couch instead of sitting up straight, I would slink away into my room. But one night, I had just had it. Instead of going quiet when my aunt criticized me, I yelled back at her. Then I stormed off, called Dor, my best friend from the Royal M's, and asked if I could come over. I even packed a bag, planning to leave permanently. Dor was game for letting me stay with her for as long as I wanted, but soon my conformist, wanting-to-do-the-right-thing side kicked in. I knew that good girls didn't just go off and live on their own or with female roommates. I also knew that the only legitimate way I could escape that house and not look or feel like I was embarrassing or abandoning my mother, and giving my aunt and uncle another reason to condescend to her, was to get married. In fact, I would be congratulated. And there was Eddie.

As I got to know him better, I liked him more and more. He was clearly the best of the lot, never trying to force himself on me or treat me like he owned me. Instead, he was always kind and thoughtful, a real gentleman. OK, he was a little too quiet, too content with staying home and reading rather than going out the way I liked to, but I figured I could live with that. I knew he genuinely cared for me, and I surprised myself by actually caring about him. This was something I didn't even realize until I noticed that when we went out, aware that he didn't have much money, I ordered beer instead of the expensive mixed drink I would have other guys buy for me. It must have been love. So I left Dor's, went back to my aunt and uncle's house, and accepted Eddie's proposal of marriage. We set a wedding date, January 12, 1952.

Ivy when she was a student at Pratt, c. 1945.

The Royal M's in Ivy's car, 1946.

The Royal M's, 1946. Ivy is bottom left.

Ivy at a shooting range with her friends, 1947.

Ivy (right) at one of her first jobs as work as a graphic artist, 1949.

Ivy in 1950.

Getting Married

ONE DAY ABOUT a week before my wedding, I woke up and I couldn't swallow food. I could chew but when I tried to get food down, it felt like somebody was squeezing my throat. For weeks before this, I had been so wound up that I always felt on the verge of exploding. But I hadn't. I managed to pull myself together, appear calmer than I was, and go through the motions of a happy bride preparing for her wedding. But this eating thing was ridiculous. It threatened to betray me, to myself and to everyone else.

I told myself I had some physical illness and, in desperation, called the general practitioner I had had all my life, Dr. Gerkin, yes, like the pickle. I explained my problem and he asked me what was going on in my life. With my reply, "Not much, but I am getting married this Saturday," he responded, "Ivy, I'm going to make an appointment for you with a psychiatrist I know. You don't have a physical problem. You have an emotional one."

I knew he was right, but this was not what I had wanted to hear. Back then, people were supposed to solve their own emotional problems. They could go to other family members, or maybe clergy, but going outside of that, for anyone to even know you were having a hard time, was shameful. Only people who were weak, or really crazy, went to psychologists or psychiatrists. But what could I do? I was a mess and terribly confused. I wanted to do the right thing, do what normal women do, be in love with a man and get married.

The problem was I still kept falling in love with women, and while I knew that I loved Eddie, I wasn't in love with him. So I didn't want to marry him. That he was probably the best I would ever get wasn't much consolation. So I made an appointment for the Wednesday before my Saturday wedding to see the therapist Dr. Gerkin recommended.

The psychiatrist's office was in Freeport, which was only twenty minutes away by car from the house in Lynbrook. But, I took the bus because didn't want to take the chance of anyone seeing my car anywhere near the psychiatrist's office. That's how worried I was that somebody would find out that I needed outside help. I was tempted to turn around once I got to the door of the building, but I got myself up the elevator to the appropriate office only to spend the next ten minutes in a waiting room arguing with myself about whether I should stay or go.

Before I had a chance to make up my mind, I was startled out of my reverie by a deep male voice calling, "Come in" from the other side of the office door. I steeled myself and was confronted by a stern-looking, pale, middle-aged man in a dark suit sitting behind a massive mahogany desk in the center of the room. I immediately felt judged as guilty. He didn't get up. He didn't ask me to sit down. He didn't even say hello, at least in my memory.

He asked why I was there, and I replied with the first thing that came into my mind, "Because I think I love women." For an instant, I wondered if it had really come out of my mouth, if I had actually said that out loud. I certainly never had before. I was terrified about how he would respond. Still, I couldn't stop myself and gushed out about how much I liked being around women, about my Royal M's' friends, and about some of my crushes.

He didn't blink. "Have you ever kissed a woman?" he asked.

"No!" I exclaimed. I had been afraid to even imagine anything like that until he put the idea into my head. Then, even in the midst of my emotional trauma, I felt the excitement of such a possibility. Shame and embarrassment swept over me. As I said, I was very confused.

The next thing I remember I was sitting against the wall in a plain, straight backed chair, the only other piece of furniture in the room, facing him.

He said to me, "You are not hom-o-sexual. Go get married. And cleave"—he actually said "cleave," a word which even in this critical junction of my life I thought ridiculous—"and cleave unto your married friends. Give up all your sports friends. And cleave unto your married friends."

I was tremendously relieved. This expert had told me that there was nothing wrong with me, that I was not unnatural or sick. All I had to do was to get married and cleave and then everything would be OK. It all seemed so simple. I would do what he instructed me to do. I wanted to get up, kiss his ring, and genuflect, but I didn't. I said OK and left. I was able to eat again.

EDDIE AND I were married in a Catholic church since that was what Eddie wanted. I didn't really care. When I was a kid, my mother had taken me to so many different Protestant churches, always losing patience with the minister or something and moving on, that I hadn't developed any great faith or denominational loyalty. Besides, I had much more to worry about than the church.

As I started down the aisle with my Uncle Phil, my heart and head were thudding so hard that I was convinced, absolutely, without a doubt convinced that I was going to die of a heart attack before I got to Eddie at the front of the church. It didn't help calm me that standing near him was Annette, my maid of honor, the woman I had so wanted to go out with that I had arranged those double dates with Eddie and others. I was in a daze as rings were exchanged, we were pronounced man and wife, and we kissed. Once we got outside, I realized I had given Eddie my right hand for my ring instead of my left hand.

With a surge of hope, I thought, "Maybe I'm not married." Then reality set in. I knew it didn't matter. I was Mrs. Edward Bottini.

Married Life — Children

BEFORE I GOT married, I was so worried about finding a guy that I could like enough to wed that I rarely thought about having children. But once married, I knew that having kids was next. In for a dime, in for a dollar. Two would be nice, I thought, or maybe even three. Not just one. Too much responsibility for the poor kid. I wouldn't do that to anyone. But having kids meant that Eddie and I would have to have intercourse, and I didn't like intercourse.

It wasn't Eddie. I was never interested in actually having sex with men. I would kiss, cuddle, and put up with a little petting, but that was it. That may have been frustrating for the guys, but, for once, I had the heterosexual value system on my side. We all, men and women, knew that the fastest way for a woman to lose a man's respect, or at least suitability for marriage, was to give in to the man's entreaties to have intercourse before getting married. If word got around that a woman was no longer a virgin, her chances for matrimony plunged. Not a good thing. Women needed that wedding ring to show, one, that they were attractive enough to get a man, and two, they were not so loose as to be unworthy of one. And without a man, a woman had little to no social standing. Of course, this didn't mean guys wouldn't try to "go all the way." That was part of their role. Our job was to stop them.

This isn't to say that I didn't have a robust sexual appetite. Eddie and I had a lot of sex, all of it pretty much initiated by me since Eddie was much more reticent than I was. Mostly it was oral sex. This was for three reasons. One, I liked oral sex and, as far as I could tell, Eddie did, too. He was certainly very eager and attentive and never complained. Two, as I mentioned before, I didn't like intercourse. The penetration it involved made me think of myself simply as a receptacle. That was not me. And three, while I wanted to have kids, I didn't want any unplanned pregnancies, and in those days, birth control options were severely limited. I mean severely, though some states were worse than others.

Thirty states prohibited the use of any kind of birth control. Even distribution of birth control information was against the law in many states. In the places where birth control was legal, neither the IUD nor the pill were available, the IUD because it wasn't widely distributed until the late fifties and the pill because it hadn't been developed yet for birth control. It wasn't approved for contraceptive use until 1960. The diaphragm, which had been around since the early twentieth century, was only available to married women with a doctor's prescription. The main sources of information about birth control for the women I knew were hushed, often urgent conversations we had with each other. From what I gathered, most depended on condoms and diaphragms, or rhythm, withdrawal, and abstinence. The last was for me. I didn't trust any form of birth control except not having intercourse. Still, if I wanted to have kids, I knew what Eddie and I would have to do.

That spring, a few months into our marriage, when we finally had the time and money to get away for a belated honeymoon in Daytona Beach, Florida, Eddie and I gave it a try and I got pregnant.

The pregnancy didn't start well. I had a terrible pain in my side that doctors didn't recognize as a pregnancy for over a month. By then, the pains had gotten so bad that I had had to give up the little free-lance graphic art work I had been doing from home after I left Lackey and Lambdin soon after Eddie and I were engaged. Once our wedding date was set, I had been in too much of an emotional tizzy to deal with the demands of the wedding and work at the same time. Besides, I knew that once we were married, Eddie was supposed to be the primary bread winner in the family. Eddie's small salary from his male secretary job in New York City, supplemented by my work, was just enough to pay for our decent-sized apartment near where our parents lived, but not enough when the pain and then the severe morning sickness forced me to stop working. Besides, I couldn't stay by myself.

We had to move, first into his mother's house, which didn't last since she was always rude to me, having never forgiven me for stealing her son away, and then in with my mother and aunt and uncle until about my sixth month when both the mysterious pain and the morning sickness subsided enough for me to be able to take care of myself. Eddie and I were able to move into a small apartment in Lynbrook. Suddenly I began to feel that this was what my body was made for and was elated and amazed at the idea that I was going to give birth to a whole other person. It was surreal but wonderful. And a psychological relief. I had given up my basketball friends and was cleaving to my husband. Never mind that this Ivy was not the person I felt I truly was. I was doing the right thing, fulfilling my role as a woman and was going to be a mother. I was being what and who I was supposed to be.

Laura was born on January 25, 1953 after thirteen hours of very difficult labor. At my insistence, I was conscious during the delivery and watched as the doctor pulled this other being out of me and flipped her onto my stomach. She was covered in goo, her arms flopping, and bald as she would remain until her ninth month. She was twenty-four inches long and weighed eight pounds nine ounces. Huge. To me, it was all miraculous. One minute there was just me and the next there were two of us.

For the next year, I spent most of my time taking care of Laura while Eddie was the usual only sometimes attentive dad. I expect I was as good and as bad as all new mothers were their first year as a parent, but I knew I wasn't as content as I was supposed to be. It's not that I didn't enjoy much of my time with Laura. It's just that I was lonely and frustrated. In the evenings, Eddie often preferred reading his histories over talking to me, and, on many weekends, he was out of commission with the migraine headaches which plagued him.

We were friendly with a few married couples, which relieved some of the isolation, but I also knew I needed other women friends when the crushes I had on some of these women brought my illicit desires too close to home. I was afraid that if Eddie got even a whiff of the nature of my attachments to women, the delicate structure of my life would collapse and I would lose my family and my reputation as a good person. Since I couldn't stop feeling them, I realized I better take these feelings farther from home. Besides, while, yes, I got satisfaction from fulfilling my womanly roles, I was losing the sense of self and control over my life that working outside the house and having a job afforded me. Luckily for me, then, we needed the money. Eddie had quit his job in the city and was working in his father's small house painting and construction business, but business wasn't great. So I could go back to work without looking like I was recklessly abandoning my child.

I couldn't find a job as a graphic artist, but looking around at all the houses being built in Nassau County, I decided that becoming a real estate agent might just be the opportunity I was looking for. It had the added attraction of allowing me some flexibility so that the times when Eddie was actually working, I could stay home with Laura. It was a good decision. I took a position as an agent at Maffucci Real Estate and found I really liked the work. I was also good at it and soon was able to support our household and to put a little money away for myself. I cheered up considerably.

Having a bit of a crush on one of the married woman I worked with also added some spice to my life. I didn't expect, or want, anything to come of this relationship. I was just allowing myself to secretly indulge in the erotic feelings I had for her under the guise of friendship. That is until I realized that Eddie was more perceptive than I thought he was and I was less discreet. One evening after I had given Laura her usual bath and had settled her into her bassinet, I was all ready to go out and visit this friend for a few hours, something I had occasionally done before. I told Eddie I was going, but before I could leave, Eddie stopped me with a worried look in his eyes.

"Are you in love with her?" he asked. All that went through my mind was "Oh god, oh, god." I had to bluff.

I managed to get out, "Nooooo." You know, like, "What? Are you out of your mind?"

I insisted we were just friends, and, chuckling at the absurdity of the idea, kissed him good bye and left. I convinced myself that he believed me. I have no idea if he did. We never spoke about that conversation again. Never. But he clearly had a suspicion about my temptations. Now and again throughout our marriage, he would say of various women, "You leave them alone and they'll leave you alone." Eddie was no fool. In a way, I was the fool to think I could go on like this.

Levittown

AFTER A YEAR or so of working as a real estate agent, I decided it was time for me and Eddie to get ourselves more of the American Dream and buy our own house. So one day in 1954 when I knew Eddie and his dad were going to be away for a few days working in the Hamptons, I took Laura and drove over to the housing development that had recently been constructed on converted farm land by Levitt and Sons in Hempstead, Long Island. This 1947 Hempstead Levittown was the original planned community, the one that became the model for the thousands that would soon spring up in new suburbs all over America. They proclaimed themselves the fulfillment of the promise of the good life made to returning World War II vets and their families. Like those that followed, Hempstead Levittown consisted of several thousand two-bedroom, one bath, single-family houses built on cement slabs along tree lined streets. Each had an attic expandable for an additional bedroom for possible additional children. All had yards with a barbecue, lawns in the front, and driveways on the side. But we had choices. There were four different styles, a few different colors, and different setbacks from the street. Garages and car ports were optional.

The community also included schools with playgrounds equipped with swings, jungle gyms, baseball diamonds, and swimming pools; houses of worship; and grocery stores and other shopping, all in accordance with the Levitt idea of a community's needs. Although I didn't know it at the time, evidently one of these needs was that the community be all white, so the first ones were covenanted for whites only. All I knew was that Eddie, Laura, and I could get out of the apartment we were living in and have a clean, spacious suburban place of our own. To me it seemed like paradise, the embodiment of the American Dream and symbol of the distance I had come from the kidney stew of my teenage years. Now my family and I could eat well cooked steak in our own kitchen filled with the latest, most modern appliances. What was not to love? That was the dream I wanted to live.

I found a house for $10,500, an affordable price for the typical one income family in 1954 when the average family income was about $5000 a year. I signed the papers an hour after I saw the place. The only reason I could actually do this myself was because I was married—I was Mrs. Edward Bottini. Even though I was earning more than Eddie, I later had to have him co-sign all the papers so we could get a mortgage. Without him, or some other man to co-sign, I couldn't have gotten any kind of credit, never mind a mortgage. No women would have been able to. That lasted all the way until 1974 when, pressured by the feminist movement, Congress passed the Equal Credit Opportunity Act that enabled a woman to get credit in her own name.

After I signed for the house, I went home, called Eddie in the Hamptons, and said, "I just bought a house." There was a long silence. I asked, "Did you hear me?"

He replied, "Yeah, I did."

I said, "You're going to love it. You're going to love it."

I DID, BUT I'm not sure he did. For one thing, he continued to suffer from migraine headaches on most weekends. Sometimes I think they were an excuse to have his mother come over and take care of him, which was what she did on those weekends, all day each day, until I finally asserted my marital rights over her and kicked her out. As I said before, we did not get along. But Eddie and I never talked about his relationship with his mother. I knew he wouldn't want me to say anything negative about her, so I knew not to bring it up. Like my feelings for women, that was one of the things we did not discuss.

This is not to say that Eddie and I didn't talk. He was quiet, but he was not withdrawn or particularly moody. In fact, we were very at ease and companionable with each, chatting at home about the weather, Laura, our neighbors, or any house or business projects we had going. He would listen, too, when I shared office intrigues and gossip with him and was fine socializing with the group of friends we developed in Levittown. While he rarely made friends of his own, he got along well with the couples I brought into our lives and would even join with the men in our group on their bowling nights and at poker games. From what I could tell, he was good at being just another one of the guys. The problem was, I didn't want a guy.

Family Life

AT THE END of 1955, I got pregnant again, and, in June 1956, after a much easier pregnancy, my second daughter, Lisa, was born. She was a healthy, little, short butterball with a full head of black hair, just the opposite of Laura. She looked like my dad, even as an infant. I was thrilled once again.

But that didn't mean I was about to give up work and stay at home. For one thing, we still needed the money since Eddie's father's business never seemed to do very well. For another, just about the time I got pregnant, I had finally gotten the job I wanted at *Newsday*, and I wasn't going to give that up. And I had had to fight in order to stay working, especially once my pregnancy began to show.

In those days, women were usually fired once it was clear they were pregnant, a practice that persisted until it was banned by the 1978 Pregnancy Discrimination Act. There seemed to be something about visibly pregnant women appearing and performing complex tasks in public that greatly disturbed men. I don't know what the issue was, but I managed to convince my boss that I would stay inconspicuous, would not do anything having to do with my pregnancy while at work, and would only be out for about two weeks once the baby was born. Maybe I had a talent for talking people into what I wanted even then, or maybe my boss just needed his graphic designers. Whatever it was, he didn't fire me, and I worked pretty much right up to delivery. I stayed home for two weeks, using up all of my sick leave, and then I was back at work.

This didn't mean that I abandoned my kids to the care of others all day long. Oh no. That would never do. That was one of the great things about my job. Since *Newsday* was an evening paper, I didn't have to leave for work until about eleven a.m. I could spend the mornings with the kids and sometimes could return home in time for dinner and for more time with them. When I wasn't around, if Eddie was working, my mother took over. She wasn't our first choice even though she was very eager to help. By that time, she was acting out again, alternating periods of passivity with hours long rantings like those she used to subject my father to. I knew it wasn't good for the kids, but there weren't a lot of other options. Home day care was hard to find, and expensive, and there were practically no nurseries, day care centers, or pre-schools to send kids to, especially for middle class women who were supposed to be home taking care of their children. For working women, a family member was expected to step in.

Besides, I had developed more sympathy for my mother as I got some distance. Instead of being irritated and frustrated at her when she wouldn't respond to my aunt and uncle's condescension to her, I focused more of my anger on them. And not just them. My other uncles and my mother's sisters who often gathered at Phil and Edna's also minimized my mother. When they weren't actively demeaning, their attitude was one of tolerating her presence as though doing so was a favor. By the time I became an activist, I hated whenever anyone talked about tolerance. To me, this was a put down, not acceptance, not respect. It wasn't enough. Not for my mother, and later not for women and for gays and lesbians.

Sometimes though, my aunt and uncle wouldn't even tolerate her. I never knew exactly what would bring on one of these crises, but from time to time for the next several years when the kids were young and we were living in Levittown, my aunt would call and tell me that I had to take my mother for a while. Eddie even converted half of the attic into a bedroom for her. For a while, she would be calm and able to help with the kids. Then out of nowhere it seemed, she would erupt into one of those moods that had haunted my father, myself, and her, I'm sure, the last years of my father's life. Something inconsequential, maybe some kind of disagreement about taking care of the kids, Eddie's family, the food we had in the house, or the dust on a table—who knows—would set her off. She would rage in a loud, high pitched, strained voice for hours, starting downstairs in the living room or kitchen and then stomping off upstairs to her room, still screaming at us. Eventually these diatribes would become monologues filled with complaints about her life and how badly people treated her and would go on for hours and hours. After a few of these tirades, even recognizing how badly she was treated at my aunt's place, I would lose patience.

"That's it," I would tell her. "You've got to go back to Aunt Edna's." She would meekly return to my aunt's for months or a year, whatever.

Then my aunt and uncle would say, "You've got to take your mother for a while." And we would. This merry go round went on and on.

Miscarriage

TWO AND A half years after Lisa was born, I got pregnant again. Eddie and I were going for that important child, a son. But, things didn't go as planned. During the second month I had a hemorrhage. My doctor told me I had to stay in bed if I wanted to have a successful pregnancy. I couldn't go to work, I couldn't do anything. I really wanted this child so I took a leave from work and went to bed. It didn't help. I continued to feel weak and sick and was in pain most of the time. It was only in the sixth month that my doctor realized I had a molar pregnancy. That meant that instead of an intact baby, only tissue parts were implanted in the placenta. There would be no baby. There was also nothing that could be safely done to end the pregnancy until the ninth month. I had to stay in bed and wait.

I was devastated. I tried my best to accept the situation, but it was hard. What was amazing, though, was that my mother came through then, just when I needed her. She pulled herself together, moved in, and, without complaint, took care of the house, Eddie, and the kids. Not one rant during that whole traumatic period. Eddie, too, was around, always attentive and caring when he wasn't at work. Interestingly, he, like my mother, overcame his maladies for the duration. During the seven months that I was on bed rest, Eddie didn't have any migraines. I don't think Eddie ever noticed this, or his earlier tendency to get the headaches on weekends when he wouldn't miss work and his mother could be around. For the most part, he was good at avoiding thinking about whatever might make him uncomfortable. Or at least talking about it. That is, until he just couldn't deny some things or keep quiet anymore. But that came much later.

EVEN WITH EDDIE and my mother tending to me, I was terribly lonely. Sometimes when I couldn't stand being in bed and alone any longer, I would drag myself across the street to visit friends. They would end up carrying me back to my house since I would inevitably start to hemorrhage. Finally, in the ninth month, teeth, hair, and other fractions of a baby began to come out of me in great globs of blood. By the time I got to the hospital, all the baby parts were out, as well as much of my own blood. I had to be given five pints of blood.

I managed to recuperate more easily physically and get back to work than I was able to heal emotionally. Somehow this miscarriage, crushing all on its own, had ruptured the wall I had erected to protect myself from my true feelings. I had thought that by compartmentalizing, by keeping all my feelings for women to myself and trying to go about the rest of my life as usual, I could manage. But then came the miscarriage and my nerves shattered. I didn't know who I was. I was terrified of being alone and having no control. I couldn't get on an elevator by myself. I couldn't drive by myself. I was also very depressed. I could feel I was closing down part of myself, especially at home. One day I was so despairing that I went into our bedroom and flopped down on my stomach on the mattress. The bed had been stripped because my mother was there doing laundry. All I could see were the gray stripes of the ticking on the mattress. Suddenly, I felt like I was melting into the mattress. I flew off the bed, certain I would have disappeared had I stayed there. I knew this couldn't go on.

I picked up the phone and called old Dr. Gerkin—yup—he was still alive. After I told him about my fears and the bed incident, he said, "No, it's not physical. It's emotional. Again." He gave me the number of a new psychologist. I started going to him. He was easier to talk to than the last therapist I had seen. Often we talked about how I felt about women, the problem I had always had.

He kept saying to me, "You love your husband, don't you?"

I said, "Yes, I do; he's a very nice man."

"And you love your children?"

"Of course I do. I love them very much."

"You don't want to hurt them."

"No . . . I . . ."

"So stay in your marriage."

We went round and round on this. I wanted it to be that simple and be happy with this solution. That idea, of doing the right, natural thing, had been enough to get me to walk down the aisle to get married. I was having a harder time accepting that now, but I was still determined to succeed as a wife and mother. I pulled myself together and learned to keep my conflicts and unhappiness in check. I stayed in my marriage. But barely.

Suburbia

AS BEST I could, I plunged back into my life. I went back to work, played with my kids and had secret crushes on women. Perhaps most importantly on the home front, I began to form close friendships with some of the other women who lived in my Levittown neighborhood. Here, when I say friendships, I mean friendships. Not crushes.

The most important was my relationship with Esther Siegel. I met Esther through my involvement in the local school board election in 1956. I was thirty years old, and this was my first political involvement. Pretty much all I knew about electoral politics before had to do with my father and his job. And that foray into politics had not ended well. But this campaign touched me. Even though the area was still pretty much segregated, a group of rabidly racist, anti-Semitic, and anti-Communist right wing John Birchers were trying to infiltrate the Farmingdale school board. (The Levittown schools were part of the Farmingdale School District.) I hadn't seen the civil rights movement for black people that was just beginning to gain national attention as my fight, but my growing sense of how hard it was when someone didn't fit in, and my memories of Ruby and Lakeview, were enough to pull me in this time. I volunteered at the campaign office and stuffed envelopes, made calls, formulated lists—all the general necessary scut work. I was not a leader in any way.

Esther wasn't one of those racist radicals, but she believed she could work with them so was running in opposition to our candidates. How naïve, I thought. Even then I understood that there was no compromising with people like that. Esther also imagined that she could convince those of us who were campaigning against her to support her. So right before the election, she stopped by our phone bank to explain her point of view. I was immediately smitten, not so much sexually but with her warmth and earnestness. Although she was misguided on this issue, I could tell that she was also smart and sensitive. And she had delightful dimples. I couldn't vote for her, but I couldn't help myself falling for her.

Even without my vote, Esther's spirit of cooperation won. I was so taken by her and intrigued about what she was actually going to do once she took office that I took to dropping in on the school board meetings when I had a night off from work. After one, she invited me out to coffee. Our connection was immediate. We talked at our local all-night diner well into the next morning covering the commonplaces of family, friends and work, and the more abstract ideas and ideals. But not, I want to make clear, my crushes on women. That was a place too private and scary to go with anyone. Nonetheless, it was the beginning of a beautiful friendship.

Esther was not the only woman in my neighborhood or the surrounding suburbs with whom I became friendly, though she was the most important. We were both part of a close-knit group—Bobbi, Claire, Estelle, Doris, Mathilda, and Millie—all married with kids. Since I didn't have to go to work until later in the day, I had a chance to hang out with them and our kids in the mornings. Some of my favorite memories are of the days the other mothers and I would sit on someone's porch and chat as we watched our children play hop scotch, jump rope, and tag in the safe streets. It was on those streets that I taught both of my kids how to roller skate and ride bikes. I can still see short, little me running along down the road trying to hold on to the back of the bike seats until the kids could balance themselves and ride off on their own.

By 1958, when many of the children had started school, a group of us would often settle down in one of our living rooms or kitchens or on the beach and chat. Mostly we told tales about how our kids were doing and complained about the small transgressions of our husbands. We rarely voiced serious complaints. If somehow discontent slipped out, we would meet it sympathetically, but often the woman who confessed her distress would laugh it off as inconsequential. What could be done anyway? Divorce would mean financial ruin for us and our children as well as social disgrace. Besides, unhappiness with our American Dream lives was something neither I nor other women could admit.

No matter the range in professional status or economic class of our families—in our neighborhood they ranged from handy man to college professor—we all had our single-family homes in our pretty much all white, safe suburban community of nearly identical houses on nearly identical streets with good schools and playgrounds for our children and supermarkets nearby. The message we got from our husbands, women's magazines, advertisements, therapists and probably each other was that if we were not happy, there was something wrong with us personally. It was our fault. All we had to do was adjust our attitudes. If we couldn't manage that on our own, we could go to a therapist and/or take pills, but those were humiliating and secret last resorts. That is certainly how I felt.

Still, with all of our secrets, with these women and at the gatherings with our husbands and children on weekends and holidays, I felt normal and could even enjoy myself. Even though I was the only one of us who worked, I still felt some satisfaction in fulfilling my roles as housewife and mother, just as I imagine they did. I knew the rules and how to fit in. I knew never to leave the house without make-up, but not with too much—blush and lipstick for most occasions, with maybe a little eyeliner.

For fancy events, like New Year's Eve, I might go so far as to add false eyelashes. I knew how to dress, too. A casual shirtwaist or skirt and sweater for outside the house. A house dress was OK for home but not outside. No one ever wore slacks, inside or outside. For those few dressy events Eddie and I attended, I had a gold lame cocktail dress that fit like a glove over my then cute figure. Generally, I shopped at large department stores where I could use my newly acquired department store charge card. These retail store cards were pretty much the only credit cards available at the time, and then only to men or married women. And then they were only issued in our husbands' names.

All my cards said "Mrs. Edward Bottini." That's who I was.

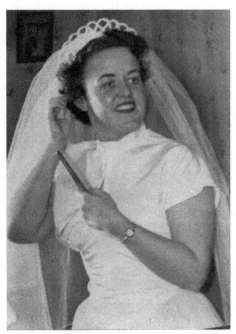

Ivy in her wedding dress, 1952.

Ivy and her mother preparing for Ivy's wedding, 1952.

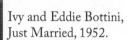

Ivy and Eddie Bottini, Just Married, 1952.

Ivy and Eddie at the beach, 1952.

Ivy with her daughter, Laura, 1954.

Ivy with her daughter, Lisa, 1957.

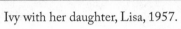

Ivy with her daughter, Laura, 1959.

Ivy with her daughter, Lisa, 1964.

Ivy in her house in the suburbs, Long Island, 1959. *Courtesy of ONE Archives at the USC Libraries*

Gallery 1

STILL, THERE WAS something missing. I didn't complain about Eddie or married life, even though I often felt depressed or empty outside of work. While I got a good deal of pleasure from spending time with my children, it wasn't as fulfilling as I had been led to believe it would be. Often it was boring. I also found myself frequently irritated at Eddie as he sat and read in his easy chair or lay in bed with a migraine. I thought at the time that my guilt over my love for women and my inability to reveal or act on it were the causes of my pain. I learned later that many other women felt trapped in lives that didn't allow them to be themselves. But in the meantime, something had to be done. Neither of the psychologists I had seen had touched the root of my unhappiness. Having a job wasn't enough. I decided to go back to painting.

I started by working in the kitchen, setting up my brushes, paints and canvases on the kitchen table, but I would always have to put everything away for meals. I kept asking Eddie to make a space up in the attic for me. He always replied, "Yeah. Yeah. Yeah." But he never did anything. So, one day I drove my little Volkswagen Beetle down to the lumber yard and bought building materials, including large pieces of pressboard that I had the sales people tie on top of the car. I dragged each piece off the car and up the attic stairs, one by one, by myself. I did my best to cut the pieces to fit the slanting roof line and windows.

The result was what might be call an "interesting" design. By the time Eddie got home, I had finished my renovations and set up my drawing board. He took one look, and, embarrassed both by my clumsy job and that his procrastinating had forced me into it, he built me a beautiful studio with straight walls, shelves, a window seat with storage, and a great looking floor, all in beautiful wood. He put in a skylight that could open and brought in light. It was stunning. I was able to set up my drawing board in a well-lit alcove.

I spent as much time as I could in that studio, some painting by myself, some with my kids. When they were very young, I would give them crayons or pencils and pads and sit them down on the floor where they would draw as I worked. When they got a little older, I taught them the rudiments of colors and some of the tools and tricks of the trade, just as Miss Abel had taught me. We all worked together companionably for hours.

Those were wonderful times, but they weren't enough to take my mind off the guilt and confusion I felt about my marriage and the crushes I kept having on women. So, in 1960, even with a full-time job, two children, and a husband, and once again spending money without consulting Eddie, I decided to do something even more extreme. I opened an art gallery with another discontented housewife and artist, a ceramist, Barbara Marx, who was on the periphery of my Levittown social circle. I didn't expect to make money. I was just hoping a foray into art and business would bring me out of myself and my depression. That's what seeing new art and talking to artists about their ideas and techniques had done for me while I was at Pratt. I missed that.

We found a little barn on Merrick Road, which was one of two main east-west highways that stretched the length of Long Island from New York City to the Hamptons, the summer resort for the city's well to do. That meant we would have a lot of folks driving by. Perhaps most importantly, we got the barn rent free from the farmer's widow, then in her late seventies or eighties, who still lived on the land and wanted to have someone around the property. We called our gallery Beyond the Blue Door in honor of the barn door that we painted a wonderful shade of medium Delft blue.

The barn was small, about the dimensions of a good size living room, and still held its old barn hay smell, which I loved. We covered the walls with burlap and set up a display of crafts on shelves along one wall and patchouli scented candles along another. We mounted a pegboard on another wall where we hung the paintings. I also set up a drawing board in a corner of the shop and would paint when I could while it was my turn to take charge of the shop. I loved having customers hang around and chat with me as I worked, but I never showed my own work in this or either of my subsequent galleries. My main goal with the galleries was to meet and give opportunities to other artists.

To find these artists, every once in a while Barbara and I would get in her car and drive to galleries in small towns or cities in upstate New York, Connecticut, or Pennsylvania. If we liked anyone's work, we'd explain that we had a gallery on Long Island where we wanted to display and sell his or her work on consignment. They'd say, "Sure, take three. You want those three? Take 'em." They were extraordinarily trusting. They didn't know us from a hill of beans. We would come home with her station wagon filled with artwork.

Galleries 2 & 3

BY 1963, A few years after we had opened the gallery, Barbara and I were getting on each other's nerves. I felt under a lot of pressure with my family, working, and dealing with my emotional turmoil. Barbara didn't have a job outside the gallery, so I suspect she felt that she was taking on more than her fair share of work. She probably was. It was not a happy time in my life. We amicably fell into closing the gallery.

But I kept painting. One painting in particular I did around this time illustrated my deep discontent. It was inspired by Bill Robinson, a painter who particularly impressed me. One painting of his that especially spoke to me featured a man wearing a business suit trying desperately to balance himself on a plain straight back chair with only one chair leg on the very high tightrope in front of a circus crowd. It opened my mind to the dangerous way I was living my life. I painted my own version in 1965 when the hypocrisy, guilt, claustrophobia, and hopelessness of my life, married to a man while constantly falling in love with women, was getting to me.

I started my painting by covering my large canvas with deep ruby red paint and then dragged a brush dipped in oil and turpentine over it to carve out a blurred whitish reddish image of a naked woman in profile. Along the left vertical edge of the painting, I wrote in caps, WE ARE BORN ALONE, WE LIVE ALONE, WE DIE ALONE. We live alone, we die alone. It was clear I was feeling more and more trapped, more and more despairing. I knew I was living the wrong life but I had no one to talk to about it and didn't know how to get out of it.

Eddie and I did make one change. After eleven years or so in Levittown, we traded our smallish Cape Cod for a larger ranch style house and a more expansive back yard in Wantagh, the town next door where Esther and her family lived, another of the sprawling suburbs that marked Nassau County at that time. This house offered more room for Laura, by then a junior in high school, and Lisa, a few years behind. There were also a lot of kids in the neighborhood and still woods nearby to play in. Both kids could walk to and from school.

Wantagh was also a turning point for my kids.

Laura, while tall and lanky like her dad, had more of an outgoing personality like mine. That didn't mean we got along once she entered her teen years. At first, she had treated me as a friend who happened to be her mother but soon after we moved to Wantagh, she became more distant, disaffected, and pouty—diva-like would describe her—and I had become the enemy. She would barely talk to me. Part of me figured this was just her being a teenager, but part of me wondered how much her attitude and behavior had to do with me not being around that much, physically because of work, and emotionally because of my ever-present turmoil about loving women.

Lisa, about nine or ten when we moved, had become close to her father. She was basically a quiet, withdrawn kid, more like her dad than me. While she had learned how to ride a bike and skate, she seemed more at ease sitting in the living room reading with Eddie in his easy chair and her on the couch. Part of this, I think, was because she had to wear clunky shoes to help straighten her turned in feet. These made her self-conscious, as did the glasses that she started to wear from first grade on. But Wantagh brought her out more, especially once she met the more tomboyish Beth. No more sitting and reading with her dad. I always knew I could find her in a tree or somewhere with Beth when I was looking for her. Lisa became especially attached to this neighborhood and didn't seem to need me much at all.

Eddie, on the other hand, was not doing well. As was often the case, around this time Eddie was out of work for days either because his father had no jobs or because of his migraines or asthma. Maybe to compensate for not being as present as I knew I should have been, I felt a deep need to do something for him and the kids. I knew he liked art and liked visiting The Blue Door gallery, and I suspected that he would like being more or less in charge of one if we opened a new one. I convinced him to convert our large garage and family room into a gallery where he could work and the kids could hang out. So, in 1966, we opened Beyond the Red Door.

It turned out that opening an art gallery in the remodeled garage and family room of a suburban ranch house, even if on a main street, was not such a good idea. We had practically no customers. We closed the gallery within a few months of it opening, but Eddie was hooked. He wanted to open another. I wanted to please Eddie. We discovered a wonderful, big windowed kiosk all by itself on a street just off the main road in Fort Salonga, a fairly wealthy town on the north shore of Long Island on a route from New York City to the vacation areas in eastern Long Island.

Eddie and I knew the place because our family had spent a good bit of time there visiting with a fellow artist friend from work, Ken, his wife Gerri, and their kids. We rented the kiosk and opened the Fort Salonga Gallery. Eddie ran the place himself, which was fine with me. I have no idea if we even made any money on this shop, but if we did, I know it wasn't much. We were wrong about the location. It was set too far off the main road. But the gallery at least gave Eddie something to do. A good thing, because our world, and our marriage, was about to split open.

Understanding Freedom

I KEPT TELLING myself that if I could stop falling in love with women, if I could only love Eddie a little more or a little better, everything would be fine. But I couldn't. I was a forty year old married, working mother, trapped in a double life, one in which I felt my true self was on the losing end. I was often afraid I would go mad. And sometimes, I think, I did. This was not a good situation.

Then in June of 1966, Betty Friedan announced NOW to great fanfare. Hers was one of the first, loud volleys of a war that I hadn't even known was going on, never mind that it could be fought. I certainly hadn't given much thought to analyzing my life as a woman, or the lives of other women. I was stuck in what I saw as my own personal dilemma. But Friedan certainly was thinking about women in general. She knew that while things might look good, something was wrong. In her 1963 best seller, *The Feminine Mystique*, she called it the "problem with no name." While Friedan would later be accused of using the situation of married, middle class, white women to represent all women, at this point in history she had struck a chord, or a nerve, depending on your point of view, with many. I might not have heard of her, but she didn't need me. Her book had become a best seller.

Even if I had been more aware of Friedan and her ideas, I'm not sure I would have seen her issues as my fight. For one thing, I knew I didn't have some of the typical frustrations of a stay-at-home mom that Friedan described because I had good, full-time job that I enjoyed. I wasn't as dependent on my husband for status, definition, and money as many other women were. For another thing, I wasn't interested in politics. Aside from that Farmingdale School Board election, the other great social movements of the day—the civil rights and the anti-Vietnam war movements—had left me cold even as they dominated the news and the conscience of the country.

As I said before, I had sympathy for the civil rights movement, but black people were too far out of my immediate life to get me engaged. Not a good excuse, I know. But I couldn't get out of my own head and my worries about my own exclusion to give energy to theirs. As for Vietnam, I had lived through World War II and the Korean War and just didn't get enraged about this war. It seemed minor to me compared to the others. Perhaps if I had had sons . . . but I didn't. Besides, in general, I had no interest in being a rebel.

Nonetheless, after that first NOW board meeting, even with my hesitancy about the relevance of women's liberation to me, I let Dolores convince me to join her and her friend Pat Trainor in organizing the first NOW chapter, NYC NOW. I was still smitten with Dolores, and Dolores with NOW. Besides, I guess something was going on in me, too. While I hadn't been able to determine if there had been any lesbians at the NOW board meeting I had gone to, I had gotten a glimpse there of women taking charge of their lives in ways I hadn't imagined possible. Theirs was a different concept of how women could live and what a woman could achieve. Evidently, I, and many other women, were ripe for a change.

To develop arguments necessary to recruit the twenty people (men were welcome) that were needed to make a chapter according to the NOW charter, Dolores, Pat, and I spent hours in coffee shops and cafés, on buses and trains, trying to get a handle on what women's liberation meant and how to explain it to others. With them, I began to think about the way society was set up. I recalled then what I had just recognized as my first feminist thought. It had to do with the Jehovah's Witnesses. I had gone to a few meetings with the woman I had had a crush on at my first job out of college, the crush that had gotten me fired. The dogma of male control over the female was so overt and central to the Jehovah's Witnesses that even I couldn't avoid seeing it. That led me to think about all the churches my mother had dragged me to and how they all shared that same ideology. That was enough to put me off of churches for quite a while. Not enough, though, for me to reject their emphasis on the necessity of heterosexuality and the unnaturalness of homosexual love. I had lost faith in the church but not my adherence to social convention.

Now with Dolores and Pat, I began to see how this hierarchy played out in all aspects of our lives, men's and women's. I considered the lives of my suburban Long Island women friends who saw and defined themselves by their roles as subordinate caretakers, as full time housewives and mothers. Some, like Esther, had entered public life part-time or did volunteer work at a local hospital or civic organization, usually something family oriented. No one worked for money but me.

Since NOW began with an emphasis on equal employment opportunity and workplace discrimination, Dolores, Pat, and I spent a lot of time talking about what work meant to us, or to anyone. I began to see how lucky I was that my father had taught me that I had to take care of myself and that I had taken that to include the financial arena. I saw how fortunate Dolores and I and the other professional working women I knew who had somehow slipped through the cracks of custom and convention were. Work got us out of the house into a larger world. If we were lucky, it challenged our minds and allowed us to be creative. It gave us a sense of self we otherwise would not have had. And perhaps most importantly, because we earned our own money, we didn't have to cede total control of the purse strings, and thus a significant amount of power, to our husbands, as I saw so many of my friends do. But even then, we women who worked were often financially stuck. Not being legally permitted to take out loans or have checking accounts or the new bank credit cards in our own names limited our access to funds and independence.

Once I began to think about women's lives and look around more, I also realized that Dolores and I, and others like many of the NOW board members, were exceptions in terms of most women who worked since we had professional positions. Later, I would learn that breaking into some professions was not enough. The few women who became scientists, doctors, and lawyers were clustered in areas like gynecology or family law, just as female college professors generally confined themselves, or were confined, to the arts and humanities and were often at women's colleges. If women held public office, they were often appointed after their husbands who had been elected had died. The term "glass ceiling" hadn't even been invented because there was so little incentive for women to even think of being in, never mind, moving up in professional careers.

During these discussions with Dolores and Pat, I thought about my mother, too, and the sense of worth she got from the few jobs she had had and about her inability to take care of herself after my father died. Of the daily humiliation she put up with because of her lack of independence and self-confidence. I was beginning to get infuriated.

Even things I had accepted before started to piss me off. All the rules and restrictions that might have seemed petty and acceptable suddenly weren't. There was taking my husband's name, for instance. I accepted Mrs. Ivy Bottini, but Mrs. Edward Bottini rankled sometimes. I began to get angry, too, that women couldn't play full court basketball and that baseball was turned into six inning games of softball for us delicate creatures. Even then we weren't supposed to be too aggressive. And heaven forbid we beat a man at anything! Their poor egos. There were also all the other rules of lady-like and male behavior aside from the obvious men work and the little lady stays at home. Men were the strong silent type, protective of women, the weaker sex. They drove, opened doors for ladies, walked on the outside of the sidewalk, and did anything physical, except carry babies and groceries. Women were strong enough for that.

Not getting married was the worst thing. That would make a woman a dreaded old maid, i.e. not attractive enough to get a man, or, heaven forbid, a whispered about lesbian. After marriage, at least one boy and one girl was ideal, but if only one was possible, a boy was better to carry on the family name. Well, actually, having a boy was just better. Thus my third, unfortunate, pregnancy.

So many rules about keeping us seeing ourselves as weak and men as strong. So many rules to keep us controlled!

BY LATE NOVEMBER 1966, Dolores, Pat, and I had enough women to qualify as a NOW chapter. Dolores had done most of the recruiting since she lived in NYC and knew a lot of people. With my family and my job, I had limited time for that. I had tried to get my Long Island friends to join. I asked them what gave or could give them a sense of fulfillment. Was it being good housewives and mothers? I doubted it. I imagined if housekeeping was boring to me, it was boring to them, too. The same with spending hours of the day with kids with little other stimulation.

Were our luncheons, our coffee klatches, our days at the beach or pool, chatting and watching over the children, our barbecues with our husbands, enough for them? Since many of these women seemed smarter to me than their husbands, I didn't think so. But when I, aglow with my new found insights, tried to convince these friends that they needed to be liberated, to go to work, that their lives could be much more than they were, they resisted. They were not interested in rocking the boat and joining NOW. One would respond, "Oh, this women's liberation stuff is just a flash in the pan. It will all blow over soon." Another agreed, "Someone wrote a book so some folks got all excited, but it will soon go away." Others nodded their heads in agreement. They were kind and patient in listening, but I knew they were waiting for me to get through this stage. Denial ran strong in them. Too scary for them I guess. I could understand that.

In the end, the folks who joined that first NOW chapter were pretty much all from New York City or close by. They were white, heterosexual, mostly married, middle class women, some with kids, some not. A few similar men were sprinkled in. Of the women, some were divorced. Most worked. There were secretaries and receptionists, teachers, writers, academics. Perhaps being employed was what allowed many of them to see the unfairness and limited opportunity in the work force up close. I don't know. Whatever it was that brought us together, by the time our chapter actually got going, I was hooked. I knew I was part of a revolution that could change the world. This was an extraordinarily powerful and motivating idea, especially at a time in my life when I was frustrated by so much else. For the first time in my life, I would be able to help other women and perhaps find more peace of mind for myself in the process.

At first, Dolores, Pat, and I and other new members of NOW were cautious in many ways. We knew that NOW and its mission were controversial and we didn't want to put people off by appearing too radical. We also already had the beginning of the lesbian baiting problem. Many, both men and women, who saw the movement as dangerous to the status quo were accusing women of being lesbians just for being interested in women's liberation. This charge was scandalous enough to scare a number of women off and to keep lesbians who were involved in the closet. Not that I knew who they were, but they had to be there. I couldn't be the only one in the world, could I? So when it came time for our chapter to elect our first president, we elected Jeanne Faust who was well-liked by the members, but perhaps more importantly, she seemed pretty clearly not a lesbian, was well-educated, and had a proper, reserved manner. She was, in other words, a lady. We thought she would be our most effective bet.

Even as I continued to work at *Newsday*, I became totally absorbed by NOW and its mission to change women's lives. I became an active member and contributed when I had time to spare after work and from my family life, but, admittedly, family began to fade in importance as my NOW participation increased. National NOW had set up seven task forces—Equal Opportunity of Employment; Legal and Political Rights; Education; Women in Poverty; The Family; Images of Women; and Women and Religion. Equal employment was really central to the movement and its appeal, so much of our early energy went into that. Women academics had just shown that women earned fifty-nine cents to a man's dollar, confirming the pay discrepancy that we all knew existed. So we set out to change this and other aspects of women's opportunities for work.

One of the earliest NOW campaigns I was involved with was to get rid of sex-segregation in want ads to open up more and better opportunities for women. This was still a time when classified ads in newspapers were listed as "Men Wanted" and "Women Wanted" with, not surprisingly, the higher paying, more responsible, prestigious, and engaging jobs reserved for men. That didn't mean just white collar jobs. The better paying, higher skilled trade and craft union jobs were also exclusively for men. Jobs advertised for women were—surprise, surprise—school teachers, nurses, secretarial and clerical positions, saleswomen in department stores, unskilled health workers, housecleaners and the lesser paying factory jobs. And, of course, even if men did the same or similar jobs, women were paid less. What made it even more difficult for women was that in all situations where both men and women worked, if there were layoffs, the women lost their jobs first because, after all, men were the breadwinners so they needed the jobs more than women did.

After repeated appeals to the EEOC to take action ended in frustration, National NOW sent out word to local chapters to collect newspapers, bundle them up in red tape, symbolic of all the red tape preventing change, and deliver them to their local newspapers' offices. *Newsday*, the paper I worked for, was not a target. It was popular in Long island, but it was nothing compared to the *New York Times* in terms of influence and circulation. I was fine with that. No point in causing trouble too close to home. Besides, if the *Times* would change, other papers would change. So I helped gather papers, bundled them in red tape, and loaded them onto trucks for delivery to the *Times'* offices. As I watched the trucks drive away, I felt that intoxicating thrill that I was learning political action gave me when a group of us crossed a previously forbidden line into power and potential. I would get that feeling more and more often over the years. I still find it irresistible.

I had to go to work at *Newsday*, but a few members of my chapter and of the NOW national board held a sit-in with the papers that had been delivered to the *Times'* lobby until representatives from the paper met with them. We won. The Times gave in and changed its classified ads policies. No more male help wanted /female help wanted distinction. We were on our way.

Other issues were also rising in importance as NOW began to feel more empowered. In 1967, at its second national conference, NOW issued a "Bill of Rights for Women" that listed passage of the Equal Rights Amendment (ERA), publicly-funded child care, and the repeal of all abortion laws among its goals. I had pretty much been all about employment issues, seeing economic inequalities and dependencies as the main factors keeping women down, until Ti-Grace Atkinson and others made me realize how fundamental women's control over their own bodies also was to their liberation. And that wasn't until I began lobbying members of the New York Legislature in the state capital of Albany on these issues with Ti-Grace and listened to her arguments. Ti-Grace had been at that first NOW national board meeting I attended looking for lesbians, and she was a member of our NYC chapter. I greatly admired her, especially her ability to see and explain to the rest of us the power arrangements that underlay issues, ones that I and others often missed. This is what she did with women's reproductive rights.

It's not that these were new issues. Battles over reproductive rights had been raging in the United States from the early decades of the twentieth century when Emma Goldman and Margaret Sanger had led campaigns to educate poor, often immigrant women, about birth control and provide them with the supplies they needed. That didn't end well. Sanger was arrested and Goldman deported. It wasn't until 1965 that there finally seemed to be some progress. The Supreme Court issued the Griswold v. Connecticut decision that prohibited states from making birth control illegal for married couples. That was a good step, partial as it was, but Ti-Grace's concerns were not just with the laws. She wanted to change the argument from one about specific issues like birth control and abortion to a dispute over who had the right to control women's bodies: men and the government, as had been the case, or women themselves. Clearly, Ti-Grace's answer was that women, married or unmarried, had that right.

As Ti-Grace pointed out to us and the legislators, if women were tied down with children, and being tied down or trapped was the way we were beginning to talk about being mothers in those days, they would not be able to take advantage of economic or other opportunities even if they were available. It was all about power. Power over women's lives. That's what we wanted to take back, or rather, get for the first time.

Taking Charge

AT FIRST, I was happy to participate in discussions and events as a NOW chapter member. I could see we were making progress even in those first two years. Women's liberation was more and more in the news and starting to be a larger part of the national discussion about civil right and justice. We also had the want ad and other victories, including getting President Lyndon Johnson to issue an executive order prohibiting sex discrimination for federal contractors and requiring women be considered in affirmative action hiring.

But while National NOW was aggressive, I felt my chapter was often too afraid of what people might say about us so was hesitant about taking strong stands on its own. Not me. Once launched, I was eager to go. What I saw as the chapter's timidity was beginning to drive me nuts. Observing what worked and what didn't, I became convinced that if we were afraid to go out on a limb, we'd never get anywhere. The limb was where to be. I knew that to make this happen, I would have to step up into more of a leadership role, just as I had when I was a kid. So, at the end of 1967, I decided to run for chapter president for the two-year term that would start in early 1968.

There was another reason I decided to run for president then. At this point, our first president, Jeanne Faust, had resigned and Ti-Grace had taken her place as an interim president. That was fine. I really respected Ti-Grace, and not unexpectedly, had something of a secret crush on her. (My unrequited heart still belonged to Dolores.) We actually had become good friends and often met in the city after meetings for dinner or drinks to discuss the ins and outs of movement philosophy, her great strength, and strategy, mine. We even went away with each other for weekend R & Rs now and again. I would tell Eddie I was leaving for a few days and he, always compliant, would agree to take care of the kids. I liked to think Ti-Grace and I learned a lot from each other.

I could see that Ti-Grace might have been fine as president except that when she started to campaign, she was suggesting what I saw as some pretty radical, and harmful, ideas about how to organize and run our chapter. She suggested that instead of a president and officers, the chapter should have rotating leaders and all issues should be discussed by the group until consensus on a decision was reached. She believed that hierarchical structure was just another instance of a patriarchal model that was at the root of all oppressions. To get rid of oppression, then, the whole patriarchal hierarchical system had to be torn down, including having a chapter with any officers. Ti-Grace was not alone in thinking this.

By this time, a number of feminists, and members of other progressive radical groups, had begun arguing that all chains of command had to go and be replaced by consensus decision making and action. Now don't get me wrong. I agreed that the patriarchal system in which men dominated women was the main source of the subjugation of women, but I didn't think that all hierarchy had to go. In fact, I thought Ti-Grace's scheme was insane, and if instituted, would make the chapter much less effective. So, even though I didn't like the idea of running against Ti-Grace, after much inner turmoil, I decided I had to act in the best interests of the chapter.

I won the election but lost Ti-Grace's friendship. She was very hurt, and not just by me. She felt that she had given much of her life to the movement and she and her ideas had been rejected. To her, this was one indication that NOW was already too moderate and heading in the wrong direction. The woman I had originally seen as delicate and quiet at that first board meeting turned out to be a real revolutionary. She drifted away from both me and NOW. I couldn't follow her. While I agreed NOW had to be pushed in a more radical direction, I didn't see how her approach would be effective. I felt bad about what had happened with her but not about doing what I thought best for the movement.

President of NYC NOW

AS SOON AS I took office in 1968, I made some changes. The movement was growing and I wanted us not just to keep up, but also to lead. After all, we were in New York City, the most influential city in the country. We had been having two to three hours long general meetings once a month during which we were supposed to take care of all our chapter business and hold some kind of educational program. That was barely enough time to have a program never mind to strategize and organize. I changed that. Soon we were having meetings of one sort or another at least once a week, sometimes twice, to supplement our monthly general meetings. There were the usual internal business committees like public relations, finance, and membership that would meet once a month outside the general meetings. Then we set up a reproductive rights committee, an employment rights committee, a daycare committee, an images-of-women in advertising committee, an education committee, an ERA committee. You get the idea. (Note, there was no lesbian issues committee—not yet.)

One week we might have an educational program or entertainment, another week it was planning for a specific public demonstration or lobbying effort. We wrote letters, marched, picketed, raised money, and educated people. We worked on equal pay and equal credit, job training, policies to help women in poverty, and challenges to discrimination against women in employment, housing, and jury service. (The jury exclusion for women persisted until the 1975 Taylor v. Louisiana Supreme Court ruling prohibited it. For many of the other issues, work is still in progress.)

We marched for five days in front of the New York headquarters of Colgate-Palmolive to protest rules that prohibited women from lifting more than fifty pounds, keeping them out of higher paying jobs. We held public accommodation actions and sit-ins at restaurants, bars, and clubs that served only men. We even had monthly announcements for all of our programs and activities in the "Calendar of Activities Around Town" in the *New York Times*. The revolution was on. The times were inspiring, exhilarating, and exhausting. The sense of mission, the camaraderie, the discussions, the learning and teaching, the strategizing, and the leading—all were consuming.

And surprising to me, at least my part in it. While I knew that as a kid I was the one who stepped in and took charge, nothing before feminism prepared me to think that I might be good at this organizing business. I don't have the brilliant analytical mind that Ti-Grace and others had, but I discovered a talent for organizing. I would get a whole picture in my mind of what had to be done and where people had to go. I could almost literally see it all in my head. It was like getting all the pieces of a puzzle to fit together.

Interestingly, I could do this in my painting, too. In Miss Abel's art classes, and even at Pratt, while others often struggled to envision what they wanted to put on paper or canvas, I could see it whole in my mind and know the steps necessary to fulfill my vision. I didn't know that not everyone thought that way until Miss Abel commented on it.

My lettering teacher at Pratt, Mr. Herman, encouraged this in me and the other students so that I got pretty good at seeing what I wanted to create, and then putting the various artistic elements together to generate what my mind had envisioned. I can still hear him admonishing us time after time, "When you put your pen to paper, know where you want to go and go there. Make sure, too, to get out of your own way." What was effective in art turned out also to be very effective in politics.

Turns out, I was also a persuasive speaker. Who knew! I had never done anything like that before my involvement with NOW, but once I was engaged, whether I was talking one-on-one, to a couple of people, to the fifty to seventy folks who came to monthly NOW general meetings, or to the crowds that swelled to hundreds, even thousands at demonstrations and rallies, I could connect. Always speaking without notes, I seemed to be able to not only get people to listen, but also to get them to act.

Consciousness Raising

ALL OF THIS was great. NOW was growing and had a great cadre of activists, but as I observed and listened to the women who were involved in NOW or were thinking about getting involved with this new movement in some way, I knew there was a problem. Many women simply didn't believe in themselves and other women. Often, they didn't know who they were outside of the identity and status granted them based on the men they lived with and the children they had. Not a surprise. That's just the way it was. To create a real revolution and get more women involved, to get them to act on fantasies about a life broader than house, husband, and children, we had to change that. Women had to get past allegiance to the restricting roles that had been drilled into them all their lives, and past the lack of confidence that seemed to be bred by these roles.

I knew those attitudes had to change for the women's movement to be successful. Maybe, I thought, if we could get women to talk honestly and openly about themselves instead of being afraid of violating some rules about how they were supposed to behave, think, and talk, they would realize that often their problems and unhappiness were not so much rooted in themselves as in the structures of society. They would see their male dominated world as what it was, a patriarchal system of control. If women recognized the root of their oppression, I knew they could rid themselves of it and claim themselves. They could become strong and take command of their own lives. They would become feminists and activists. But changing laws would accomplish little if we didn't also change ourselves.

I got this idea of setting aside time for women to talk together honestly about their lives from the discussions within lesbian groups in New York City that I had begun hearing about. By this time, while I was staying firmly in the closet, a few lesbians and gay men had begun to organize and had made the Firehouse in Greenwich Village, an actual converted firehouse, their de facto headquarters. Some feminists who were lesbians had joined their ranks, affiliating themselves with gay men rather than deal with organizations like NOW that did not welcome them if they insisted on being out and speaking about lesbian issues. At that point, that was fine with most people in NOW, including me. These gay people were too far out there for us, too dangerous, too threatening to our image as a mainstream movement.

But I liked what I heard about their consciousness raising discussions. Evidently, they had been going on long enough for Kathie Sarachild from New York Radical Women to have presented *A Program for Feminist Consciousness Raising* at the First National Women's Liberation Conference near Chicago, Illinois in 1968. But I hadn't heard of her program or others. Word on the street was just that these women got together to talk as honestly as they could about their lives, not to debate about issues or strategies or complain about others. This seemed a pretty radical idea to me considering that many of these women, like me, had spent much of their lives ashamed of and closeted about their feelings about women on the one hand. On the other hand, they had been taught to distrust other women. From what I understood, these discussions left the participants feeling more self-assured, and that the trust they had established in their groups gave them more courage to be the activists they wanted to be, to change their lives and the lives of others for the better. We sure could use some of that empowerment in NOW and among women in general.

But I wanted something more than the freewheeling discussions I had heard about. I wanted women to find their own truths and power by recognizing the true nature of their oppression. If they didn't, they would never be able to combat the forces that kept them from living whole, fulfilling lives. I knew there were thousands of women waiting and wanting to be their own truer selves and to change the world. This transformation would be fundamental to the success of the movement. What I came to call feminist consciousness raising (CR) became one of the most effective tools to make that happen.

I got to work. I started with a few basic principles and guidelines. I decided on no more than twenty women sitting in a circle with each woman taking a turn talking. This way women who had been trained to be quiet would be able to speak up about themselves. There would be no cross talk until everyone had spoken, and even then, each person could only speak about herself. A women's experience was her own experience and it was not to be questioned or challenged. Meeting once a week for eight weeks with one topic a session seemed about right to cover the areas I believed were important to create aware activists. These included topics ranging from women's feelings about each other, their relationships with their children, husbands, and family, especially mothers, to body image, sex, money, and work. The only time I would come into the discussion was to make sure the women focused on their feelings and experiences, and that the discussion didn't devolve into a bitch session about men. My hope was that these women would see that it wasn't just individual men or themselves that needed to be changed. It was the entire system.

And it worked. Way better than I ever dreamed. Starting with New York City NOW's executive board as a trial group, I saw the move to insight at our very first meeting in the basement of a church on 33rd Street that often lent its space to progressive groups.

I started us off with something that was fundamental to the movement and the success of any CR group, "Do women like other women?" This was not about loving women—lesbianism was still pretty much forbidden as a topic in these early NOW groups—but do we like each other? As the women went around the circle speaking, each woman claimed, of course, to like other women, were best friends, etc. But then, about half way around, there was a change in the air. It was as though they suddenly understood that they weren't telling the whole truth.

Finally, one announced, "You know, I don't like many other women. They are the competition."

That was it—the breakthrough. It was like a flood of revelation.

"We don't like each other," some exclaimed, "because we have to compete with each other for men. Men give us our status, so we all go after the same high status men."

Questions came. "Why do we define ourselves by the men we are with? Who made those rules? Why do we fight each other?"

Then the answers. "This needs to stop. We are not each other's enemy. The system is messed up. It's a set up to turn women against each other just to please men."

Even these feminist members of NOW had come to a deeper understanding of the predicament of women. That was what we came to call the "ah ha!" moment, the instant that occurred time after time in a group when the members saw that the whole patriarchal system was rigged to keep them second class citizens. Once this first group got to that, I knew we were onto something powerful.

But before the juggernaut that CR became, one glitch had to be remedied. There couldn't be any men in a group. It's not that there were that many in NOW itself or who joined one of these early CR groups, but having even one man in the circle threw off the whole dynamic. The behavior of the women changed. Energy often focused on the man or men. In some cases, it was angry, with women lashing out, demanding, "Why do you do this to women?" or "Why are so many of you rapists?" Other women became silent, unwilling to talk about themselves in front of or to the men for whatever reason—shyness, not wanting to offend, fear. It didn't take too many meetings before women began to complain to me, "These groups are for and about women. Why are men allowed?"

Warren Farrell, a young member of NYC NOW who attended some of these early CR meetings was sensitive enough to see the problem and came up with a solution. He suggested to me that he take the men in the various groups to his apartment. "We'll meet the same night the women meet and we'll discuss the same topics. What do you think?" Sounded good to me. So the ten men or so who were in various groups started meeting at Warren's. Warren went on to set up hundreds of such groups, essentially founding the current men's movement. He later became the only man to be elected three times to the Board of Directors of NYC NOW, from 1971-74. There were indeed some good men.

AFTER THE BOARD group, I started offering CR to the NYC NOW membership. Soon, other NOW chapters from all over the state started to ask me to come and facilitate groups for them. It didn't take long then for CR groups based on my model to spring up all over the country. Other organizations, from newly created women's centers, professional women's organizations, houses of worship—anywhere women gathered together as women—began to sponsor groups.

One of the most interesting things about these groups was that without my prompting, the participants generally came to the same conclusions through a similar line of thinking.

Just as the topic of women's friendships turned out to enlightening, the money discussion was particularly revelatory. The married women often started by singing the praises of their generous husbands—"My husband lets me get my hair done once a week" or "He's so generous, he let me buy two dresses this week" or "He gives me a good allowance, even a little over household expenses so I can get something for myself." But as the session progressed, the women began to ask themselves, "Why are we so grateful? Why does he just dole out the funds like we are children? We do as much or more work than he does. Why aren't we seen as equal?" Then, "It's not just husbands or fathers. It's the whole system. I mean, why can't I have my own checking account or get my own credit card?" I liked to imagine how conversations at home might have gone after these meetings.

"Rape—the Tool of the Oppressor" turned out to be a powerfully transformative session also. In part, this was because too many women had personal experiences with rape, outside and inside of marriage, and many found themselves able to talk about their experiences for the first time in these groups. Almost invariably, they had blamed themselves for the assault whether they were ten years old or twenty-five or fifty-five, whether the rapist was a stranger, acquaintance, friend, relative, or husband. We had all internalized that it was the women's fault, and that meant that we had to be careful about how we dressed and behaved and not to go out alone after dark without a man to protect us.

Then would come the revelation. Who were these men protecting us from? Other men! Why wasn't anyone asking the men to change their behavior? And who made laws about sexual assault so that rape was almost impossible to prosecute when an eye witness was required and the shame and blame was almost always on the victim? Why, too, was it legal for a husband to rape his wife? Rape remained legal in marriage until 1993. Guess who made the laws? Guess who started to realize they didn't have to go along with this anymore?

But the issue of sexual violence was not the only aspect of sex that came up for discussion. Many women disclosed that they often felt that sex with their husbands or boyfriends was not very satisfactory. Sex was something expected of them, not something to be enjoyed. But that situation began to be questioned. Why weren't women having orgasms? What would help? What should their men be doing? What could they do?

The discussions of a woman's right to her own sexual pleasure became so wide spread that mimeographed pamphlets like "The Myth of Vaginal Orgasm" by Anne Koedt began to emerge and circulate in 1968. Women were being told that they deserved to have sexual pleasure, too. The point was to change women's attitudes toward their bodies by giving them more information about how they worked. With the help of CR and other sexual pioneers, women, as Ti-Grace had put it, began to take control of their own bodies, learn about their own sexual pleasure, and refuse to take the blame for being harassed or abused.

An interesting side effect was that the frustrations women admitted about sexual relations with men later led a number of women to experiment with lesbian sex. But not then. That had to wait a while. For the most part, up through the early seventies, heterosexuality could be dissected, but discussion of lesbianism wasn't even considered, nor were admissions of any same sex desires outside of the few groups exclusively for lesbians who were brave enough to come out. For most women, some truths were just too hard to disclose, too shameful and too scary even in these truth telling CR groups. I understood that. Openness would come later.

OF COURSE, NOT all of this happened in all groups, and for many it took weeks or even months of meetings for trust to develop, truths and secrets to be revealed, and understanding to be achieved. In many cases, women continued to meet as a CR group after the initial eight meetings, sometimes for years, continuing their own discussions but still using the guidelines I established. But whatever the case, early on or months later, at these meetings, women struggled to figure out the differences between how they were supposed to live and the way they wanted to live. In the process, when it worked the way it was supposed to, they learned to trust their own experiences, feelings, judgment, and strength. They discovered themselves. Once that happened, there was no going back to old ways of thinking. The genie couldn't be put it back in the bottle.

Many of these women came to see that to be the free and independent people they deserved to be, they would have to change not just themselves but the world. With other women. Sisterhood was powerful. That was how CR became fundamental to the growth and direction of the feminist movement. It was a first, necessary step toward empowerment and a rejection of the status quo. CR was obviously an idea whose time had come. By 1973, at the height of CR, over a hundred thousand women in the United States belonged to a CR group.

Coming Out

NOT SURPRISINGLY, AS my activist world consumed me, the situation at home was deteriorating. As you can imagine, between NOW and my job at *Newsday*, I was rarely at home. That meant mentally as well as physically. All of my emotional energy was going either to the women's movement or to Dolores, an easy overlap since Dolores was easily as deeply involved in NOW as I was, perhaps even more. Even on the days I made it back to Long Island from the city after a meeting or an action, I often wouldn't go right home. Instead, I'd stop by the night owl Esther's. We would have strudel and coffee at one o'clock in the morning before I could get myself to go home. Other times, instead of going home after work, I would drive with Dolores straight from *Newsday* in Garden City to a NOW meeting in the New York and stay over at her place. I'd even drive myself into New York now and again when there were no NOW obligations or activities so I could spend time with Dolores.

As 1968 progressed, I found myself staying in New York City three, maybe four, up to five times a week. I persuaded myself that Eddie didn't need me, and either he could take care of the kids or they were old enough to take care of themselves. I told myself that they would be asleep when I got home anyway. Eddie grumbled now and then, but never really complained. He wasn't someone who liked confrontation. That worked for me. I didn't want to confront him or my situation either.

Part of this was because I was reaching a crisis point around my sexual desires. The kind of unrequited love I had for Dolores and others was getting me down. When I visited Dolores in the city and we went to dinner or to her place to talk and drink our J & B scotch on the rocks in her tiny living room, I would be filled with desire. When it was my turn to pick up the liquor, I'd think, "Maybe if I get her drunk enough . . ." but nothing ever happened. I wanted to touch her but I couldn't, both because I wasn't out and I still thought she was straight. Or I was just scared. Whatever it was, I couldn't make a move. She'd be lounging on the couch and I'd be in the chair, too far away. I was always too far away. Even when we were in the same bed.

Dolores's $72 a month apartment in Greenwich Village wasn't any bigger than my living room and it had only one bed, a double. So, on those nights I stayed over, we slept together, which meant I really didn't sleep much. It was a kind of exquisite torture for me. My heart would pound and my body tense in my efforts not to touch her. OK. OK. I cheated when I could. If I was sure she was asleep, I would slowly, slowly move my foot over to lightly touch hers, just a little. Not enough to wake her. It was pathetic. And it left me exhausted. The next morning, I'd get up early, go home, get the kids ready for school, and pull myself together before I left for work again to start my eleven a.m. to six p.m. shift.

Not only was this suppression of my desire frustrating, it was getting mortifying. The feminism I was teaching other women demanded they come to an understanding of the oppressive forces in their lives to find their own true selves and develop the courage to combat them so that they could reach their full potential. Why wasn't I doing this? In 1968, emboldened by this rhetoric, more women had been coming out, but I hadn't. I always had an excuse for myself, mainly that I could lose my husband, my kids, my job, my status in the movement. Besides, I was afraid of losing my reputation as a good person in society in general. The problem was that by letting the fear of those losses prevent me from coming out, I was risking losing my own self-respect, never mind my mental health. I really, really wanted to get to the other side and be out, but I was paralyzed. I needed help, but I didn't want to go to someone in the movement. Somehow revealing my awkwardness around the lesbian issue would be too embarrassing. And threatening. I knew Friedan and many others believed having lesbians associated with NOW would destroy the organization as well as the movement. They would not be pleased.

Then I thought of my old basketball buddies, Dor, Sharpie, and Joan, those "sports friends" who that first therapist had advised me to give up when I got married. By this time, I had realized that the "difference" I saw in how Dor and some of the others acted with each other was that they were lesbians. Luckily for me, while I had limited my contact, I hadn't cut them off completely. Since my marriage in 1952, once every few years, I'd call Dor and we'd get caught up on ourselves and friends. Then I wouldn't speak to her again for another year or two. But somehow, in my current situation, I felt I could trust her discretion and understanding. So, I called her. We chit-chatted for a while. "Ah, Joan's sorta drifted off somewhere, haven't seen her in months, but she'll be back" or "Sharpie's very depressed."

Then, maybe somehow sensing that I wanted to do more than catch up, Dor broke our pattern and asked, "Why don't you come over for a drink?"

I didn't hesitate. "OK," I replied.

I got in my car and drove to her place which was only two towns away. I soon found myself in her living room, me on a chair and her across the room on the couch. The story of my life at that time. I was always across the room—safe.

We were making small talk until finally she asked, "Why are you really here?"

I replied, a little hesitant and embarrassed but also determined, "I want you to take me to a gay bar."

She smiled. "God, we thought you'd never get there."

Ooh. I was furious for a moment. I thought, "Why didn't you say something before?" But she was smiling at me, and I had to smile back. I knew it hadn't been her fault.

Together we drove to Jan's, a gay bar in Locust Valley, a wealthy community on the north shore of Long Island, an area I didn't know well since most of my life I had lived on the poorer south shore. Not that the closeted me would have known about the bar anyway. When we got there, there were a number of young men hovering over each other at the near end of the smoke-filled bar, mostly slender and white, but my eyes slid over them to focus on the women who were crowding the rest of the bar, tables, and dance floor. Oh my God! There they were, lesbians. I was instantly overwhelmed. Even though not everyone looked like me in my plain skirt and sweater, there was a feel to the place, to the energy between the strong faced, good looking women with short haircuts and male style shirts, slacks, and shoes and the highly made up women dressed in tight, shimmering low cut dresses and high heels that I recognized. I was home. Finally, at forty-two, I had found a place where I saw others like me and could be myself.

Dor walked me to end of bar and found two seats that looked out onto dance floor. We sat, drank, talked, and watched women dance, me observing it all with a combination of incredible relief, anticipation, and sexual thrill. I was particularly entranced by one blonde woman who was a great dancer. I couldn't keep my eyes off of her, but I couldn't approach her either. Or anyone else. I was too shy, too unsure of myself in that setting. Still, I was in paradise.

After a few hours of my being quietly blissed out, we went back to Dor's to decompress and have another drink. I was exhausted but elated.

She asked, "Have you ever had sex with a woman?"

Nervously, I replied, "No."

She said, "Come on."

She took me into her bedroom and initiated me. I felt a little hesitant at the beginning, but then I realized that in many ways the mechanics were not all that different from when I had sex with my husband. I knew what I wanted done and what to do, and to do it with a woman seemed totally natural. That part was amazing. I would love to say the sex itself was great, but really more it was fine. I mean, I knew there would be no romance with Dor. I knew I was not in love with her, and she was not in love with me. It was an initiation and nothing more. For that I was grateful.

The next night, a Sunday, I returned to Jan's alone. I couldn't stay away. I was intoxicated by a sense of freedom and possibility I had never before experienced. I also very much hoped that the blonde dancer who had caught my eye the previous night would be there again, and that I could get up the courage to ask her to dance. I sat at the bar nursing my drink until I spied her among the women weaving on the dance floor. She was small, my height, about five feet tall, with just the right amount of flesh on her bones. She was hard to miss, though, because she had a habit of shaking her head when she danced so that her long, bleached blonde hair went around and around, playing peekaboo with her very fair white skin, blue eyes and straight, pointed nose. Gorgeous, I thought. I kept watching her. That I considered myself a pretty good dancer helped me finally get up the courage to ask her to dance. She told me her name was Nancy and warned me that she already had a girlfriend, Martha, who was there but didn't like to dance. Fine. I didn't care. Off we went. We danced for what seemed like hours. I was ecstatic and in love, not just with Nancy and even Martha, but with the whole scene. I was at a lesbian bar dancing with an out lesbian! Wow!

After that evening, as was the way in those days, Martha and Nancy took me under their wing to show me the ropes. On nights when I didn't have NOW obligations, I would leave Eddie and the kids at home and go with them, eventually visiting the eight or so lesbian bars on Long Island that they knew about, being introduced to a world in which lesbians were not hiding and being tortured about who they were, or, if they were tortured sometimes, at least they were also having fun, romance, and all the typical dramas of dating and relationships.

It was the flip side of Radclyffe Hall's 1928 novel *The Well of Loneliness*, a book I had picked up on a weekend trip to Montauk, a resort town on the eastern end of Long Island, I had taken with Ti-Grace in 1967 when we were still friends. On the way, we had stopped at a small store to pick up snacks. Even though I was not out and didn't want Ti-Grace to know I had had lesbian crushes, I couldn't resist buying the paperback once I spied it in the book rack. After all, how could I resist a book with a cover that featured one woman with short hair and one with long, looking yearningly but unhappily at each other. I had never seen anything like it.

I started it immediately and immediately knew I also had never read a book like this before. I didn't know it at the time, but this novel was notorious in many lesbian circles. After having been banned in England upon its publication, it was allowed distribution by its U.S. publisher in the United States when an American court declared it not obscene. The book had provided many closeted women a literary introduction to the joys and horrors of forbidden and unnatural lesbian love, just as it was doing for me as I read it. While I was not as tortured or as masculine as the butch hero Stephen was, nor a femme like Mary, the woman she loved, I recognized myself and some of the other women I had known. I suddenly understood, with great relief, that there were whole little societies and communities of women like me. And here in these Long Island bars, I had found them. I was not alone and I was not crazy. Those excursions with Nancy and Martha were exhilarating and freeing.

Still, even with all this new, exciting world opened to me, I was not ready to leave my husband, kids, and home. The result: I began to feel even more trapped than I had before. How could I choose between my respectable family life and the movement and being a lesbian? I was stuck. My solution was to try to keep my NOW and lesbian activities separate from my domestic life. But that didn't always work. One particularly confusing cross over came in that volatile 1968.

Dolores had been at the 1968 Democratic convention as a reporter and had come from the airport to sleep at our house so she could get to work more easily the next day. Eddie and I had closed the art gallery that had been attached to the house and turned the gallery space into a lovely large bedroom. Dolores started using that room now and again when she and I had no NOW meetings or obligations in NYC and she didn't want to bother to drive back to the city only to have to return to Long Island for work in the morning. I thought of it as her room. I even bought a metal military locker and painted an abstract design in bright colors on it so she could have a place to leave some of her things. Of course, I was elated to have her there. Whenever she stayed over, I would abandon Eddie and the kids, and she and I would lounge on her single bed, the only place in the room to sit. We'd break out a bottle of J & B scotch and talk for hours into the night. I was still very much in love with her, but I didn't expect anything to go further than our half drunken conversations.

That night after the convention, I was down in her room visiting her, both of us sitting close together on the bed as usual, drinking as usual. She was in her slip. I was fully dressed. After a while, there was a pause in the conversation. She leaned a little closer to me, looked me straight in the eyes, and asked me if I had ever slept with a woman. I was totally taken aback, but then more than a little aroused. Where was she going with this? Maybe, maybe, we would we finally do something?

I managed a "No" even though I had had that one experience with Dor. That didn't count for me. It was just sex, not love.

Dolores mildly replied, "OK, you can have sex with me, but no kissing."

I was so stunned both by the proposition itself and the prohibition on kissing that I fell off the bed.

Just at that moment, Eddie knocked on the door and asked, "Are you coming to bed?"

He never opened the door. I knew I couldn't stay. I breathed out a yes for him, not sure if I was more relieved or disappointed. I pulled myself off the floor and left.

Dolores and I never talked about that night. Nor did Eddie talk about what he might have heard outside the door. In fact, Eddie never said a thing about all the time I spent with Dolores or with NOW or even out of the house when I was running around with Nancy and Martha, just going to clubs, I had told him. Instead, it seemed to me he purposely turned away. He didn't want to know, so he didn't. Sometimes I wished he would say something so that we could talk, even if there was an explosion. Maybe that way we could reduce some of the tension in our relationship, but for months he never brought anything up. Neither did I.

IT IS PROBABLY no surprise that during this time of emotional confusion, I was having panic attacks, especially driving over bridges or through tunnels between New York City and Long Island. Pretty symbolic of the passage from one of my worlds to the other I see now but certainly didn't then. Sometimes, just before entering the Midtown Tunnel to get to the city, I would have to stop my car at the pull-off just after the toll booths until I could catch my breath and let my heart stop pounding. I sat there many long minutes. I even had to pull over one time when Lisa was with me. I wouldn't even think of driving over the Queensboro Bridge because there was no place for me to pull over if I had an attack. The funny thing was I loved to drive and appreciated cars. I had even traded in the Volkswagen bug that Eddie had given me for my birthday in 1967 for a red Karmann Ghia sports car that I spied when I took the VW in the next year for muffler repairs. I guess that trade should have been a hint to me about which direction I wanted to go, but I was still too scared to make the leap.

IN A WAY, Eddie made the leap before I did. A few months after the Dolores incident, Eddie reacted. Nancy drove him to it. Two or three months after I had started hanging out with Nancy and Martha, they broke up. Their breakup had

had nothing to do with me. Honest. I had feelings for Nancy, but I hadn't let on about them, something I was pretty good at after so many years of practice. But after Martha was out of the picture, I kept hanging around with Nancy even though I wasn't sure what I wanted or expected from her. I was still pretty shy in the lesbian world. Then one night, Nancy and I and a bunch of others went out to a party which included a lot of drinking, very common in those days. Unfortunately, when the drunk Nancy started to drive the also drunk me home, it was snowing. She skidded on the snow and hit a tree, boom. Luckily, we weren't going very fast, so the only injury was me having a badly banged up leg from having smashed it under the car's dashboard. The car, on the other hand, was not drivable.

We called a tow truck, and without thinking, I asked the driver to take us to my place rather than Nancy's, which was closer. Nancy came into the house with her arm around me, helping me because of my damaged leg. That I was injured didn't matter to Eddie. I guess something broke in him. As soon as he saw us, he turned, went to our bedroom, got his pillow, and left me, Nancy, and the children at the house and drove over to his mother's place. I admit I was a little ashamed at the situation I had put him in, and a little guilty, but mostly I was relieved that he was gone, the kids were asleep, and I was there with Nancy.

Nancy and I went up to my bedroom and we made love. I count this as my first real lesbian sexual experience because it was the first time I had sex with a woman I was in love with. This time as before, I knew exactly what to do, but it was not like being with my husband, or with Dor. This time it was tremendously arousing and filled with passion. Afterward, as I was lying gratified and fully satisfied next to Nancy in bed, I kept thinking to myself, "Here I am. I finally made it." My relief was incredible. I felt like I had been running a long race and had finally gotten to the finish line victorious. It was a wonderful feeling.

Nancy stayed. I had been told by my doctor to keep my leg elevated for four to six weeks so that the hematoma on my injured leg could heal. That meant I didn't go to work and ended up lying around most of the day, waiting for Nancy to come home from work and take care of me. By this time, the kids were old enough to take care of themselves, so I left them on their own and they left me to Nancy. She did a good job of looking after me. In all sorts of ways. Let me tell you, you can still make love even with an elevated leg. It was a great interlude.

But as so much in those days, there was no pure happiness. I was deeply sorry that my marriage was turning out the way it was. I hadn't wanted to hurt Eddie, but here I was doing just that. More confusing, I wasn't even sure how

I felt about him. An incident that took place one evening shortly after Nancy moved in and Eddie moved out reveals just how crazy I could get. That night I got a call from Lisa who was staying with Eddie and her grandparents for the weekend.

"Mom," she began, sounding disturbed, "Daddy has gone out to visit Gerri."

Gerri and Ken, our old friends from Fort Salonga, had been divorced for years, but I had no idea Eddie had stayed friendly with either of them. I don't know why, but once Lisa told me about this rendezvous between Eddie and Gerri, I was filled with a jealous fury. Where did all that emotion come from? I had no idea.

I immediately rushed out of the house, abandoning Nancy with no explanation except an "I'll be back."

In a rage, dragging my injured leg, I drove the fifty minutes to Fort Salonga. I parked in the woods next to Gerri's driveway and waited for Eddie and Gerri to return from their date or whatever, growing even more agitated as the minutes passed. After about a half an hour, they drove up in her car. He walked her to her door. I couldn't see exactly what happened there. It didn't matter.

Once he started back to his car, I called out to him from the dark, "Get in my car."

"How dare you come here! We're separated," he hissed back.

Still, he got in and we argued for about thirty minutes, me whiningly complaining about him going out, him responding that I had no right to say anything about his life outside of the kids. Finally, I let him go and I drove back to Nancy, still upset, telling myself I must be crazy.

Separation

AFTER A MONTH with me, Nancy started to see Martha again. I was heartbroken. This was not something I could tolerate. Eddie would never betray me like that, I thought, knowing at that point that his rendezvous with Gerri had been basically innocent. I was ashamed of the way I had treated him. I made Nancy leave and called Eddie and asked him to come home. He didn't hesitate, and we never spoke of our short separation again. I thought that we could go back to where we were before and I could maintain my marriage. Ha ha.

For one thing, after about a month, Nancy and Martha broke up again. Nancy called and without apology or anything, as though nothing had happened, asked if I wanted to go dancing. I should have known better than to say yes, but my infatuation with Nancy, and my love for dancing, got the better of me. I thought that if dance together was all we did, I would be safe. So I said yes, and boom, Nancy was back in my life as a lover. She didn't move back into my house, but we would escape for romantic weekends at small resorts within driving distance where no one was likely to recognize us. I would tell Eddie I was going away with a friend and he would accept that. I guess he was in as much, or more, denial about the state of our marriage than I was.

While these weekends were fun and exciting and the sex and dancing were good, this liaison with Nancy wasn't really working. I wasn't totally into it, in part because I was always worried that she would go to back to Martha, but mostly because I didn't want to hurt Eddie or my kids. I knew I was emotionally not in my marriage anymore, but I couldn't leave. I also couldn't stay. I was caught between two lives.

Part of me was thrilled with being a lesbian and part of me was terribly guilty and ashamed. It was not so easy in those days, and probably for many now, to just say to yourself, "I'm a lesbian or gay. Oh, OK" and go with it. Before I could make the break with my old life and fully embrace being a lesbian, I had to get over a lifetime of comments and asides in conversations, movies, TV shows, and books about how unnatural, unattractive, and immoral lesbians were. I also had to deal with the damaging lesbian baiting that surrounded the women's movement from the outside and the discomfort among some straight women and lesbians about out lesbians in the movement from the inside. And I had to get over the fear of what would happen to me and my kids if I came out to everyone, to come to terms with the knowledge that I could lose Lisa and Laura and everyone else I loved. It got to be truly horrible. I was dying inside.

ALL THIS CAME to a crisis very early one morning in late October in 1968. I had stayed overnight in New York for a NOW event and was coming back on the Long Island Railroad to check in at home and then go to work. It was snowing, really a blizzard, and I was beside myself. It was like I was going to explode, just go pakooey. I felt trapped, unable to make a decision. I couldn't go home to Eddie and couldn't go see Nancy. I was so jittery that I couldn't even stay on the train, so I got off early at Garden City. I picked up the pay phone at the station and called the therapist I had seen after the miscarriage. The physical and emotional pain of that pregnancy and all the unresolved conflicts in my life had kept me going to him for about two years. It obviously hadn't helped. When I had tried to talk to him about my love for women, all he did was to try to keep me in my marriage.

When I called from the train station, he picked up the phone. I remember thinking, "Doesn't he have any clients? Is he sitting there, waiting for a phone call?" Therapists pretty much never pick up the phone. Even then I thought it was a funny thing to have flit through my mind as miserable as I was. I'm not sure what I even expected when I dialed his number.

He simply said, "Hello."

I said, "It's Ivy Bottini, and I can't go home anymore."

He replied, "I'm sorry, I'm in session," and he hung up. That was the end of that relationship.

The snow was coming down hard. It was cold, and I was on an empty platform. I stood there for a few seconds before I screamed, "Fuck you!" I picked up the phone again and called Esther. I knew I would be safe with her. The love I had for her was different than the love I had for Dolores, Nancy, and others. Besides, I knew I could trust her. Absolutely. No matter what I told her about myself.

When she picked up the phone, I said, "Esther, I just got off the train, and I can't go home anymore."

She replied with hesitation or comment, "Well, come here." So I took a cab to her house. The only thing she asked when I got there was, "How long do you think you want to stay?"

I answered, "I honestly don't know."

"That's fine. Use the bedroom upstairs. It's yours. Go and come as you want. You've got a key." She never asked me another question. Not one. She just accepted me.

I was at Esther's for a day—it might have been two days—when I called Eddie. When he picked up, I simply said, "Hi, it's me. I'm at Esther's."

I guessed that Ben, Esther's husband, had called Eddie earlier because Eddie didn't seem surprised. He didn't ask why or when I was coming back. He just said, "Yeah."

I continued, "I can't come home anymore. I just can't."

He asked, "You mean ever?"

I replied, "Ever" and hung up. I'm ninety-eight to ninety-nine percent sure that he had known for years that I was a lesbian, but he never asked directly. He would ask me if I was in love with various women, but I don't think he really knew, or admitted the possibility of a sexual attraction to himself until the night I ended up bringing Nancy to our house. I don't know what he thought this time since I was at Esther's, but I'm pretty sure he knew our marriage was over.

I stayed with Esther for two weeks. I was too low to be very good company. I couldn't even talk to her about what was going on with me. I just couldn't come out to her. So I didn't volunteer any information, and she didn't ask any questions. She just was there, patient and considerate, sitting with me when I needed it, leaving me alone when that was required. I managed to keep going to work and take care of the most pressing NOW obligations, but otherwise I pretty much kept to myself. Finally, I called Eddie and told him I wanted to go home and be with the kids. I missed them terribly. I asked him to leave the house. Always one to avoid confrontation, never fighting me then or ever, Eddie said OK and moved into his mother's house. He stayed for the next ten years as the world changed around him. I moved back into our house.

I had and still have lots of guilt around Eddie. The pain I had in my stomach for months thinking about him after our split only gradually went away. I know I hurt him very, very deeply. I very much regretted this. He didn't deserve what happened. The break up wasn't his fault. He was a nice guy, and we had some very good years during our sixteen together, but we also had been miserable too much of the time. I certainly had been. In the end, I had to leave. I couldn't continue repressing my love and desire for women. The only way I could save my own life was by accepting who I had always been.

That doesn't mean I didn't fall back. It was not easy to just plunge into homosexuality, even once I had had a taste of it. After Eddie and I split up, I got a little close to one guy I knew from work, Warren. He was a very funny, nice guy who was one of the group of folks who would go out drinking when we were waiting for our turn to design the pages. One night at the bar he asked me to dance. That began an innocent flirtation that lasted about a month. I guess maybe I just wanted to see if I could still attract men before I gave them up. Maybe I was trying to test myself to see if I might like another guy. I don't know. As I said, it was a confusing time. For us all.

Eddie, Laura, Lisa, and I all went into therapy. Eddie and I went to the same psychologist but separately. We did that for a few months. We were trying hard to be cordial with each other for the kids. Eddie and I even had dinner a few times the year after we split up, and then no more. The girls had a child psychologist who they said was really stupid. I'm sure the whole situation was difficult for both of them, but neither ever overtly expressed anger toward me specifically over the breakup, or later when they knew I was a lesbian. It seemed that at least for Laura that part wasn't a surprise.

According to Lisa, shortly after the split, she asked Laura, "Why are mommy and daddy getting divorced?"

Laura, who was fifteen, replied, "Lisa, you're so dumb. Mommy's a lesbian."

Lisa, at thirteen, didn't know what lesbian meant, so Laura explained simply, "Mommy loves women."

Maybe the split itself was expected by them, too. In many ways, I hadn't been emotionally present even when I was around. And they probably had already gotten the idea that I did what I wanted to do. Whatever it was they were feeling, they kept it inside.

I KEPT THE kids with me. I had it figured out. Laura was old enough to be in the house by herself, so she could take care of Lisa when I had to go to work. Then I would either be home for dinner with them or leave something prepared. Again, if I had to go out in the evening, Laura could be in charge. Unfortunately, that only worked for a short time. A few months after the separation, Laura, who had always been very headstrong, became moody, defiant, and reckless. I don't know how much of her behavior was rooted in my splitting from Eddie or in her age—probably both. I was having a hard time dealing with her. Then came the incident with her friend Sharon, a girl I didn't trust.

One evening when Laura and Sharon were supposed to go out together, Sharon hadn't shown up, so Laura went on ahead. When Sharon later arrived looking for Laura and slid her gaze from mine and rushed off after I told her that Laura had already left for wherever they were going, I became suspicious. I followed her to a house a few blocks away. As Sharon got out of her car, I jumped out of mine and ran toward the house I sensed she was heading for. I got there first, knocked, and, without waiting, pushed open the door to see my fifteen year old daughter sitting in a bare bones living room with four men, all who looked to be in their mid-twenties, all in business suits. Their attire didn't reassure me. All I could think was that four adult men sitting in a room with my teenage daughter couldn't be good. They all stared at me, including Laura, the girls holding their breath. No one said a word. I moved to the middle of the room, pulled myself up to my full five-feet, and glared at the men.

I turned to Laura and said, "You, get out. Go get in my car."

She left quietly.

I stood there for a moment more before I snarled, "If I ever see you with my daughter again, i will . . . kill . . . you." Then I turned and left and thought, "Oh, God."

I realized at that point that I couldn't control or trust my daughter. I was upset by the level of trouble she could have gotten into, but I was more terrified of a future I could see in which she could get herself into more dangerous and damaging situations. With my job and all the other things on my plate, I couldn't be around to watch over and protect her. I was flooded with anxiety about her. I know it was not entirely rational, but I couldn't handle it. I drove Laura to her dad in Lynbrook. By then, it was around nine o'clock at night.

When Eddie answered the door, I blurted out, "Eddie, here's your daughter; you're in charge of her now. I can't trust her. And I can't watch her all the time. I have to go to work. Between you, your mother, and your father, you can keep a better eye on her."

"OK."

Laura walked by me into the house without a backward glance. I hated feeling like a failure as a mother, but I couldn't figure out anything else to do in that situation. It was a horrible, painful day.

Transition — NYC

ONE DAY LATE in November in 1968, shortly after Laura went to live with Eddie, Dolores called and told me that an apartment in her building was available. That year, Dolores had left her position as a reporter and editor at *Newsday* to become National NOW's first full-time executive director. She had moved into a wonderful two-story apartment uptown on West 93rd street. The building was one of a group of seven attached brownstones, each building a little different from the others. I knew a women architect had designed them, which gave it a special appeal. It also helped that the other apartments were occupied by a collection of artists and young professionals. But most attractive, the rent was a manageable $350 a month and it would put me closer to the center of the feminist action. So, without actually seeing that particular apartment, I took it. I was right to have jumped at it. The place was gorgeous, and large: three bedrooms on the fourth floor, and a gourmet kitchen, balcony, even a dark room on the fifth floor.

Unfortunately, though, I lost Lisa to Long Island and her father. She didn't want to move with me to Manhattan. I think that this was the right decision for Lisa. All her friends were on Long Island and she was a country kid. She loved the woods that area of Long Island could still offer. But the almost sixteen year old Laura was very eager for big city experiences. Even with our disagreements, she wanted to move to Manhattan with me. With her promises of good behavior, I pushed down my fears about her and conceded.

The situation was never great. I was so caught up in the movement at that point that, between that and work, I rarely was home until late. Some evenings Laura and I would have time to talk, but most of the time she would be asleep. In the morning, I'd only see her for a short time before she'd have to go to school. Still, even without much supervision, she stayed out of trouble. She knew that if she didn't, she'd go right back to back to Long Island and her grandparents' house. I didn't like that I had so little time with her, but that's how it was.

Or rather, that's how I made it. Without me being conscious of it, the pattern that came to haunt all my personal relationships had already been set. Given a choice between time and energy committed to the movement or to a relationship, I chose the movement. For me, when the kids were teenagers and second wave feminism was in first flower, there was no question. I gave my time and energy to the movement first. We were freeing women and transforming the world. I sincerely believed that, and I still do. It's just that my dedication to this vision took an emotional toll I hadn't reckoned with.

As it turned out, Laura made the decision to move back to Long Island herself. After six months or so in New York, she informed me, "You know, Mom, I'm not learning anything in school because the kids won't shut up. They're always interrupting the teacher. I think I'm going to move back to Long Island."

I knew she had liked the insolence of these students when we first arrived, attracted to what she saw as their independence. She had told me as much. So I was impressed that at her age she was mature enough to decide that education was more important to her than rebellion. I also was relieved that she wasn't moving away because of an issue between us.

I had been calling Lisa regularly at her dad and grandparents' place once I moved to Manhattan and continued my calls when Laura moved back. But keeping in touch wasn't easy. If my mother-in-law answered and I asked to speak to one of the kids, she would put down the phone—not even hang it up— and never come back. The weekends during the first months of our separation worked better. When possible, I would clear my schedule of meetings and demonstrations, pick them up and bring them back to the city to hang out. No movement stuff with them on those occasions. Movies, dinners, the Village. If I was going to be with them, I was going to be with them. Still, much as I missed them, I would be lying if I didn't admit that not having either of my children living with me was freeing. I wasn't constantly worried about them or feeling guilty about not running home to be with one or both of them. And I was much more able to take advantage of this new world of women and revolution I found myself in. The world was my oyster.

California Vacation – NOW Logo

IN THE MEANTIME, though, things were not going well with Dolores. The problem was not between us. It was her job. She accepted that her salary would drop significantly when she took the position of executive director of NOW in 1968, but she didn't expect that this job would require a hundred percent plus of her time and total devotion. But that's what happened. NOW pretty much immediately became the leading feminist organization in the rapidly growing women's liberation movement and Dolores gave it her all. She did everything, establishing NOW national headquarters in NYC, serving as an editor of NOW's national newsletter, *NOW Acts*, and directing membership drives all over the country.

She was so dedicated, she would pay the $5 dues out of her own pocket for women who wanted to but couldn't afford to become members. Even when she was able to hire a small staff, she was overwhelmed with work. To make things worse, Betty Friedan, the national leader of NOW for whom Dolores essentially worked, was often nasty, yelling at anyone she felt she had any power over, especially Dolores. By the end of the first year or so of NOW, she was physically ill and close to a nervous breakdown. She had an almost total collapse at the time of the 1969 NOW national board meeting, barely able to answer questions or leave her hotel room and get down to meetings. I kept telling her she needed to quit her job. She wouldn't listen. So I begged the NOW board to fire her because she was so emotionally sick from all the work and the unpleasant working situation. They didn't.

By the summer of 1969, I knew Dolores had to get away. It wasn't a bad idea for me either. My marriage had broken up, and I was exhausted from the lesbian life I had begun to live. With no children with me anymore, I had felt free to roam this new world that had just been opened to me. I found lesbians at bars, women only parties, through friends, and among more and more out women at events and meetings. I became a real Dona Juana, more androgynous than butch but the initiator of the action nonetheless. When I was on the prowl, which was often, I would approach a woman I thought was attractive and knew to be a lesbian (I wasn't into seducing straight women), flirt for a while, and end up suggesting we go over to her place or mine. I must have had something because over and over again I went or they came. Oh my God, I had so many one-night stands. It was really pretty horrible of me, but fun, and exhausting.

And there was still Nancy. She was really getting on my nerves. Through all my fooling around, she was still in my life. That might give you an indication of how crazy it all was. She insisted on coming over to my place a couple of times a week. I had given her a key during one of our happier times, and she sometimes just let herself in and waited for me if I wasn't there. As you might imagine, this really cramped my style. Besides, I hated that I was supposed to be somewhere or with someone when I didn't want to be. I didn't like the situation, and neither did she.

So, the idea of a break from my frenetic love life, Nancy, and my obligations as president of NYC NOW, as well as a chance to help save Dolores, was appealing. Neither of us had much money, but we had met two women from Los Angeles at the 1969 NOW national board meeting, Toni Carabillo and Judy Meuli, who had invited us to stay with them in their Santa Monica house anytime. All we would have to pay for was the plane fare. So in August of 1969 Dolores and I headed for two weeks of sun and surf in southern California. This was to prove a very significant trip. For one thing, it was during that trip that I designed the well-known NOW logo.

The idea for a logo was suggested to me by Aileen Hernandez, then one of national NOW's vice-presidents. One evening when I was hanging around by myself in the small design studio Toni, another graphic artist, had attached to their house, I got a call from Aileen asking about some NOW issues. After we had taken care of business, we continued to chat.

"What are you doing?" she asked.

"I'm sitting here at Toni's drawing board just doodling."

"You know, NOW could use a logo," she replied. "Why don't you design one?"

Great idea, I thought.

We hung up and I hunkered down. I wanted a clear, strong image that matched the straightforwardness of the organization's acronym and conveyed female power and unity. After two days of drafting, I came up with the circle, a long time symbol of women, enclosing the name of the organization. Aileen loved it and the board adopted it. The popularity of that image led me to other political designs as the movement progressed and other organizations splintered off. Among them was the logo for the National Women's Political Caucus which I designed in 1971. The success of the NOW logo also inspired me to start designing t-shirts for the movement, something I ended up doing for many years. One of the earliest images that I put front and center on brightly colored t-shirts was the women power symbol of a raised fist contained in a women's symbol. It was very inspirational.

The other significant thing about that trip was that I got to know LA and its women's community better. I didn't know then how important that would be to me, but all in all you could say that that break in LA was very fruitful. I rested. Dolores rested. And we were both ready to go back to the war.

Coming Out Wars

I SHOULD MAKE it clear that while I was playing around with other women and still with Nancy, in early 1969 I wasn't totally out. I was out within the lesbian community but not to the world. Not even in the movement. This was not unusual. Many people, then and now, came out to other lesbians but were not out anywhere else in their lives. If I had a fling with another NOW activist, we kept it quiet. NOW was definitely not welcoming to such affairs, and I was devoted to NOW. I didn't want to lose my place in it. But just as I had to get up my courage to risk my family and reputation and leave my marriage, I knew it was only a matter of time before my conscience wouldn't allow me to stay quiet in NOW. And the time was coming fast. There were a lot of cracks developing in the solidarity of the crusade for equal rights for women. One of the widest at that time for NOW had to do with the increasing number of women who were coming out as lesbians, or, in the process of rejecting traditional roles for women, were also rejecting heterosexuality and experimenting with same sex affairs. If men were the oppressor, why not just have relationships with women?

The problem was that Betty Friedan, still the most influential feminist leader in the country, had made it clear that she didn't want lesbianism associated with feminism. I don't know that she had a problem with individual lesbians themselves. It was just that she and many other feminist leaders were convinced that anything involving "those deviant lesbians" could easily be scorned and dismissed by mainstream society. The lesbian baiting accusations that all women's libbers were lesbians had been enough to frighten some women, even straight women, away. Real live out lesbians in the movement, Friedan and other leaders were convinced, would kill the cause. Friedan was a little crazy on this topic.

I thought Friedan was wrong about lesbians. I knew we had contributed a lot to the movement and could continue to do so. But I hadn't had the courage to challenge her anti-lesbian doctrine. I had been too scared of being out myself. Over time, though, especially as so many came out, I began to get uncomfortable with my acquiescence. I could see that my silence, like the silence of others, actually made me, all of us closeted lesbians, party to this anti-lesbian policy. Besides, the movement should include us. After all, weren't lesbians women, too? Shouldn't attention be paid to their set of issues, problems like child custody disputes, job loss, and the emotional toll of social rejection? How could I stay a part of this neglect of a whole segment of women? Women like me?

I decided it was time that NOW as an organization confronted its own homophobia and acknowledge and address lesbians' concerns. I knew as the president of NYC NOW, I had a position I could act from. So, in the summer of 1969, I suggested to the steering committee we sponsor a lesbian program. At first they were shocked. NOW had never used the word lesbian in any of its activities, pronouncements, or publications. But I convinced them that it was important. With their backing, I began to organize a panel on lesbians in defiance of Freidan's wishes.

With this attention to lesbians, I was on to something that was in the air, but I hadn't realized it. The riots at the Stonewall Inn in Greenwich Village had taken place at the end of June that year, but, at the time, I, and many others, didn't take a lot of notice of them. In fact, on the first night of the uprising, I had been in the Village, driving uptown on 7th to pick up the Long Island Expressway to go back to Lynbrook when suddenly I heard a commotion. I opened my car window and realized that what I was hearing was shouting. Just then, I passed the side street that seemed the center of the tumult and saw that the road was filled with police cars with flashing lights. I also caught a glimpse of men lined up on one side of the narrow street yelling at something or someone across the street. That was it, just a flash. The next day, I read a small article about the riots at the Stonewall Inn. All I remember thinking was good for them. They were challenging attitudes that I was also in the process of challenging. It was a local event that only later took on a mythic quality.

WHEN I OPENED the NOW public forum entitled, "Is Lesbianism a Feminist Issue?" in September of 1969, I knew we had hit a nerve. The basement room of the church on West 83rd street where we sometimes held our monthly NOW meetings was packed with two hundred-and-fifty to three hundred women instead of the fifty or so who usually attended our programs. I was pleasantly shocked. I had never seen most of them before and had no idea where they had come from. I hadn't had a phone tree or any other special advertisements for this event. Maybe they heard about it from the monthly announcement of our activities that we published in the *New York Times* and the word had spread. I had no idea. Whatever it was, lesbianism in the women's movement was clearly an issue whose time had come. The excitement, the sense of being at a transgressive, transformative event, was palpable.

Fourteen women were on the panel, all active feminists, plus me as the moderator. Among them were academics, activists, and journalists. Some were members of the NYC NOW chapter. Some were not aligned with any women's organization. Only two of the women on the panel were out lesbians, Barbara Love and Sydney Abbott, who later in 1971 published *Sappho was a Right On Woman*. I didn't introduce myself as a lesbian. I had the courage to host the forum at that point but not to go public myself. Along with the possible social disapproval I was not yet quite prepared to face, there was the fact that I was still not officially divorced and I didn't want any trouble with Eddie on issues of child custody. The divorce was not final until Eddie served me papers in 1972.

Not without some anxiety on my part about what we were about to do, I began. The panelists took turns speaking. All agreed that yes, lesbianism was a feminist issue and homophobia was wrong. All knew that there were lesbians in the movement and that they were often deep in closet. From that baseline, the discussion became an exploration of what the panelists did and didn't know about the lives and situation of lesbians. Often, comments were prefaced by, "I heard this story," or "Someone told me." A panelist would then go on to tell of a lesbian who lost her kids in a custody dispute. Others would then chime in, "Yes, I heard it happens all the time." Other panelists would add, "I know somebody who got fired." "I have friends who have two bedrooms made up, and when company comes, they each sleep in separate rooms." "Gatherings could be raided by police, in bars, or at private parties where cops come just to frighten people with bogus complaints about music being too loud." "She couldn't even visit her partner in the hospital." "She lost her job." "They turned to drink. "She had a nervous breakdown." The list went on and on. It was as though each statement was a great discovery. And for many women it was. "Oh really, I hadn't thought of that," was echoed throughout. Somehow talking about it at all in such a public forum, even with all the traumas of lesbian lives, was electrifying.

The panelists didn't ignore the way people who didn't like the women's movement were throwing around the lesbian label to scare women away or from coming out. The panelists named this lesbian baiting for what it was, another illustration of men's contempt for women and another method for men to manipulate and control women and have them do what men want. In a way, like many of the insights that the movement gave rise to, most women already understood this on an unarticulated level. They knew they were being controlled. So once the power dynamic was named, the recognition was instant, and a crack in what had been accepted truths and ways of doing things was opened. The crack this panel opened was eventually wide enough for many straight women to refuse to be intimidated into silence on the issue and for lesbians in the movement to come out.

But Betty Friedan wasn't squeezing through this crack and wasn't pleased. From that forum on, she disliked me for publicly associating NOW and the women's movement with lesbianism. If I had done a painting of Friedan at that time, it would be more of a caricature. Her features would be outlined in black. There would probably be a lot of red. She would look really angry. This is when she first became associated with the term "lavender menace" to describe women in the movement who were lesbians. Even though the term was used by a journalist interviewing her rather than being a term Friedan originated, the phrase has stuck with her as her invention. No matter what, though, it reflected her attitude and made the split between so-called mainstream feminism and a more radical lesbian feminism public.

IN THE MEANTIME, I was going through my own transition. Even as I was indulging in many one night stands and continuing to be involved with Nancy, I had fallen in love. In October of that year, 1969, about a month after the panel, I met Helen Hotwood. She had been coming to NOW meetings for a few months, but I hadn't really noticed her until a Sunday picket I had arranged at Gracie Mansion, the traditional residence of the mayor of NYC. We were marching because of Mayor John Lindsay's poor record on women's issues. I spied Helen and her stunning bright red hair and pale skin right away, but it wasn't until after the march and we were on our way to our somewhat distant subway stop that I had a chance to talk to her. There was something about her. I was totally entranced and lost my usual cool. I could only manage small talk. She didn't help.

When we got to the station, since it was a late Sunday afternoon and the trains were few and far between, we ended up waiting and waiting. We eventually slid down against the wall and sat on the cold platform and found ourselves talking more intimately and honestly about our lives. Then, boom, a jolt of attraction shot between us. We sat looking at each other silently, absorbing the shock until the train finally came. We boarded silently, and silently stood next to each other, still shaken. She got off at her stop and then I got off on mine.

I WENT BACK to work the next day, Monday, and called Nancy. I told her flat out, "I've met someone else. You and I won't be seeing any more of each other." I know that that wasn't a very nice way to break up with someone, but that's what I did. Looking back, I realize that's how I leave something that no longer works for me. I make quick and clean breaks. At least for me they're quick and clean. At that time, I believed that easy moving on was one of the side benefits of being a lesbian. If I was not happy in a relationship, I could go, unlike in my marriage where I had been stuck. Not the greatest attitude I admit, but it worked for me, at least for a while.

Helen and I got together again shortly after that subway moment and then didn't waste any time. Within a month, Helen and her thirteen year old daughter Valerie moved into my West 93rd street apartment. The Valerie part was a bit of a surprise. I had heard about her from Helen, but I hadn't met her since she had been living in Texas with her father. When Helen mentioned bringing her along, I said OK. Valerie was about the same age as my daughter Lisa, so I figured that I was familiar enough with a girl that age for it to work. Besides, I thought that maybe with another girl around her age here, Lisa might come and visit me in the city more often. By that time, I wasn't seeing Laura much since she had her own teenage life. I had given up trying to get her to visit, but I hadn't given up on Lisa, a much more compliant child, even though I knew she was bored when she was with me in the city and I was off doing my NOW things. In fact, having Valerie there worked. Lisa came to the city more often with the promise of someone to hang out with. It seemed like a win-win.

Movement Divisions

IN THE MEANTIME, the divisions in the movement were getting more serious. Lesbians weren't the only issue. The moderate feminists, the Friedan ones, the ones most afraid of the effect of lesbians being associated with the movement, seemed to be focused mainly on workplace issues such as equal employment opportunities and equal pay. Many others thought those were concerns mostly relevant to middle class heterosexual women and left out other more fundamental issues. For instance, that a woman's right to control her body was paramount, so discussions of sexuality and sexual pleasure; reproductive rights such as abortion and birth control; rape; and even breast feeding should take priority. Some felt that black women, and later all women of color, were being ignored so demanded more attention to race. Others focused on economic class. Some were Marxist feminists, others were anarchists. A faction believed that for women and all other oppressed people to be truly liberated, the patriarchy had to be dismantled and society reorganized along non-hierarchical lines. Other feminists proposed giving up on men altogether and founding all women communities.

Being pulled in all these directions, the movement began to erupt in anger, frustration, name calling, and accusations of betrayal. The arguments within feminism were getting so bad that they threatened to fracture the movement and slow any progress. This really bothered me. We had to find a way to work together, or at least not fight each other. We couldn't have issues within the movement taking up all the time and attention of the movement. As usual when I saw a problem that I thought needed to be solved, I got to work. By November of 1969, under the umbrella of NYC NOW, I had organized and convened the (first) Congress to Unite Women. My aim was to find a way to fuse moderate and radical feminists. Pretty naïve, huh?

At first, things looked good. It seemed like I was not the only one who wanted to heal wounds in a movement that had expanded exponentially over the past few years. Over five hundred women packed the public school auditorium we had secured for the weekend. Emotions were running high. Everyone knew that there was a lot at stake, that while we might seem to be talking about abstractions and theories, we were talking about women's lives.

There were panels, break out groups, discussions, and performances. Through Friday night and Saturday, people yelled at each other, cried, walked away, and hugged, not necessarily in that order.

By Saturday night, we organizers knew that feelings and emotions for that evening's plenary session would be running very high. So, Rita Mae Brown, at the time one of the most prominent members of NOW, the first out lesbian in the NYC NOW chapter and editor of its newsletter, and I were patrolling the aisles in the packed auditorium to be available if anyone needed assistance. We both carried boxes of Kleenex. That was the kind of conference it was.

The radically oriented Cell 16 was up that night. Roxanne Dunbar, one of the group's leaders, began the program. She directed six women with very long hair onto the stage and had them sit facing the audience in a row of straight-back chairs. Their expressions were determined, some also looking tense, some frightened. Behind each woman stood another intent, serious woman, each with a pair of scissors. All lights in the auditorium focused on these twelve women. No one spoke. Everyone, women in the audience and on stage, seemed to be holding their breath.

At some signal, the women with the scissors began to cut the long hair of the women sitting in front of them. We all understood by then that long hair was one of the many body and clothing expectations that turned women into sex objects. It was part and parcel of the objectification of women. So, cutting hair was an exercise in women taking back control of their appearance and bodies, in de-objectifying themselves. We weren't going to let our appearance be driven by what men would find attractive any more. That meant, along with short hair, we would not use makeup and would wear loose fitting tops—I and many others came to favor blue work shirts, jeans, and heavy shoes, boots, or Birkenstock sandals. No more cleavage, tight clothes, or high heels. Through the seventies, this became the sign of rebellion and the uniform of the movement, but not, I should say, early on, the way of everyday life. I and others still wore skirts and dresses to work and when we needed to look respectable, such as when we met with legislators and other government officials. That would change, but it hadn't yet.

But even for a good political principle, cutting off hair that had taken years to grow and that still represented attractiveness to the world at large, was not easy. As their hair fell to the floor, many of the women on the stage, still sitting straight, cried, as did many in the audience. Rita Mae and I found ourselves walking up and down the aisles handing out Kleenex to sobbing women.

Brown and I were partners in another aspect of the hair cutting ceremony, but one that was much more covert. Interest was high in our movement at that time, so there were many media people who wanted to cover this conference. I wanted the coverage, but I didn't trust a lot of the reporters to be respectful of the women attending the Congress and our cause. So when Marlene Sanders, a member of our chapter who was a highly regarded TV reporter at that time, asked for an exclusive on the conference, I agreed. I had a condition, though. I knew that there would be times when things would become too highly charged and personal for public exposure, so I would determine what could be filmed and what not.

The hair cutting was in the what-not-to-film category, so I was pretty angry when I noticed Marlene's camera man on the other side of the auditorium from me filming the whole thing. I couldn't stop him without causing too much disruption, but I was determined not to let that film get out. I kept an eye on the camera man and saw him deposit the reel I was interested in in a box with the other full reels.

I grabbed Rita Mae and explained the situation. We devised a plan. My job was to pull Marlene and the camera man away from the area of the box of film reels, which I did by promising them an exclusive interview with me. How could they refuse? While they were distracted by me talking, I glimpsed Rita Mae and another woman, running bent over Groucho Marx style, sneak over to the box, grab the whole thing, and creep away. I guess Rita Mae figured in for a dime, in for a dollar. It was hilarious, like watching a comedy sequence, but I couldn't crack a smile. I couldn't crack one either when a few minutes after the interview, I heard the camera man cry, "What's going on? Where is all my film?"

A while later, Marlene tracked me down. "I can't believe it. Someone stole all the film. We searched and searched and can't find it anywhere."

I feigned shock and concern. "Oh, that's horrible. What could have happened?"

Later, when I met up with Rita at a local bar, I asked her what she had done with the film. "Unfurled and exposed it and threw it into the sewer."

I laughed, but now I wish we had it. What a great historical document it would have been.

WHILE THERE WERE many dramatic ceremonies and gestures such as the hair cutting and much heart felt discussion at this conference, unfortunately there was little resolution of our conflicts. In fact, instead of reconciling differences, it seemed to harden the stance of some like Friedan. She didn't play a major role at the conference, but since she was the titular head of NOW and known as the leader of the women's movement to the general public, her views were very influential. She could not get over her belief that man-hating radical lesbians were ruining the movement. Not only was simply having lesbians as NOW members damaging enough, she traced what she saw as the movement's other dangerous radical elements, the ones that demanded a total transformation of society rather than equality within it, back to trouble making lesbians. So she initiated what famously became known as the lesbian purge, the systematic exclusion of lesbians from leadership positions in NOW, including getting rid of those already in office, many having been dedicated members and workers for years. She also refused mention of lesbians and their concerns in all NOW activities and publications. Tempers flared. Arguments broke out. Ultimatums were delivered.

In February of 1970, because of NOW's efforts to banish lesbians and lesbian issues, Rita Mae resigned, taking herself out of the organization. Things got even uglier. Shortly after her resignation, Brown published a scathing article about NOW in a broadsheet she published labeling NOW's membership as garden variety menopausal women. Friedan and many others were enraged.

But out lesbians in the movement was a juggernaut Friedan and others could not hold back. In May of 1970, shortly after the NOW lesbian purges, NOW sponsored the Second Congress to Unite Women. I wasn't able to attend the conference, but I sure heard a lot about it later. From a variety of reports, I learned that in the middle of the opening session on the first night, May 1, when all four hundred delegates were gathered in the auditorium, twenty women suddenly stormed to the front of the hall, faced the startled audience, and tore off their sweaters or shirts to reveal purple T-shirts emblazoned with "Lavender Menace." It seems that many of these women had been in the same lesbian consciousness raising group and had decided that action was the appropriate next step after talking. Go CR! The group was led by the ex-NOW lesbians, Rita Mae Brown and Karla Jay.

The women on stage began to speak, announcing their anger at NOW's exclusion of lesbians. They wanted a less heterosexual, less male-centered version of the movement. In the meantime, other t-shirt clad women were distributing mimeographed copies of their manifesto, "The Woman-Identified Woman" that basically made the same points. It outlined a new feminist agenda to promote lesbian pride, advocate for lesbian rights and visibility, and fight against homophobia within and outside of feminism. There were boos and applause and a somewhat riotous informal speak out. I gather it was all pretty chaotic. Whatever the immediate reaction, I heard that the Lavender Menace sponsored dance that night was crowded with boisterous delegates from the conference. I wish I had been there. I love that in your face attitude. To me, that is really the best way to go to get something done.

These women were pioneering a new way to be a lesbian. It was a part of a rejection of the traditional gender roles. After all, if men were the oppressive forces in our lives, if heterosexual roles and rules kept us from being our own true selves, if women were wonderful, why give men priority in our lives? Why not turn to women for all our needs, sexual as well as emotional? Suddenly, being with another woman was a thing to consider. But first, for many of these women, there had to be a change in what it meant to be a lesbian. The butch-femme model that lesbian feminists found when they began to flock to the bars was a throwback in their view, a sad, dangerous, and destructive mimicking of patriarchal heterosexuality. All the trappings of heterosexuality and patriarchy had to go. These lesbian feminists wanted women loving each other equally, without any roles. No male-female. Only equality. Only androgyny. While few would admit it at first, many of the old bar dykes later confessed that they liked these new possibilities, that they had been thrust into butch-femme roles because they were the only ones available. But others resisted. For them, though, mostly it was a losing battle. The appeal of a lesbian feminism that offered visions of liberation as well as a community of support to women who loved women was strong. That and sheer numbers.

I wasn't sure that it was necessary to throw out all the old ways. After all, they were what I had come out into. But I was all for the overthrow of the patriarchy and its roles for women. And I was comfortable in the androgynous wardrobe of the lesbian feminists. Besides, I was totally taken by the openness, energy and enthusiasm of this new world of women-identified women that was blossoming. It was totally exhilarating and inspiring. At least it was to me and many other feminists.

AROUND THIS TIME, just as the Radicalesbians, the name the Lavender Menace took for themselves, were declaring their presence in the movement, I finally had the courage to come out beyond my circle of lesbian and feminist activists. My conscience was telling me that I was failing myself and other lesbians by allowing myself to be intimidated by homophobia, especially with so many others coming out. I had organized the panel but I hadn't declared myself there.

I made the move in late 1970. Kate Millett's book, *Sexual Politics*, had just been published. Just about all of us in NYC NOW were pretty familiar with her book because Kate was a member of our NYC NOW chapter. In those days, there were no personal computers and typists were expensive, so we had pitched in and helped type the dissertation her book was based on. Even from that limited exposure, we knew the book was revolutionary. No one had ever called the portrayals of women in the works of a number of the most revered male writers, men like D.H. Lawrence and Norman Mailer, sexist, or suggested that these authors were presenting not objective or universal truths but a limited, male point of view. Millet's analysis was taken as the attack on the entire literary establishment that it indeed was.

Millett's book got a lot of press coverage, which gives you an idea about how in-the-news feminism was in those days. Millett was even on the cover of *Time* magazine in August of 1970. That was fine, but not much later, since her critics couldn't argue with her points, an article in that same magazine denounced her personally, hoping to shame her by emphasizing her avowed bisexuality and that she was living without benefit of marriage with her lover, a non-white, Japanese man. Many feminists, including me, were furious at this attack with its fake high morality, homophobia, and racism.

So, as president of NYC NOW, I decided to hold a news conference and invited the movement's movers and shakers to condemn the media's efforts to dismiss Millet's book through this kind of vilification of its author. Representatives from TV, radio, and print media came from all over to listen to well-known feminist leaders such as Gloria Steinem and Flo Kennedy speak in defense of Millett and of the book. This was the first time the leaders of the women's movement addressed the topics of bisexuality and lesbianism in a mainstream, public forum. While I was the moderator of the panel and never said anything specifically about being a lesbian, I was there. I knew that was enough. It was guilt by association. I considered that press conference my public coming out as a lesbian.

And it clearly was. That afternoon, after the news conference, I went to work at *Newsday* as usual. Once I got there, it came to me that since our panel had gotten a lot of coverage, all my co-workers would know about me by now. They had to have seen the news. After all, feminism was controversial, big news in those days and *Newsday* was a news organization with TVs broadcasting news all over the place. I took a deep breath and went straight to my desk. Nobody said anything. I got to work.

Later in the day, as usual, I went to check the mockup of the pages that I had designed before they were actually printed. This involved walking through two heavy, leather doors into a large room filled with the din of linotype machines. Generally, when I came into the room, the machines would be making a racket. The men who worked at them would whistle in a friendly way at me as I walked toward a desk at the end of the hall where Joe Kelly waited for me to check in. This day, as soon as I opened the doors and walked in, the machines went quiet. There was no whistling. As I plodded down the long corridor, I thought to myself, "Oh no, they're going to kill me for being gay." I finally got to Joe who was in his usual blue shirt with, as usual, a cigar in his mouth, wearing the square paper hat made out of a sheet of printed newspaper that marked the folks who worked in the actual printing of the paper.

He looked at me, leaned back in his chair, took the cigar out of his mouth and said, "Hell of a press conference, Bottini." He brought his chair back down and showed me the pages printed from the chase for me to check. The machines went back on.

I breathed a sigh of relief.

Exit Dolores

THE WEIRD THING about this time period was that while Friedan had not forgiven me for the lesbian conference of the previous year, I was still part of her NOW inner circle, as was Dolores. For some reason, Dolores and I, and a few others, were the only people Friedan felt comfortable traveling with, and she traveled a lot. Besides this, Dolores and I often served as support staff for her in general, accompanying her to conferences, board meetings, and speaking engagements. But Friedan wasn't easy to work for. She had no hesitancy in yelling at people if she thought they had somehow failed her. She would not listen to reason. Because Dolores was NOW's executive director, she took the brunt of a lot of Friedan's belligerence and meanness. Often Friedan's mode of communicating with Dolores was just to complain and scream at her.

Sometimes I got caught in the middle. For instance, in 1970, Friedan was preparing the speech she was to give to the congressional committee to help derail G. Harold Carswell's nomination as a justice on the Supreme Court of the United States. About six a.m., Friedan called Dolores to come down and take dictation for her speech so Dolores could type it up, one of Dolores's many jobs. I should mention here that at the time we were all living in the same apartment complex. Just at that moment, Dolores was working at the mimeo machine in the spare bedroom of her apartment which also served as NOW national headquarters. She had already been working almost non-stop for a couple of days and had been going pretty much all night. Not unusual for her. Her work load was gigantic. Not only was she at Friedan's beck and call, she was also still the chief administrator of National NOW. She was writing and mimeographing newsletters and remained in charge of the exploding membership, all with very little increase in staff. She was constantly swamped and harried. When Friedan called Dolores that morning, Dolores complained to me that she was exhausted, but she said OK to Friedan anyway. I couldn't let her do that.

Since I knew shorthand (thank you Peg Wilson), I volunteered to go down to take the dictation so that Dolores could get some sleep. When I got to Betty's apartment Betty was not happy. I wasn't good enough. She called Dolores again and insisted that she come down. Dolores dragged herself over.

When she arrived, Betty, who was half way up the stairs to the second floor of her apartment on her way to the dining room where she had her papers, looked down on Dolores, stamped her feet like a child having a tantrum, and screamed at her, "When I call you, I want you to come."

That was the last straw for the depleted Dolores. She replied, shouting herself, "Fuck you lady. Fuck you." Then she turned around and walked out.

I just stood there.

Betty was furious, shaking her head, muttering, "Nobody talks to me that way."

To mollify her, I repeated what I had said before, that I could take the dictation. Finally Friedan calmed down enough to agree. She said she would need it typed in a few hours because she had to leave to get to DC. I said fine and got it done.

Dolores was very angry but went back to work the next day. The movement was more important to her than her personal work situation. But after the fuck you incident, Friedan became even meaner to Dolores. I pleaded with Dolores to resign but she wouldn't. Again, I urged the board to fire her to save her health. She was an emotional and physical wreck. By May of 1970, both the board and Dolores had had enough. They let her go.

1970 — More Activism

EVEN WITH ALL the dissension in NOW and Friedan's antagonism toward me, I was not about to abandon the organization or the movement that at that point was gaining adherents, visibility, and effectiveness at an incredible rate. 1970 was promising to be banner year. The EEOC had been convinced to expand equal pay by prohibiting employers from changing a job title to justify lesser pay for women. And the battle for passage of the Equal Rights Amendment (ERA) was finally fully engaged.

The ERA simply stated, "Men and women shall have equal rights throughout the United States and every place subject to its jurisdiction. Congress shall have power to enforce this article by appropriate legislation." Doesn't sound all that radical, right? Yet, until 1970, the ERA had been stuck for twenty-five years in a congressional committee controlled by Emmanuel Cellar, the Democratic Congressman from Brooklyn. Twenty-five years! The ERA couldn't even be considered as a constitutional amendment until it was out of committee and passed with a two-thirds majority vote in both the House of Representatives and the Senate. Only then would it be sent to the states where pro-ERAers had seven years to get the approval of two-thirds of the State legislatures. (Generally an amendment only had five years for passage in the states, but a loophole was discovered by feminist activists later in the campaign that gave the ERA seven years.)

To get the ERA going, my chapter organized a picket line at Cellar's home. After a week of demonstrators in front of his house from early morning well into the evening, Cellar finally invited another NOW member and me in to negotiate with him. I guess he saw the angry women and the handwriting on the wall. We got him to release the ERA from his committee so that it could be voted on. That was 1970. By 1972, it had been approved by both the House and the Senate and was ready for state by state approval. The ERA brought women into the movement in droves and took over NOW's focus. Alas, it fell three states short of getting all the states it needed by its June 1982 deadline. Nothing was easy or guaranteed.

ANOTHER ONE OF our significant actions took place in early August of 1970 at the Statue of Liberty. In the spring of that year, I was back working with Dolores and Pat Trainor on the Women's Strike for Equality and the Fiftieth Anniversary of Suffrage march which were to take place in NYC later in August of that year. Dolores, even though she was out of NOW, had gotten very involved in the anti-pornography, anti-violence against women movement that was emerging as a force. So, because the march was not just a NOW event but one that was aimed at drawing in all women, Dolores was willing to give her time and energy. And she was still one of my closest friends and advisors.

As we had done when recruiting for NYC NOW in 1968, Dolores, Pat, and I, and sometimes others, often went out after organizing meetings for a few beers. One of our favorite places was Remo's, a local bar in the Village. We even had our own table in the back far away from the other patrons who gathered at the bar closer to the front. One of these nights when Dolores, Pat, and I were sipping our beers, two of our young lesbian NOW members came striding up to our table, visibly angry. Another Pat, the more vocal of the two, explained that they were both very disturbed about a monument and fountain in Queens that they passed to and from work every day. The marble statue, about seventeen feet tall, featured a muscular nude man with a heavy sword on his shoulder, his privates barely covered by carved decorative vines. Two twisted, trapped figures with the heads and torsos of women and the tails of serpents were being crushed beneath his giant feet. The statute was provocatively called "Civic Virtue."

Unbeknownst to me or the other women at the table, when this statue was first erected in front of New York's City Hall in 1929, a mere nine years after women had gotten the vote, it created a furor for its misogynistic depiction of women. But there it stayed until Mayor La Guardia, who reportedly was more disturbed about looking at a naked man's rear end every day when he left his office than the negative image of women, had it moved to outside the newly erected Queens Borough Hall. This is where it was when it so enraged our two young feminists.

I could sympathize with their anger until young Pat ended her description saying, "I'm going to blow it up."

All my excitement at the raised consciousness of these young women disappeared. I thought, oh, oh. That would not be good.

"Yes, the statue's offensive, but blowing it up isn't a good idea. It would be bad for the movement. Besides, it's not a major statue. You'd get in trouble and few people would notice," I responded.

Pat hesitated, pondering my comments. "OK. Then we'll throw paint on it." Yikes! Again, I advised her that that would probably hurt us more than help. "Well, let's do something spectacular," she replied.

Trying to keep her from going off and doing anything reckless, I threw out what I thought was an outrageous idea, but one that would at least be a distraction. "Why don't we take over the Statue of Liberty?"

"Wow," she replied. "That's a great idea."

I was relieved. I had gotten her over the blowing up and paint throwing ideas and was confident the Statue of Liberty proposal wouldn't fly since it was so over the top. She and her girlfriend then sat down and helped us finish off a few pitchers of beer. No one mentioned the Statue of Liberty again that night.

The next day, I was at work when young Pat called. She had remembered our conversation about Lady Liberty and was ready to get going. I was still interested in directing her energies in a productive rather than destructive way, so I agreed to call a meeting. A number of women showed up, and with young Pat and others as leaders, they proceeded to set up all the committees they thought necessary for such an action. OK, I thought to myself, let's see where they go with this. I had to trust the youngsters. Besides, I was spending most of my energy on preparations for the big Women's march. I managed to keep abreast of their efforts by checking in with Pat now and again. I was confident she at least would not blow up or deface anything.

In the end, I was enlisted to lead part of their action. On August 10, 1970, one hundred or so women gathered at the lower Manhattan pier to take the tourist boat to the Statue of Liberty, splitting up onto two boats to be less conspicuous. When both groups arrived on Liberty Island, I took my larger group up the hill from the boat ramp to the grassy area at the foot of the statue. One of the women with us took out her guitar and we started to sing popular songs that we had rewritten with lyrics for the movement. The women from the other boat, looking pregnant with bulges under their clothes, received very solicitous attention from guards and were able to either walk up the stairs or take the elevator to the top of the pedestal level.

As I looked up from the ground, I saw the fifteen or so women gather on the pedestal. I could see a lot of bustling movement as they removed their bulges, which were actually sections of an oil cloth banner that they had wrapped around their bodies in pieces. They then attached the segments and stretched them out along the top of the pedestal. Within minutes they had dropped and hooked to the railing a forty-foot long, four-foot high banner that commanded in giant letters, "Women of the World Unite." They raised their fists. It was spectacular. Even I thought wow. That was until I saw three police boats and two fire boats coming toward us.

For the first time, it occurred to me that we were on federal land and could go to federal prison. That would be big trouble. I also noticed that no other boats were coming or going from the island. Yikes! What was happening? What were they going to do to us? I held my breath as the police boats landed at the wharf.

From the deck of one of the boats, one police officer yelled up at us through a megaphone, "What are you doing up there?"

I shouted back, "We're walking and singing," even astounding me at my cheeky composure.

His reply, "How long do you think you will be?"

"I think about another half an hour will be OK."

He said, "Fine. We'll be here."

"OK, you'll be there and we'll be here. That's a good arrangement." They never got off of the boat. They left us to our singing, banner, and fists raised in the air. Got through that, I thought, kind of amazed.

But the surprises weren't over. A few minutes after this conversation, the fire boats began to shoot streams of water out into the air just as they did at times of civic celebrations, and then these boats and the police boats started their sirens. They were joining our demonstration! After about three hours, during which no tourist boats came or went from the island, we told the police we were ready to go, got on one of the boats that had been stopped on the island, and returned to Manhattan, exhausted and exhilarated.

To my surprise, even though we had alerted the press that we were going to have a major action at the Statue and that the police and fire department had joined in with us, it didn't get much press coverage. In later years, I sometimes asked myself if it really happened. I really wasn't sure. But a number of years ago, around the end of the last century, as I was gathering materials for a celebration of NOW's pioneers for a National NOW conference in Beverly Hills, someone sent me two postcards with photos by Ann Brady of the Statue with the banner on it. I was relieved to find that it had indeed happened after all.

THE EVENT THAT did get a lot of press was the August 26 Women's Strike for Equality and its accompanying march, the project that had kept me so busy during the planning of the Statue of Liberty caper. The idea was to have women all over the country go "on strike" from their regular activities for the day and rally and march against women's inequality instead. As President of NYC NOW, I was one of the major coordinators for the New York City march, expected to be the biggest in the country. It was quite a job. It took months of preparation to coordinate with the city and all the different women's organizations that wanted to take part. Yes, all these disparate feminist factions were finally united about something. Even the socialist women's groups, formed in response to the sexism those women experienced in their own leftist organizations, were eager to join us even though they had previously labelled NOW as too bourgeois and accommodationist. Black women's organizations that had seen NOW and the women's movement in general as pretty much exclusively concerned with the issues of white middle-class women also became a part of the march.

Another group that unexpectedly took an interest in the march was the FBI. They tried to recruit Jill Ward, one of the women training to be a march marshal, to be an informant. Their method was not very subtle. During the training period for the marshals, Jill lost her wallet. She was greatly relieved, then, when, a few days after it disappeared, she got a call from a guy who said he had found it. He suggested they meet at a local café where he would return it to her. That was fine with her. She went. This man did indeed have her wallet, but he also had an agenda. It seems he had somehow stolen the wallet in order to get to talk to her. He informed her that he was FBI and offered her $750/month, a lot of money in those days, to spy on NYC NOW. National NOW was kind of the public relations wing of the movement, but my chapter, NYC NOW, was the center of many of the large, organized actions. We have no idea why the FBI chose her. Maybe the FBI knew she had little money and thought she could be tempted. They were wrong. Jill refused the offer and came back and reported it to the chapter. Such attempts at infiltration were scary and disturbing, but at least they meant we were making some of the people who had power in the country pretty uncomfortable.

Jill Ward was also a central character in another significant occurrence associated with the march. She finally brought Dolores out as a lesbian, something I had wanted to do for years but had not managed. Dolores and Jill were at the same training meetings for marshals, but from what I heard, they didn't pay particular attention to each other until the march itself when they ended up working together. Clearly, sparks had flown because shortly after the march, Jill seduced Dolores and they became lovers.

THE WOMEN'S STRIKE for Equality was extremely successful. Hundreds of thousands of women actually left their homes and jobs for demonstrations and marches in cities and towns all over the country. In New York City, an estimated fifty thousand women rallied and marched along Fifth

Avenue, carrying placards and loudly chanting for women's rights. Some of the women pushed strollers and baby carriages, some were in wheelchairs, many were dressed in white to honor the twenty-five thousand white clad suffragists who had marched on this very same street in 1915. We were a giant mass of beautiful, strong women. It was a glorious day.

Although I was exhausted by all the work the rally and march had taken, I was exultant and deeply moved, especially when I stepped out of the street and stood on tip toes on the sidewalk as the march turned a corner to head for the rallying point. Stretched in front of me and behind me, filling the streets in all directions from sidewalk to sidewalk, were marchers who had joined in our cause. We had indeed created a serious and joyous—at least that day— movement and I had been a part of it. I was almost brought to tears. The anti-Vietnam war and Civil Rights movements were important, but this, I thought to myself, was the real revolution. We were changing people's lives. Everyone's.

NOW logo that Ivy designed in 1969. It is still in use.

Demonstration at the Statue of Liberty, 1970.

Ivy (left, front) at a NOW demonstration, c. 1972.

NOW Election — Being Purged

NO MATTER HOW successful any of the actions I helped organize or led were at generating publicity and progress for the movement, I was still in trouble with Friedan and a number of other women in NOW because of the lesbian issue. I knew some lesbians had left the organization because of its anti-lesbian stance, but I had no intention of going anywhere. NYC NOW had had some great successes while I was its president, and I knew there was much more I could contribute. So I was stunned when I discovered the lengths to which the anti-lesbian forces would go to get rid of me.

During the preparations for the strike and march, I heard from the two out lesbians who had been on the lesbian panel, Barbara Love and Sidney Abbott, that there was a campaign against me that had started a few months after the symposium.

They both warned me, "Her [Friedan's] people are spreading horrible stories about you. They're making phone calls, saying that you are a predator and that you're making passes at all the women."

They were worried that these rumors would hurt me during the upcoming chapter elections in which I was running for reelection as president. I was astonished and disturbed at these accusations, not just because they weren't true but also because Friedan had resorted to the stereotypical lesbian as predator image. I might have been a player when I first came out, but I never preyed on anyone. I never forced or pushed. Besides, since Helen, I didn't even have any inclination to play around. How low could Friedan go!

Love and Abbot went on. "They're going to rig the elections with a lot of new people and members that never come to meetings. Paper members. But we've got thirty lesbians ready to go join to be able to vote. We'll have your back."

I've done a couple of stupid things in my life. My response to these friends was one of them. I answered, "Thank everybody for being willing to do that, but that's not fair. Those women aren't members. I bet they're not even interested. They're only going to join to be able to vote." And then I said, "I trust the membership." Now that's the stupid part. I trust the membership.

The time for chapter elections came around a few months after the march. Normally we had forty or so women in attendance at the actual election, but this time the room was packed to overflowing with maybe two hundred women, all ready to vote. I had never seen ninety percent of them. One face was conspicuously missing, though: Betty Friedan's. She had left her henchwomen to do her dirty work.

I hadn't really thought much about the election. In spite of Barbara and Sidney's warnings, I was sure I would be re-elected. With me as president, the chapter had had a lot of successes. And my slate was the one put forth by the chapter's nominating committee. I wasn't even expecting any opposition. Was I wrong! I was stunned by this turn of events. It soon became clear that there was another group running against me and my steering committee and that many of the new "members" were carrying slips of paper listing alternative steering committee names. I soon realized that my slate might be in trouble. The way the election worked was that the voting was actually for the fifteen-member steering committee. The person who got the most votes to be on the steering committee became the president. Everybody had five votes, and each person could cast all those votes for one person, for five different people, or anything in-between.

One woman was pointed out to me across the room. "That's the woman who's running against you, the one who all these women were brought in to vote for."

I thought she was indicating a woman I had been casually introduced to earlier that night as Valerie. I certainly had never seen or heard of her before that evening and had no idea where she had come from. By that time, I was bewildered into a kind of paralysis, barely able to process the betrayal that was emerging in front of me.

The fourteen members of my steering committee were more together, though. Once they realized the danger to my presidency the opposition slate posed, they all publicly stepped down from running for reelection so I would be the only one on our slate against the opposition. All of our supporters could cast all five of their votes for me. Even with that, it wasn't enough. I ended up losing by seven or so votes—I was so disturbed, I never got the exact vote count. I also didn't realize until just recently that there was no Valerie who had been chosen to depose me. In fact, Jacqui Ceballos, an active member of NYC NOW and later founder of the Veteran Feminists of America (VCA), was head of the opposition slate and was elected president of NYC NOW that night. That I hadn't processed this for so many years shows just how stunned, dazed and angry I was and ultimately how alienated from NYC NOW I became.

The vote devastated me. The chapter board election was still coming up that night, and one of my steering committee members nominated me. I was elected to the board, but I thought, "What the hell has happened here? Somebody that I've never seen before is now president of the New York chapter of NOW! So now I was elected to the board of directors. Big deal."

I went home. Every day after that for the next few weeks after work I'd sit in my rocking chair going over what the hell happened. I couldn't do anything else. I was paralyzed, miserable and angry. I appreciated that my steering committee had stood behind me, but that was the only bright spot in the whole affair. Sure, there were issues and splits and often feelings ran high, but I never expected this duplicity from the organization I had dedicated so much of my life to. What I didn't know at that time was that the two women who told Friedan all sorts of stories about the lesbian Bottini this and the lesbian Bottini that were two nurses who were in my NOW chapter and had been deep in the closet. We had been friends. So I thought.

The nurses' social life had consisted of entertaining at home with the few couples or individuals they trusted. Earlier that year, once they realized that Helen and I were a couple and they had decided they could trust us, they had invited us over to their place now and again. We would have a lovely time dancing to tunes in their collection of big band, jazzy recordings. But we never mentioned our friendship to anyone else. That was how it was for many lesbians in those days, especially the older ones who had come of age during very homophobic times.

I think these two women spoke to Friedan because they were afraid that if I was out as president of NYC NOW, or NOW in general got a reputation as a place that harbored lesbians, they would be dragged out of the closet, too. As I said before, guilt by association. I could almost forgive them. Terrible things could happen to gays and lesbians back then when their secret lives were revealed. They both could have easily lost their jobs. There was little room for lesbian nurses in the world. (Lesbians and gay men can still lose their jobs for simply being gay in many states. They are not fully protected against employment discrimination to this day.) But they should have known that it was never my intention to paint the movement as any more lesbian than it was or to force others to come out. It was all very sad. It was like all the folks in Europe who betrayed their neighbors during World War II out of fear of what the Nazis would do to them. I know that sounds extreme, but the idea is the same to me. I don't want the enemy to destroy me, so I'm going to go help them destroy others like me.

What got to me most, though, was the discovery that four or five long-time friends and members of NOW, women I had worked with for so long and with so much commitment, had been the ones making the phone calls that smeared me and helped get all those paper members to the meeting to vote for the other candidate. I had believed in the movement and I had believed in these women. This was my personal introduction to horizontal hostility, the phenomenon of people in an organization turning against each other instead of fighting their real enemies. It was not the last time I would experience it. Since it happens in all movements and is often directed by some members against the leaders in a group, I was going to be subject to it again. It was inevitable. I was a leader. That it happens all the time doesn't help. That first time, and often later, it felt like betrayal.

TWO OR THREE weeks after that horrible election night, I got myself out of my chair and went to the first meeting of the new board. Some of the members were new but many were old. I knew some of them had had something to do with my defeat. When my chance to speak came, I lashed out. I was really, really angry.

"I've worked with you for four years. You know me. How you could support what was said about me? I thought I could trust you. Obviously, I can't, so I'm resigning." There was a shocked hush but no argument. That was the end of my official association with NYC NOW, the chapter I had co-founded. My lesbianism and others' fear of it did me in.

BUT IT WAS not only at NOW that things were getting out of control in my life. Just as things were falling apart for me there, my situation at *Newsday* was taking a final bad turn. It probably didn't help that I might have been seen as stirring up the women in the office. I was so involved in the movement by that time that I couldn't help but bring its ideas to work with me. For instance, as I mentioned before, at the NOW and other meetings, most women wore slacks or jeans, a change from the unwritten dress code for women that had required us to wear skirts and dresses in any professional or formal setting, including public meetings, work, and restaurants. My own NOW outfit consisted of jeans, a blue work shirt, and comfortable shoes.

This move to slacks was not entirely new. In fact, sometime in 1967, long before Eddie and I broke up, *Newsday* had actually done a feature on the then just emerging women-in-pants phenomenon. A *Newsday* reporter friend, Marilyn, invited Eddie and me to go with her to test out how local restaurants would react to a more casual look, that is a woman in slacks. Eddie and I went as a married couple, which we were, with him in a sports jacket and me in a dress. Marilyn came with us dressed in a pink pants suit. At the first restaurant, Eddie was given a tie to wear, but even then, one look at the pants suit and we were not seated. Similarly, in our forays into two other white table cloth restaurants, even with Eddie in the tie he had kept on, we were denied admission. The pink pants suit had struck out.

Now it was 1971, four years later, and I was fully ensconced in the women's movement and feeling feisty. It didn't make much sense to me that I couldn't wear comfortable and practical pants to work. So one day, I came in wearing bright yellow jeans with fringe on the bottom and a nice, simple white blouse. Nothing happened. So I continued to wear slacks to work. I was expecting some response, maybe not a reprimand but at least a comment. I knew people, men and women, noticed. I could see their eyes go down to my pants, and then they would look away. No one said anything to me. OK. I guess a woman wearing slacks was not as big a deal as I thought. But about a week or so after I started to wear my jeans, other women in the city room, both professional and clerical staff, started to come to work in pants. I heard later from Audrey, a friend from work, that all the women had been talking about my wardrobe challenge from the first day but had waited to see if I would be fired. Once it was clear that I was not going to be, they were emboldened to wear slacks, too. That was fine with me. After all, progress was progress.

Even though I had this small victory, a serious challenge to my tenure at *Newsday* was coming to a crisis. It started with an incident way back in 1967 that I never told anyone about, certainly not Eddie or anybody at work, but which had haunted me ever since. The summer of that year, Eddie and the kids and I went to Fire Island, a resort island off the coast of Long Island, with my boss, Paul, and his wife, Ursula, for a weekend. This was not unusual as we sometimes socialized together. On Saturday night, after a nice day at the water, I had put the kids to bed and Eddie and I had gone down to the beach to sit with Paul and Ursula around their bonfire. Before long, Eddie went back inside because he had one of his migraine headaches. That left Paul, Ursula, and me sitting on our beach chairs around the fire, chatting, relaxing, enjoying a few drinks. Or, maybe more than a few for one of us.

Without warning, Ursula came over to me, sat on my lap, and kissed me on the lips. She announced, "I'm in love with Ivy." She then stood up, ran to the ocean and threw her wedding ring into the water.

Paul and I were aghast. I was terribly embarrassed and Paul was furious. I swear I never encouraged Ursula, before, then, or after. But there was no explaining anything to Paul. Paul dragged Ursula away. I didn't see them again that weekend until the boat ride home the next day when Paul was barely civil to me.

Life went on. I went back to work and neither Paul nor I nor Ursula spoke of the incident again. Ursula disappeared from my life. But, a few years later, Paul came to me at work and told me he wanted to try something new. He was going to create the position of art director for the news and editorial pages, a post we had not had before, and he wanted me to take it. His offer was flattering and tempting. The problem was that instead of my current eleven a.m. to six p.m. time slot, I would have to go into work at six or seven p.m. and not get off until two or three a.m. I knew that would wreak havoc not just on my activism but also on my just budding relationship with Helen. I didn't want to mess that up, so I told Paul that I didn't think it would work because I was starting a new relationship.

He replied, "Let's just try it for three months. If it doesn't work out, I promise you can go back to your old job. No problem."

What could I do? In the back of my mind, I wondered if he was trying to get back at me because of Ursula, but I wasn't sure. Whatever it was, he was insistent. He kept assuring me that it was just a trial. I said yes.

So I began going in around six or seven p.m. and leaving at about two-thirty or three o'clock in the morning to drive back to the city. I was exhausted all the time and unable to give attention to my activism, Helen, my kids, or anything else. So I went back to Paul after the three months and told him I would like to get my old job back.

His reply, "So sorry. I filled that position."

I was stunned and angry. He had promised. I kept asking him for my old hours back and he kept coming up with excuses about why he couldn't give them to me. I was getting more and more furious. I grew certain this was payback. I managed to maintain that schedule for a while, but eventually I just couldn't continue with it. I was getting more and more physically and mentally sick. In the end, just as I felt I had been forced out of NOW, I felt I was maneuvered out of *Newsday*. I left the job. Of course, *Newsday* claimed I quit so refused me the right to collect unemployment benefits. That left me pretty high and dry.

In the meantime, NOW and the job situation were not the only things putting me in a very down mood. By that time, there were also severe problems with Helen. For quite a while before this, Helen and I had been doing well. Not only were we movement compatriots, we also had fun together. Especially dancing. At the lesbian bars we frequented, it wasn't unusual for all the other women to step back and watch us move. Helen would throw into the mix of new and old the dance steps she learned in Plano, Texas, where she grew up, and I would add some of the steps I still remembered learning from Ruby and her friends. We were great together. I loved those nights at the bars. We had a lot of them, too, drinking and dancing and then going home with both of us amorous. "This is a good life," I had told myself.

It took me four or five months to see that something was wrong. When Helen was drinking, which was often, she'd laugh and dance and just have a great old time. She would be very sexy and flirty. When she was sober, she would close off and barely respond at all. She'd just give one of those thousand-yard stares. At those times, I couldn't read her at all. I would have no idea what she was thinking. It was like she was two different people. I had overlooked some of this before, but during those traumatic months in early 1971, her drinking and split personality were getting old.

Besides that, her teenaged daughter Valerie had become a problem for us. While it was pretty clear that Helen loved Valerie very much, Helen only showed it when she was drinking and in her gregarious and loving state. But when she wasn't drunk, she was withdrawn and guarded. This made Valerie very insecure, really desperate for her mother's love, and very jealous of my relationship with Helen. It was understandable but annoying once Valerie started pushing herself, literally, between us. If Helen and I were sitting next to each other on the couch, Valerie would forcefully wiggle her way between us. When Helen and I were in a conversation in the living room or wherever, Valerie would call for her mother to get her attention back on her. At restaurants, she made sure Helen and I would not sit next to each other. There hasn't been a word invented to describe how clingy she was.

Even with all the tension among the three of us, I wasn't ready to leave Helen. She was at least one steady thing in a life that felt like it was all falling apart. But I clearly needed a change. It took me a month of grieving about what had happened with NOW and my job before I pulled myself together. Helen had previously lived in southern California for a few years and was eager to go back, so I decided, why not try Los Angeles. It had been good for me before, maybe it could be good for me again.

The Move to LA

HELEN, HER DAUGHTER Valerie, my daughter Lisa, and I left New York City in July of 1971. We spent about two months driving cross country, stopping along the way to visit friends and relatives. I wasn't in a hurry. I had no idea what was ahead. When we arrived in Los Angeles in September of 1971, I rented a guest house for all of us in Venice behind the home of a lovely husband and wife. I had saved some money from my *Newsday* job, and I was planning on appealing their decision not to allow me unemployment benefits. I was hopeful about that as income. Helen had no money—none—zero—and no plans to make any. Lisa stayed with us for about a week and then flew back to New York as planned. So, there I was with Helen and Valerie.

I wasn't sure how that was going to go, but in the political realm, things were looking up. Just around the time we arrived on the west coast, the NOW National Conference was convening in Los Angeles. I was still interested in NOW and decided to drop by. By this time, really only a year or so after the Friedan engineered eradication of lesbians, portions of NOW had begun to repudiate Friedan and her anti-lesbian stance. At this conference, the organization had even passed a resolution proposed by the LA chapter that validated lesbians and their issues as being integral to the women's movement and NOW, declaring "that a woman's right to her own person includes the right to define and express her own sexuality and to choose her own lifestyle."

I walked into the convention just after the passage of this resolution and one supporting lesbian mothers fighting for custody of their children. When people recognized me, I was greeted with a loud, raucous, standing ovation. It seems I had become a hero for many because I had been a high-profile part of Friedan's lesbian purge.

What a difference a year and a drive cross country could make. That the pro-lesbian resolutions had been proposed and lobbied for by the LA NOW chapter also gave me great hope. From what I could gather, the LA group, just a year younger than NYC NOW, was much more progressive than the chapters on the east coast. Good for them. It looked like Los Angeles was going to be a good place for me as an activist.

AND IT WAS. Encouraged by that greeting at the NOW convention, Helen and I both became active in the LA chapter of NOW pretty much right away. The group had just opened a women's center in an unattractive storefront on Pico Boulevard in West LA. It was not very inviting. The walls needed painting, and there was little decoration or furniture besides the very functional. Mostly, it was being used for administrative work. I knew I was new in town, but I really thought that the community would be better served if the center was a place where women could meet, work together, and just hang out.

Toni Carabillo, the friend Dolores and I had stayed with on our earlier California vacation, was the president of LA NOW. I suggested to her that we put together some work teams to improve the place. She agreed. A few of us chipped in for paint and other supplies, and before we knew it, the place had been patched, painted, and decorated, transformed into a comfortable and welcoming meeting place. From then on, the center became a hub of feminist activity, from the political and organizational to the social.

This is not to say everyone around was happy to have us there. Since the center was in the middle of the block, often women would park across the street and just walk over, not bothering to cross at the cross walks at the corners. At that time, the LA police were notorious for giving jaywalking tickets, but they seemed to take special glee in giving out ticket to women coming to the center. Officers would lurk around corners or in doorways and pounce. We soon learned to be good citizens and cross at the cross walks.

BUT AS USUAL for me, the personal and the political were different stories. While the political was finally going well again, the personal was about to go into crisis mode. Since I was busier with my activist work than Helen was, I decided that I would help her find some friends in LA so she wouldn't be lonely. I remembered that she had an ex-girlfriend, Joy, a woman she had really liked, who lived somewhere in the Venice area. I thought that it would be a nice surprise for Helen if I could arrange for her to see Joy again. Sometimes I'm so stupid. I asked around and discovered that Joy was a big bar dyke. I got her phone number, called her, explained who I was, and suggested we meet at a small bar I knew of where she could surprise Helen. She said, "Great." So, that Thursday night, Helen and I walked into the bar, and there was Joy, about a foot taller than me, with straight, chin length blonde hair. She had a very tough, butch manner. Wearing a gray sweatshirt and white slacks, she looked lean and mean to me.

When Helen saw her, she was all "Oh my god." They ran toward each other and were hugging and kissing. I was got that little uncomfortable itch in my stomach. I had expected a quick reunion, maybe the two of them making arrangements to meet some other time, and then Helen and I would be off to one of our favorite bars, a place in Venice called Brothers. But when Joy suggested she meet us there, there was really no way I could object.

When we got there and settled, I had a few dances with Helen and then Joy asked me, all polite as was the custom in those days for old time dykes like Joy, "May I dance with Helen?"

I said, "Oh, god, of course."

Old friends dancing? Fine. But I was left standing alone at the bar for a good hour while they danced and danced and then talked and talked. Since I was obviously irrelevant, I decided I might as well leave them while they caught up with each other.

After what seemed like another hour, I elbowed my way, literally, between them at the bar, and said, "Helen, it's getting late. Why don't we wrap it up?"

She replied, "All right. Just give me a minute to say goodbye."

I agreed to meet her outside.

I was standing on the sidewalk outside the bar talking to the woman owner who was taking a break when suddenly, from out of nowhere it seemed, I got a fist in my face. On my jaw. Neither the owner nor I had seen Joy coming. I was staggering back with no time to get my fists up when Joy hit me again. She then turned around and walked back into the bar. She didn't say a word. That's just what some bar dykes did in those days. Things were changing, but it was there. If a butch thinks, "She's mine," about the femme she is with, you don't even talk to that woman. It was kind of a caveman ownership mentality. That was the kind of thinking the feminists objected to. I got it. I was lucky Joy didn't have the jagged neck of a broken bottle with her.

Helen didn't come home that night or the next. While my jaw was not broken, my heart was. I knew we had not been getting along, but this was too much. By this time, Valerie had gone to live with her father in Plano and I felt very much alone and miserable. I called Toni and Judy, my closest friends in this city I was still relatively new to, and asked them if I could stay with them while I figured out what to do. After a few days with them, I was still very low and convinced myself that this Los Angeles experiment wasn't going to work. I called Dolores for help.

"You stay right there," she ordered me. "I have to take care of a few things and then I'm getting on a plane and I'll come and get you. I'll be there. Just hold on."

She arrived a few days later, but that was a few hours too late to save me. The Sunday Dolores was due to arrive, Helen called me and told me she was back home at our place in Venice. Foolishly, I was just as relieved as I was angry. I was still in lust. Just her voice made my body come alive.

All I could say was, "Are you back to stay?" No recriminations.

She replied, "Well, of course."

That's all we said. Really. That was it.

Later that night, Dolores arrived at Toni and Judy's where I was waiting for her. I couldn't look at her, embarrassed to have had her come all the way out here for nothing.

"Helen came back," I murmured.

She just gazed at me like I was out of my mind. She sighed. "So you're not coming home?"

I said, "No, I wanna stay."

"One of these days I'm going to kill you."

So Dolores went back to New York City and I stayed in California with Helen.

The Store

ANOTHER CRISIS LOOMED. Shortly after coming to LA, I had hired a lawyer and sued *Newsday* for my unemployment benefits and had won a $14,000 settlement. I also started to receive monthly unemployment checks. The benefits were due to end in late 1971, so the pressure was on for me to find a better way to support us. First, realizing I would be better off buying rather than renting, I bought a small house on Nowita Place in Venice, not far from the beach. With its three bedrooms, a small den, a dining room, two baths, and a garage, I knew it would be perfect for Helen and me. I used some of the money from my settlement and the little savings I had put away while working at *Newsday* as my ten percent down payment on the $24,500 price tag. I was confident I could make the monthly payments once I got another source of income. We moved in around Thanksgiving in 1971.

Now I had to earn money. I liked the idea of being my own boss so I could have some flexibility in my schedule and continue my activism. I also wanted to use my experience as a commercial artist and running my art galleries to get something going. Since I still had some settlement money left in the bank, I began to check out business opportunities. One day I noticed an ad in the paper about a stationery store on Ventura Boulevard in Van Nuys up for sale for $8,000, including inventory. I was hesitant, but Helen said she would help out as the salesperson so I bought the place. I really had no idea what I was doing. I needed to spend even more money to stock the store because the inventory was pretty sparse.

To help pay the rent and maybe bring in more customers, I also offered a guy I knew the opportunity to rent the space in the back of the store for his printing business. As I did in my first gallery, I set up my drawing board in public view, this time in the window of the store. We hoped that would draw folks into the store for graphic arts or other merchandise and printing services. We started to attract some business but not enough to live off of. Helen volunteered to try to drum up printing and graphic arts customers in the area.

As it turned out, instead of selling, she was going over to the LA headquarters for the Presidential campaign of Shirley Chisolm. In 1968, Chisolm, an ardent feminist, had been the first black woman elected to Congress, and now she was running the first ever campaign of any woman or black person for President. I don't know why Helen felt she couldn't tell me. Perhaps she thought I would be angry at her for not doing her job. I probably would have been. We needed the business. But maybe a compulsion to lie was just part of her personality. Whatever the issue, she never brought in any customers to help us out.

OUR BUSINESS WAS not the only thing Helen was stepping out on. She was also stepping out on me. Again. By this time in late 1971, we had gotten to know a lot of lesbians in the area. One of them was Arlie, a woman who lived in West LA and was part of NOW. She was not the ownership type of butch like Joy was, but she had a sense of control and power about her that made her very attractive. She oozed energy and confidence. I should have known then that trouble was coming when she came up to me at the NOW center one day and told me she had recently gotten to know Helen but only a little.

She continued, "Helen's really nice, isn't she?"

I replied, flattered about my girlfriend, "Yeah, she really is."

"She's got a great figure."

I smiled. "She's got a dynamite figure." I was willing to brag. After all, she was my girlfriend. A stupid move. Arlie nodded and walked off. I didn't think anything of it, but I clearly should have.

Shortly after my conversation with Arlie, Helen and I hosted a Christmas get together at our house. We had invited just about all the lesbians that we'd met in Los Angeles and had quite a large crowd. The party was going really well until I walked into the dining room at the wrong time. The way the house was set up, a large mirror on one wall of the dining room reflected not just the dining room but also one of the bedrooms right off of it. When I stepped into the dining room from the adjoining living room that night, I glanced at the mirror and saw the reflection of Helen and Arlie standing near the bed kissing. It was over in a second. I am pretty sure that no one else saw the kiss. Certainly no one said anything to me about it. But I saw it. That was enough. I thought, "Oh, god, not again," but I didn't say anything about it to Helen or anyone else. The party went on with me miserable.

A couple of days later Helen told me she was going to go out and do some shopping. Fine. No problem with that. After she took off, in a car I had bought for her by the way, I also left the house to run some errands. I stopped to get gas. While I was filling the tank, an image of Helen's car in front of Arlie's house suddenly appeared in my mind. I mean a clear, complete picture. Trees. Street. A gorgeous southern California day filled with sun and brightness. I immediately stopped what I was doing, got into my car, and drove over to Arlie's. Sure enough, there was Helen's car in front of the house just as I had seen it in my vision. I parked and went up to Arlie's door. I knocked.

Arlie called out, "Who is it?"

I said, "It's Ivy."

I heard rustling noises. I just stood there. Three or four very long minutes later, Helen stepped out of the house.

All I said was, "I'm following you home."

She got into her car, I got into mine. I followed her home. We went into the house. On the drive back, I had decided that I couldn't live with someone who betrayed me like that, twice, once with Joy, now with Arlie.

There was also her drinking. I told her, "I want you to move out."

She whined, "I have nowhere to go."

I answered, "That's really not my problem."

Well, it became my problem. I couldn't put Helen out onto the street. I just couldn't do it. And she wouldn't move. She . . . would . . . not . . . move. I decided the only solution—are you ready for this—was for me to move. But with the mortgage I was already paying by myself, I couldn't afford a separate place on my own.

Finally, a friend, Pat Demslo, invited me to stay at her place. She was a life saver. She was at least twenty years older than I was, but we were good friends. OK, OK, we become lovers for a short time. This was another one of my emerging patterns. An almost immediate rebound relationship. Or more likely, an affair or two. Maybe at those times I needed reassurance that I was still an OK person. Fortunately, Pat and I both recognized pretty quickly it wasn't going to work. We remained friends and roommates.

In the meantime, I kept calling Helen to tell her she had to move, but she wouldn't budge. None of my reasoning, pleading, or threats worked. After about three months of this, I came up with the only solution I could think of, a pretty drastic one. I would sell the house. Then she would have to move. This shows how desperate I was. So in 1972 I sold that nice Venice house and made a $3,000 profit, a goodly amount of money for me in those days.

Helen ended up not moving in with Arlie as I thought she might, but with Lynn Harper, a stunning, very elegant, very confident looking black woman we both knew. Before Helen and I had broken up, I had watched Helen and Lynn share a number of dances at a lesbian dance at a bar on Santa Monica Boulevard that Helen and I had gone to. I worried some about it but not too much. Helen was attractive. Women often asked her to dance. Helen and I went home together, and I assumed that was the end of Helen and Lynn.

From what I heard, when I sold the house, Helen called Lynn and told her she had no place to go. Lynn took her in. Evidently, they had made more of a connection than I had realized. I guess it worked for them. They stayed together for about five years.

Progress

BY THE EARLY seventies, we in the movement were feeling pretty good about the progress we were making. The constant demonstrations, lobbying, letter writing, and educational efforts had borne some significant fruit. In addition to the spate of victories in the late sixties and early seventies having to do with women and work, the fight for women's reproductive rights was finally moving ahead.

In 1970, both New York state and Hawaii gave women the right to have safe and legal abortions. Other states soon followed. Then, in 1972, in Eisenstadt v. Baird, the Supreme Court forbade limitations on the distribution of birth control or birth control information to any woman, married or unmarried. The Baird in this case was Bill Baird, one of the male heroes of the birth control movement. In spite of being thrown in jail a number of times, he didn't give up on his campaign for accessible birth control for all women until he reached the Supreme Court. The Court based its decision on a women's right to privacy, which paved the way for another landmark case. In its 1973 Roe v. Wade decision, the Court legalized abortions throughout the country. The sexual revolution, for better or worse, was on.

There was more. With our almost constant lobbying, we finally got Title IX of the Education Amendments of 1972, passed. This regulation basically prohibited sex discrimination in all aspects of education that received federal funding, which covered just about all schools, kindergarten through universities. Perhaps its most visible, and to me wonderful, effect was in women's sports. Because of Title IX, women's athletic programs had to receive the same amount of funding as men's. This meant girls and women had many more athletic opportunities opened to them. While this wasn't enough to change the Neanderthal image of some of female athletes as overly masculine and probably lesbians and certainly not date material, it gradually got a lot more women involved in sports and positively changed women athletes' views of themselves. All female athletes should thankful for Title IX.

In the meantime, in 1970, a group of women from Boston put together a mimeographed booklet on women's health called *Women and Their Bodies*. It was republished the next year, 1971, by the New England Free Press, as the revelatory *Our Bodies, Ourselves.* Made up of testimony from everyday women and women health care providers, it took the power to determine the truth about women's bodies away from the patriarchal medical establishment and gave it to women, becoming kind of a bible for women and their bodies. It's still in print, in a number of version including for kids and the elderly, today. In more ways than Ti-Grace had imagined, her dream of women controlling their own bodies was becoming a reality.

AROUND THAT TIME, I was getting friendlier with Gilda Cohen, a newly budding feminist who had been my lawyer in my unemployment benefit case against *Newsday.* Gilda and I were talking one day when she suggested we start a women's publishing company. After all, I was a graphic artist and I had a printer with a press at the back of my store. Our idea was to publish books by and about women that reflected real women's lives and thoughts, not the pap that was generally published in the mainstream press. We named the press Wollstonecraft Publishing after the eighteenth century feminist most famous for her essay, "A Vindication of the Rights of Women" and opened our doors in 1973. I hadn't heard of any other presses with the same mission when we started, but I guess we were part of the spirit of the times. Those years saw the creation of a number of women's and lesbian presses, including one of the earliest, The Feminist Press which started in New York in 1970 and is still in business. Women were on the move.

Gilda handled the business end, and I worked as the press's creative director, designing and illustrating the books we published. My favorite of all those we worked on was *Ms.ery* by Anne Wittels, a critique of views of housework that the women's movement was revealing as false. Anne wrote lines using the clichés about women and I illustrated scenes to match. An example was a little boy asking his mother why she doesn't work. My illustration featured a harried looking woman in a housecoat and apron surrounded by a vacuum cleaner, mops, brooms, and other household tools. I was particularly proud of this publication because I'd been asked to illustrate it by Anne. I was also proud because Anne had been a member of one of the CR groups I had recently facilitated in Palos Verdes, a wealthy community on a peninsula jutting out into the ocean south of Los Angeles. I was pretty sure that if it hadn't been for consciousness raising, she never would have written the book at all.

The Palos Verdes groups I ran represented an important breakthrough not just for Anne and other women in the groups, but also for me. By that time, early 1973, I had been conducting consciousness raising groups at the LA Women's Center, local NOW groups, and for other nearby non-profit women's groups, much as I had done for NOW in New York. I never charged anything. Then I got a call from Flo Zeigler.

"You don't know me," she said, "but I heard of you and your CR groups from a friend. I have a proposition for you. I'll get a group of women together if you will come and do consciousness raising in Palos Verdes."

It hadn't occurred to offer CR in private homes, never mind in such a privileged neighborhood. "Why not?" I thought. Then I had a radical idea. These women in Palos Verdes had money. I needed to make money. Why not charge them?

"I'd love to do it," I replied. I took a breath. "But I'd have to charge $2 a person for each session." With a full complement of twenty women, that would give me forty bucks a session, a significant amount of money to me.

Flo didn't hesitate. "That's fine."

Soon after that, we began our eight weeks of two hour sessions at Flo's luxurious hilltop home. In a short time, word about this group spread within the community, and before I knew it, I was facilitating about seven or eight sessions a week split between days I could get off and evenings. By the end of these sessions, for the first time many of these women saw themselves as autonomous, intelligent people deserving lives beyond the roles and social expectations of them as upper-class wives and mothers. Some started businesses. Some went back to professions they had once trained for or pursued new ones. One fulfilled a dream of becoming a radio broadcaster. A number went back to school, got degrees, and started their own careers. And some, like Anne, became active feminists. That was the transformative power of CR.

THAT FIRST YEAR, I thought the press was doing well enough. We weren't putting out a lot of books, but I was enjoying working with writers, helping them with design and illustrations as needed. Gilda wanted more. With my reluctant agreement, she brought in a friend who had been an editor for a big publishing company to try to bring in some other authors. She was very sure of herself. All right, she was arrogant, and she was backward. A few months after her arrival, she called me aside and said that, for the sake of the press, I couldn't go out and talk about being a lesbian as I had been doing in my activist work. Flashes of the bad old days of NOW and others being afraid of the lesbian label! I was furious.

"I'll continue being out as a lesbian as often and wherever I want to be," I spat back at her.

She retreated then but wouldn't let it go. She kept hounding and hounding me about this. I got angrier and angrier and more frustrated. All the joy went out of the enterprise. Finally, as I did sometimes when I felt something could not be worked out, I walked away. I had had enough. I hired a lawyer and sued for all the assets of the Press, which were primarily the remainders of the books we had published. There had only been one or two besides Anne's book that had actually gotten out the door. I won the suit. The Press folded. It had lasted about eight months. I was proud of what we had done, but still very disappointed.

In the meantime, the stationery store was barely making any money aside from the few jobs I had designing and printing business cards, stationery, and other printed matter for some of the local businesses. It was not enough. I sold the place to the man in the back with the printing press. I got my $8000 back, but I considered that venture pretty much a total failure.

Mary Carol, Acting, and Illness

IN EARLY 1972, a year before the Wollstonecraft project got started and around six months after I had split with Helen, a dark blonde with a round face, freckles, and a big smile caught my attention at one of the CR groups I was moderating at the women's center on Pico. Cute, I thought to myself, very Irish and very wholesome, with not a wrinkle on her face. This was Mary Carol Riley. She was thirty-eight to my forty-five but looked much younger. We got together for coffee a few times after CR meetings, sparks flew, and we started sleeping together. She had a wonderful positive energy that I couldn't resist after all my difficulties with Helen.

By that time, I had moved out of Pat's place because she had gotten herself a girlfriend and there was just not enough room for all of us. I rented an apartment on Laurel Avenue, just above Sunset, in one of those very LA, two story apartment complexes with outdoor corridors, a pool in the middle, and parking underneath. That's where Mary Carol moved in with me after we had been going together for about a month. I was sure this relationship was going to work better than the last. At the very least, unlike Helen, Mary Carol worked. It wasn't always very much. Before I met her, she had been on TV as a teacher in a Romper Room type show in Baltimore and had been trying to get back on TV since then. In the meantime, she drove a cab and did some work in TV commercials. Hope springs eternal.

Mary Carol was particularly significant in my life because she introduced me to acting. In 1974, after we had been together for about a year, Mary Carol began to ask me to read and rehearse with her for her auditions and the work in commercials she had been getting. I guess I was pretty good at it because one evening, after telling me she thought I was better at the acting stuff than she was, she invited me to come with her to a Lee Strasberg lecture the next week.

"Maybe you can get some work, too," she suggested.

I knew from Mary Carol that Strasberg was an innovative acting teacher and cofounder of the Actor's Studio of the leftist Group Theatre. Good politics, I thought. That was a start. And it was show business. Even then I was still really a country bumpkin when it came to some of the Hollywood aspects of

LA. I had been very impressed, for example, that the apartment complex we lived in was owned by the well-known singer and comedian Dean Martin. I still loved the Hollywood sign and got a kick out of comparing Judy Garland's tiny shoe prints in the cement in front of Grauman's Chinese Theatre to mine. So why not?

The auditorium was packed. I couldn't get very close to the front, but once Strasberg started talking about Method Acting, everybody else sort of faded away. I felt like he was speaking directly to me. His idea that actors must tap into their own emotional experiences in order to portray the emotions and actions of the people they are playing mesmerized me. I was fascinated by the need for total concentration on the role—physical, psychological, and mental—that he described, a practice that forced the actors to both get into themselves and out of themselves. Old fantasies about performing that I had secretly indulged in while at Pratt came flooding back.

In those Pratt days, most lunchtimes I would cook up my carton of macaroni and cheese in the butler's kitchen on the second floor of the original Pratt mansion (interestingly called the women's building) and carry the steaming bowl down the ornate staircase to the building's ballroom and its grand piano. Every time I saw the piano across the ballroom, in that moment, I knew I could play even though I had only had piano lessons for a short time when I was a child. Such lessons were common for girls who came from middle class or middle class aspiring families like ours. There was something about the piano that attracted me, so while I didn't take ballet lessons, I accepted piano instruction. The problem was my piano teacher would hit my hand with a ruler every time I made a mistake. I couldn't take the constant hitting, so I stopped. Nonetheless, at Pratt, I'd open the piano and pound the keys. To my endless surprise and disappointment, only noise would come out. How could that be? After all, I loved music and was a good dancer. I'd finally resigned myself to not being able to play, but during those lunch times I sang my heart out anyway, whether anyone was listening or not.

The only other performing I had done had to do with my job at *Newsday*. Every once and a while, we staffers got to propose a story. So, when I was still with Eddie, thinking about my young kids, I got permission from the paper to illustrate a story about what it was like to be a clown. "The Greatest Show on Earth," the Ringling Brothers Barnum and Bailey Circus, the largest, most popular circus of the day, was just then performing at Madison Square Garden. One of its professional clowns agreed to take me under his wing. I didn't tell any of this to my kids because I wanted them to be surprised when I came into the circus ring as a clown when they were in the audience. I was so nervous on the day of the performance that I sipped Pepto Bismol all the way to the Garden. Once I arrived, I put on the clown costume I had designed for myself. I had learned that every clown had his or her own look. Mine was baggy overalls over a white shirt, a big red nose, and a red wig topped with a black derby hat. I carried a fake glass of beer that looked full and on the verge of spilling and a fake talking parrot attached to my shoulder.

The management had given Eddie and the kids prime seats, right next to the circus band. Poor Eddie. He had a migraine that day. Getting over my nervousness once I was in front of the crowd, I frolicked along the perimeter of the arena with the other clowns a few times, capering around as I had been instructed, keeping the audience in a jolly circus mood. Each time, I made a point of stopping in front of my own kids and clowning around, but they didn't recognize me. When they still hadn't by the last go round at the end of the performance, I again stopped in front of them, but this time, I took off my nose and wig. Their mouths dropped open. I still have a picture of the kids like that, mouths open. Laura and Lisa each wrote her own version of the circus with their mother as a clown which I illustrated. We got a double page spread in *Newsday*.

ENTRANCED BY STRASBERG and always eager to try out new things, I went down to the Strasberg Institute as soon as I could. Since the courses were pretty inexpensive and didn't require auditions, I signed up for acting, improvisation, and singing for actors. I was eager to get out of myself while getting in, or getting into myself by getting out. Either sounded good to me.

It totally worked for me. I loved my classes. Through the Method exercises, I was learning to be more emotionally self-aware, taking the risk of plunging into the chaos of my feelings and desires and turning them into performance. I also was learning how to move my body easily and more self-consciously at the same time.

Unfortunately, these lessons were abruptly cut short in November of 1973. During one of those improv class sessions in which we walked around the room for a while with our eyes opened, and then with our eyes closed—the idea was to learn to sense rather than see who was there and not bump into anyone or anything—I suddenly felt an overwhelming fatigue. My legs trembled so badly I had to sit down. I couldn't continue the class. I managed to get home to rest, but over the next few days, I got worse. I could barely stand. I finally dragged myself to the nearby Queen of Angels Hospital where I was admitted for tests. They couldn't find anything wrong so just sent me home.

That didn't mean I felt any better. I could hardly get out of bed. I felt horrible overall and had no energy and no appetite. I mean really no appetite. I lost twenty-four pounds in one week. You could literally almost see the weight melt off of me. With no diagnosed physical reason for my condition, desperate for a cause so I could find a cure, I concluded that the problem must once again be, as Dr. Gerkin would say, in my head. Maybe I was responding psychosomatically to Los Angeles. Maybe I would feel better if I moved back to New York. I'd been having pangs of missing the city and knew Mary Carol would be pleased. She thought she would have a better shot at the kind of acting she wanted to do in New York than in LA. I decided we should move.

I wasn't one to hang around once I had made a decision. So, as soon as I could gather a little energy, we packed everything we could into Mary Carol's car and took off for New York. Within a day, I was exhausted, dizzy, nauseous, and feeling pretty rotten all over again. I could hardly sit in the car. We were near Las Vegas so found a room in one of the large casino-hotels. I managed to drag myself into bed only to have Mary Carol abandon me to try her luck in the casino.

"If you need me, have me paged," she breezily told me as she walked out the door.

Well, by the middle of that night, I needed her. I was burning up. I guess I was in pretty bad shape because as soon as she got back, Mary Carol called the house doctor, and he called an ambulance. Even in that feverish state, or maybe because of it, I remember that my first ambulance ride was pretty exciting with us speeding down the road with the siren screaming and the bright lights of Vegas flashing by.

I ended up being admitted to the hospital, but once again, no one seemed to be able to figure out what was wrong with me. So it was something of a surprise when early the next morning, an anesthesiologist came in and told me I was going to be taken down later for surgery to remove my gall stones. Sure, whatever, I thought, too sick to really process what was going on.

When Mary Carol came to visit me that morning and asked how I was doing, I responded downheartedly, "Aaaah, they're going to operate later."

"What for?"

I said, "Gall stones."

"You don't have gall stones."

"I guess I do." I was so sick, I didn't care. They could have cut my head off.

Mary Carol knew that wasn't right. When a couple of orderlies came in a short time later to roll me to the operating room, Mary Carol wrapped her arms around the iron bed frame and me. "You're not taking her. You have the wrong patient. She doesn't have gall stones."

"We have our orders," one of the men replied, tugging at the bed.

"Well, she's not going."

The orderlies began trying to physically pry her from the frame. She held on, telling them over and over to check my chart. I just lay there only half aware of what was happening. Finally, one of the orderlies picked up their orders and my chart. Uh oh. Turned out that the orders were for Mrs. Ivy, not Ivy Bottini. They sheepishly apologized and left us still without a diagnosis. At least I didn't have gall stones.

BY THIS TIME, my kids had been told that instead of being on my way back to the east coast and them, I was in the hospital. The next thing I knew, Laura had flown out, got me discharged from the hospital, and flew me, in a wheelchair, back to New York and my aunt, uncle, and mother's place in Lynbrook. Mary Carol was left to drive our car and possessions the rest of the way cross country by herself.

Laura managed to find a doctor through her contacts at the medical supply company where she worked. This doctor knew what he was doing and gave me a diagnosis. Finally. I had Graves' disease, a thyroid problem. How had all the others missed it? I don't know. All I know was that I was put on medication and slowly started getting my strength back. But once again, I was trapped in Lynwood and would stay that way until I felt better and could take care of myself or until Mary Carol arrived and she could take care of me somewhere else.

Return to New York — My Show

MY RETURN TO New York brought the next step in my activist career: performing. Within two weeks of my arrival, I got a phone call from a woman from New York City NOW. Even with me ill and exiled to Lynwood, word had clearly gotten out that I was back.

"I have a proposition for you," she began. "We're doing a seven-week theatre series at Town Hall called *Women for Women*, and we hear you have an act. We'd like you to perform on opening night."

"Well," I thought with a good deal of satisfaction, "I guess I'm not *persona non grata* in New York anymore."

A lot had to have changed for me to be getting this phone call. And it had. But not just for me personally. At the same time as legislative and judicial struggles continued, women, led by lesbians in many instances, were creating a whole new women-centered intellectual and cultural universe. San Diego State College announced the first of many women's studies programs in 1970, an acknowledgment, just as black studies departments had been, of the bias in scholarship and what had passed as academic truth. In 1971, *Ms.* Magazine published its first issue as an insert in *New York* magazine. That same year Jeanne Cordova, who later became a good friend, began publishing *The Lesbian Tide*, the first nationally distributed lesbian journal after *The Ladder* which had begun its run in 1955. Olivia Records was formed in 1973 to promote lesbian music. A year later, in 1974, The Michigan Womyn's Music Festival, a mainstay of women-only cultural events until 2015, began. 1973 also saw the founding of Naiad Press which was dedicated to publishing and distributing lesbian authored works to the increasing number of women's bookstores around the country, as well as to any other outlets that would stock them.

There were women's events of all kinds, from workshops and panels on topics ranging from resume writing for women entering the workforce for the first time to vaginal self-exams and masturbation. "Women," or the more radical "Womyn" as part of the title or description of an event became code for lesbian. If you were one, you understood that. But women of all sorts and desires flocked to the movement and these happenings. This invitation from NOW was my chance to take part in this cultural wave and use whatever acting talent I might have to benefit the movement.

There were two problems, though. One that I was sick. The other that I didn't have an act. My guess was that news of my taking acting lessons had morphed into me having an act. But this NOW offer was too good an opportunity to miss.

"When is the show?" I asked.

"March 4, 1974."

That was a few months away. I made a quick calculation. Yes, I convinced myself. That would give me enough time to fully recover from my illness and create a show.

"OK, I'm free." We talked a little more about what was expected and then I hung up. What had I been thinking?

Shortly after this call, Mary Carol arrived in Lynbrook. We didn't last long there. I was getting my strength back and was eager to move to Manhattan, the center of feminist activism in New York City. We found an apartment to sublet near the Columbia University campus on West 93rd Street in one of those wonderful old buildings where the windows are high and wide and let in a lot of light. The interior was spectacular with huge, marble fireplaces, columns, and counters and two gracious sized bedrooms. This is where I developed and honed my show.

As March 4th got closer and closer, and I had no ideas for my performance, I began to panic. Strasberg saved me. I thought back to some of the methods I had learned and started improvising. I visualized myself in the womb, floating with the cord attached, letting my body silently act this out. Soon, I imagined myself bored with this drifting.

"I gotta get out of here. I've been here so long, I'm just so tired of this." I looked around. "What's that? It's a tunnel. There's a light at the end. I'm outta here. But what will I take with me? Oh, I'll take my blanky."

All of this was pantomimed. I started miming pulling the placenta down around and off me. I finally got out. I acted out being picked up by the doctor and held upside down. I could see the doctor and thought happily, "Oh, there's a big me" until he slapped me. My introduction to life and men. "What the hell! What are you doing?" But then I looked down at my hands, smiled, and said, "Oh, these are going to be fun!" That was the beginning of my one woman feminist show, *Everywoman*.

Once I got going, I was pretty pleased with my progress, but as the date of the performance got closer, I began to get more and more anxious. This was to be my big stage debut. What if I flopped? Mary Carol tried to calm me down but that wasn't enough. I needed someone who had experience on what was the fast developing women's performance circuit to reassure me, and maybe be my opening act. That turned out to be Maxine Feldman, a six foot four inch tall, three hundred pound feminist singer-song writer and good friend from Los Angeles. With her large body covered with blue farmer overalls, and her untamed, dark, curly hair, I knew she would make an impression and take some pressure off of me.

Once I got NYC NOW's agreement to have Maxine be my opening act, I invited her to New York to stay with Mary Carol and me in our spacious apartment. That way she could be close by when I needed her coolness. Or when I needed a distraction. While a real professional when it came to performing, she was also something of a wild woman. One particularly memorable night, Maxine decided to give streaking, the then popular craze of running through public places naked, a try. She chose the feminist restaurant, Mother Courage, for her streak. Opened in 1972 by Jill Ward and my old crush Dolores on West 11th Street, two blocks above Hudson in Greenwich Village, this eatery was the first of its kind established to serve women, at least as far as any of us knew. In no time, lesbians and feminists from all over, high-profile and low, rich and poor, began to gather and feel at home there, including me. It was *the* feminist hangout in NYC. A welcoming hotbed of organizing and feminist activity, it gave comforting proof at a time of much movement infighting that sisterhood could work.

As planned, the three of us, Mary Carol, Maxine, and I, drove to the restaurant in my Volkswagen Beetle. Mary Carol and I parked in front of the restaurant, went in, and sat down, leaving the clothed Maxine in the car. A short while later, a totally naked Maxine, all three hundred pounds of her bouncing around, came running through the restaurant. She was so fast, I barely even got a glimpse of her. After an astonished silence, the whole place burst into laughter. That was Maxine. Maxine ended up living with me and Mary Carol for a few months until she found her own place in NYC.

EVERYWOMAN BECAME THE story of a young tomboy who is forced to give up baseball, the game she loves, and conform to what is expected of girls. In due course, she marries and has kids. Her husband, ironically the manager of a baseball team, is often away, leaving the main character to raise their children and take care of the house on her own. The children grow up. The husband dies. His two sons are too alienated from him to come to the funeral. The daughter and granddaughter come, though. The grandmother then gets the bat she has never thrown away, gives it to her granddaughter, and tells her, "Never put it down unless you really want to.'" After the Town Hall performance, I was swamped with tearful praise and gratitude. I had hit a chord. Women were hungry for entertainment that exposed the truths of their lives, but which also offered hope of empowerment and change. The leaders of several different NOW chapters immediately invited me to do my show for their chapters. More chances at consciousness raising. And at performing. How could I say no?

The first time I got money for one of my performances was from a NOW chapter in New Jersey. They paid me $300. That was a lot of money, especially for doing a thirty-five minute show that I had been doing for free at NOW chapters around the northeast. It hadn't occurred to me that any of these chapters would be able to pay me. New Jersey doing so was a revelation.

"Wow!" I thought. "I could make a living with this, do well and do good at the same time."

But I knew that my audiences deserved more than a half hour show for $300 dollars. I remembered that I had been pretty good at improv in my classes at Strasberg and thought the techniques I learned there could work well at these shows. Besides, improv would give me a chance to interact more directly with the women in the audience. So, once I began to get paid for my performances, after I did *Everywoman* I would come out onto the stage and shout out to the audience, "Give me a topic and see where I go with it. Give me an idea. Come on, come on, come on." I would take the responses I thought had some potential for humor and a feminist twist and create a scene. I called this expanded show, *The Many Faces of Woman.*

Probably the most popular piece came from the suggestion from a shadowy form way up in the balcony who yelled out in response to my call for ideas, "Do inserting your first Tampax." OK, I thought. This could be good. After a few moments of consideration, I started miming opening the box and taking a tampon out. I looked it over, sniffed it, and then began playing with it, you know, like it was a cigar or a spinning top. I even mimed it as a bomb, pretending I was lighting its string and then making an explosive kaboom sound. But what got the most laughter were my efforts to insert it. I'm missing, poking around, not being able to find where it goes. Finally I'm moving it in . . . oh, it feels pretty good. I start wiggling my hips, dancing a bit of a jig, singing, "If you want to see me do my thing, pull my string." The audience would howl with laughter. After a while, that routine and others that had been frequently requested ceased being improv and became part of the act itself. I ended up performing *Many Faces* all over the country over the next few years. But more on that later.

One of Ivy's head shots, c. 1975.

Ivy (right) on stage with singer-songwriter Harriet Schock, c.1975.

A flyer for Ivy's show, c. 1975.

A flyer for Ivy's show, with an announcement for a consciousness raising workshop, 1975.

Ivy onstage during her show "Many Faces of Woman," 1975. *Courtesy of ONE Archives at the USC Libraries*

The sleeve of Ivy's comedy record, "Women's Lip," 1976.

Mary Carol Exits

AS WAS OFTEN the case in my life, when one aspect of it was on the rise, another was going in the opposite direction. During the time when my show was evolving, my relationship with Mary Carol was going downhill. One of the things that was getting to me was her drinking. By the end of 1973 and in early 1974 or so, Mary Carol would drink just about anything alcoholic, and in large quantities. This would sometimes make her very rude. But even when she wasn't drunk, she had started acting in what I considered unacceptable, tactless, and sometimes very hurtful ways, especially once we were back in New York. I don't know why that city brought out the worst in her, but it did. One of the most disturbing incidents happened shortly after we were back in the New York area but still in Lynbrook. It had to do with Peg Wilson.

I hadn't seen Peg for probably fifteen years. I had kept in touch with her while I was in college and continued seeing her now and again, often around Thanksgiving or Christmas, even after she got married. Yes, she had gotten married during my last year at Pratt. I had known about Bob Hinkle, the man she married, since 1944, my senior year in high school. That's when he had started corresponding with her. He had been one of her students ten or fifteen years before that, when she was just starting out. By the time he was writing these letters, he was in his late twenties and a soldier. She'd get his letters and read them to me. They were not romantic at first, just newsy. I wasn't really worried or jealous because of the age gap. She had to be about five or ten years older than he was. I thought he was just another lonely soldier. But he began to get more affectionate and personal in his letters, writing things like, "I can't wait to see you" and "You're so important to me." I know, not very sexy, but still. I had no idea what Peg thought of him, but she was at the very least pleased to receive these letters. For that, I hated him. I just hated him. I was so jealous. "Don't come home," I thought to myself. Mean. All I knew was that this guy might be a threat. I didn't want to share Peg with anyone.

Much to my annoyance, once he was stationed back in the States, Bob was often at Peg's place when I was. And just as I had hated him when he was writing letters, I hated him in person. Once I was in college, I wasn't as dependent on Peg as I had been when I was in high school, but I was still very jealous. I also didn't understand why Peg liked him. He appeared to be a nice guy, but he seemed so effeminate and he spoke with a lisp. Really. Even I could take one look at him and recognize him as one of those gay people. So what was he doing with her and her with him? A number of years later, when I was more experienced with the ways of the world, I guessed that Bob knew he was gay, Peg knew she was a lesbian, and they wanted cover and companionship. I really think that's what happened. Whatever their reasons, they got married.

Whenever I saw them after that, they seemed to get along fine. I finally managed to accept that and be happy for her. But I never warmed to Bob, and I don't think he warmed to me. Often, he would disappear when I came over to visit even after I was married. But all that had been a while ago. I hadn't seen Peg since my kids were about three and five and our lives just went in different directions.

Now here I was back in Lynbrook with Mary Carol. Mary Carol and I were out at a local restaurant when I noticed Peg and Bob. Peg and I recognized each other immediately. She still had her great laugh and the twinkle in her eyes that I loved. Aside from a few gray streaks, she looked like she hadn't aged. The love and gratitude I had felt for her came flooding back. As did my jealousy of Bob. Still, I was very happy to see her, and she seemed equally pleased to see me. We exclaimed and hugged. Then things got awkward, at least for me. I didn't know how to introduce Mary Carol. At this point, I was just about certain Bob was gay and Peg a lesbian, but I wasn't sure how Peg would feel about me being out to her, especially given one big secret of our past.

Nothing seriously bad had happened, but she had come on to me once at the end of the summer after I graduated from high school. I had come over to her place and let myself in as usual. I announced, "Peg, it's me. Where are you?"

She replied, "I'm in the bedroom."

I said, "OK." In all the times I had been to her place, I had never been in the bedroom. I moved into the living room to wait for her to emerge.

This time she called out, "You can come in." So, I walked into the bedroom and saw Peg standing on the other side of the bed in a robe. It wasn't buttoned and parts of her breasts were showing.

I couldn't help but notice this but that it was odd somehow didn't register. I didn't think anything of it. I simply asked, "What are you doing?"

She opened her robe more. She had nothing on. She nonchalantly stated, "I'm sun bathing." I could see a chaise lounge on a little balcony behind her.

I went, "Oh."

Now I was shocked. I didn't know how to react. I knew there was something I should do but I didn't know what. I turned around and walked into the living room, sat on the couch, and waited. Once my surprise subsided somewhat, I realized that that had been an invitation, but I was too innocent and naïve, young and confused, to have any idea what it was I would have been expected to do if I had been able or willing to do anything. In a few minutes, Peg came out of the bedroom fully dressed. We never talked about the incident and, unbelievable as it might sound, we went on as we had been before. I needed it to. My home life was still such a mess that I wasn't going to risk the one stable, comforting relationship I had in my life. I have no idea what was in her mind.

Over time, for me it was almost as if that episode had never happened. Then later, once I understood my own sexuality and acted on it, and Peg hadn't acted on hers, or at least had married Bob, I was afraid she might think badly of me. Now in this restaurant, years later, I was still afraid. I ended up introducing Mary Carol as a friend. I just couldn't say anything else.

Since we had all had gotten to the restaurant at the same time, we decided to have dinner together. Peg and I pretty much spent the entire dinner ignoring the others and catching up with each other. She had retired by this time and seemed quite happy. I somehow managed to give her a summary of my life without mentioning the lesbian part. That ruse, though, didn't last, thanks to Mary Carol. Maybe she was jealous. Who knew with her.

After dinner, Peg suggested we all go to their nearby house for drinks. So, off we went. It started fine. We had settled in with our drinks and were sitting in their living room talking and having a nice time. Then, in the middle of the general conversation, for no apparent reason, Mary Carol got up out of her chair, walked across the room, sat on my lap, and kissed me on the mouth. I'm that irresistible. I looked over at Peg and Peg looked like I had slapped her. I pushed Mary Carol away. She flounced back to her seat with a little smile of satisfaction on her face and sat down. I kept looking at Peg who was just staring at me. I was hoping to see some forgiveness or understanding. There was none. I was totally embarrassed and ashamed.

I got up and said, "I guess we better go."

Peg and Bob came to the door with us. I gave Bob a hug and then Peg. She was very stiff. I understood. We left. That was the last time I saw Peg. She was an amazing woman. She was tremendously caring. I can't imagine who I'd be had she not been in my life. I assume she's long gone now.

Even with her bad behavior, I couldn't let go of Mary Carol, at least not then. It's like some women, including her, put a spell on me.

In early 1974, to save money we had moved to an apartment in Chelsea that we shared with two women who worked for *Ms.* Magazine. This was another gorgeous place. It had recently been redone and had large living and dining rooms and plenty of bedrooms and room for my art supplies. A huge back yard surrounded by a tall wall gave us a lot of privacy.

That summer, Mary Carol got a job at the overnight summer camp she had gone to and been a junior counselor at when she was a kid. That was fine with me. I needed some time to work on refining my show. All was good until I noticed the name Louise kept popping up in the phone conversations we had every other day. My trouble radar went off, but I didn't say anything. Then one day when I called, Louise answered the phone. This time all the alarm bells went off.

When Mary Carol got on the phone, I demanded, "What's going on with you two? What's she doing there?"

Mary Carol calmly retorted, "Louise was one of my campers years ago. She's a counselor now. It doesn't mean anything. Don't worry."

I didn't believe her. I knew, just knew, that Mary Carol and Louise were lovers. That betrayal was the breaking point for me. I told Mary Carol, "We're done." But I wasn't finished. I was furious. "And you better get some help for yourself. You're an alcoholic and you need help."

This time we did break up. And she did get help. She's been sober ever since.

New Love

AFTER BREAKING UP with Mary Carol, I moved from the apartment in NYC back to Long Island where it was cheaper. All I had to support myself was the revenue from the shows and from sales of the t-shirts I designed and sold at the events. CR was bringing in some but not much. But overall, I felt good because I was away from the Mary Carol drama and on the prowl again. And the dark cloud that had shadowed my departure from NYC a few years earlier was totally gone. I was the toast of the town and the surrounding area with *The Many Faces of Woman.*

That's when the west coast called. Literally. In early 1975, the California NOW state coordinator invited me to be an mc/speaker/performer at their April 1975 conference in Sacramento. This meant doing the welcome and keynote on Friday, conducting a CR demonstration on Saturday morning, and then performing my show on Saturday night. They were offering me $300. "Well," I thought to myself, "they sure want to get a lot out of me for $300." But I said yes since they were paying the air fare. I arranged with them to fly me in and out of LA so I could spend some time there and connect with friends. Maybe I could also squeeze in a quick Strasberg seminar to hone my skills.

I arrived on Wednesday, spent a few days in LA, and then I drove up to Sacramento with a couple of women from LA NOW. Friday night I gave my keynote on consciousness raising. I may have been biased, but I sincerely believed, and still believe, that a number of the legislative and judicial victories the women's movement had seen in the few years before the conference came about because of CR enlightening women and inspiring them to push for their rights. So, in 1974, the Equal Credit Opportunity Act (ECOA) had passed, giving single, widowed or divorced women the opportunity to get credit on their own without having to have a man co-sign their credit applications. Then 1975 saw the end of the exclusion of women from juries simply because of their gender. That was the gist of my address that night: that CR could change lives and the world. It was well received, so I was confident that the CR workshop on Saturday would draw a decent crowd. I was wrong, but in a good way.

The room the workshop was to be held in filled way beyond its thirty-five person capacity almost as soon as the doors opened. Women filled the chairs, the floors, and the aisles, sitting or standing wherever they could. Finally, the organizers closed the doors because of fire department regulations. But one brazen woman sneaked in at the last moment and jammed herself in on the floor against a wall. If she hadn't done that, I don't know if I would have noticed her. But I did and was immediately taken by her beautiful face with its high cheek bones and peaches and cream complexion set off by her shoulder length dark brown hair. Not to mention her very nice figure.

It was like I was struck with a lightning bolt. I could see she was younger than I was, but that didn't matter. I managed to get through the day-long worship without giving her undue attention, but it was a struggle.

That night, I got to the venue of my evening performance a little early. I had a plan to get her attention. Once I spotted her, I settled myself nearby, not too close, not too far. I didn't talk to her. When I was introduced to the crowd from the stage, I stood up and started stripping, removing my vest, then my top, and then my pants. I twirled each item around my head before I tossed it in the direction of this entrancing woman. I could hear women murmuring with alarm at this very un-feminist activity, "What's she doing? What's she doing?" But it had the result I wanted. As I climbed the stage in my full body leotard, I saw the woman I hoped would soon be my beloved gather my discarded garments with a knowing smile. Success, I thought, as I stepped onto the stage.

After the show, I retrieved my clothes and we introduced ourselves. Her name was Dottie West. OK, Dottie. I got a name, but that was about it. I was famished and exhausted from my show so went off to get something to eat, too flustered by her presence to even invite her along. I was certainly off my game.

Later that might, a couple of women from the conference invited me to a casual gathering in their hotel room. I thought it would be a quiet, good way to unwind, but when I opened the door, I discovered about thirty women filling the room, sitting on the bed and chairs and against the walls, the dresser, the closet door. And there was Dottie leaning on the wall at the far end of the room. My heart skipped the proverbial beat, but I wanted to be cool and not make it too obvious that I was intensely interested. I didn't go over to her and say hello. I just waved. Almost immediately, a bunch of women began peppering me with questions and trying to engage me in conversation. I couldn't maneuver my way over to Dottie casually as I had planned. So, I came up with a strategy to get me closer to Dottie without it being obvious what I was doing. At least, that's what I thought.

I broke through the chatter and said to everyone at large, "I'm going, but before I do, I'll kiss everybody goodnight." A very feminist performer thing to do. I stood up, and, starting at the end of the room away from Dottie, gave everybody a peck on the cheek. Goodbye, goodbye, goodbye. I work myself all the way down to Dottie. Very crafty I thought.

As I was leaning in toward her, she whispered in my ear, "Very clever."

She knew what I was doing! It startled me so much that I backed off and didn't even kiss her. I left.

I went back in my room thinking, OK, now what do I do? I couldn't ask her to come up here and stay overnight with me. That would have been my usual style. But she didn't strike me as that kind of person. Besides, I didn't want to make any missteps with her. Breakfast maybe. Yes, breakfast. That would work. So I called her room after I thought the group would have broken up. After much hemming and hawing, I asked her to have breakfast with me the next morning.

She hesitantly said, "OK."

She brought her calendar with her to breakfast, one of those books bulging with all sorts of papers slipped in, from phone numbers to recipes. I saw that as a good sign. So after I managed to converse with her in an adult manner for a while, I asked her for a date. "You know, how about dinner, next week, maybe, when we get back to LA?"

She looked a little startled that I would still be around since everyone knew I lived in New York. "Well see," she replied and I had to hang on to that hope.

I was so far gone that once I found out she was flying back to LA, I ditched the women I had driven up with, booked a ticket on her flight, spending money I didn't really have, and even finagled my way to sitting next to her on the plane.

But my plan for a seductive airplane conversation didn't work out once she started telling me about her boyfriend, John. A boyfriend? Where had that come from? And they were talking about getting married. I immediately hated him. I didn't have to meet him. I just hated him. Not only that, she had been divorced twice—West was her second husband's last name—and had had another long term boyfriend she had broken up with. She wasn't even a lesbian! That should have been a deal breaker since I had pledged to myself never to come on to or get involved with a straight woman. Or someone much younger. Like Dottie. She was nineteen years younger than I was. But I just couldn't help myself with her.

We said good bye at the airport, but I called her the next day asked, "Can you have dinner tomorrow night?"

She responded, "Wait a minute." I heard rustling and I envisioned her going through her date book. Finally, "Yeah, I can do that." I was ecstatic.

THE MOST IMPORTANT information that I got from Dottie during that dinner was that she was open to being with a woman. "Why am I ruling out women? Half the world? Other women aren't," she explained to me. "That's what the lesbians in my San Fernando NOW chapter tell me. So why not try?"

We both knew the answer. There was no reason not to. She put her hand on mine across the table, and I knew I was not the only one feeling the heat between us. We spent that night together. She might have thought it was safe since she knew I would be going back to New York, but I thought paradise had come and I wasn't going to give that up.

Alas, Dottie continued to date John. I think she held on to him because she was frightened of the ledge she was jumping off of with me. And I lived in New York. Why give up this nice, conventional commitment for me, then? Well, uh, sexual attraction? Love? Whatever it was, she insisted that John and I meet.

"He's important to me," she pleaded. "I want everyone I care about to get along."

Give me a break! But I was so desperate to stay on Dottie's good side that I agreed, as long as our get together was in a neutral place. So we met in MacArthur Park near downtown LA and sat on the grass, one of my least favorite things to do, uncomfortably making small talk. This was at least acceptable.

Then the conversation plunged downhill with John declaring, "I'm not worried about your relationship with Dottie because you're a woman."

I replied, "That's exactly why you should be worried."

He just stared at me open-mouthed. Then, rather than hit him, I stood and left the park.

I was right. Dottie and I began a torrid affair. I might have been Dottie's first woman lover, but she took to sex with a woman as eagerly and naturally as I had. We were so infatuated that we could barely keep our hands off of each other, which might have been embarrassing in front of others if we cared. We had a lot, a lot of sex. But that didn't stop her from going away for a weekend with John a few weeks after we first got together. Old bonds and habits are hard to break. Well, I am no angel. The Saturday of the weekend Dottie was off with John, I called a friend from Strasberg and invited myself over to her place for an afternoon of sex. That was the kind of thing I had done a lot in my pre-Dottie single days. It didn't mean anything to me except fun. Mostly, I admit, in this case, it was tit for tat retaliation. In the end, that escapade was more comical than anything else as Kathy and I spent the afternoon sliding off of her satin sheets trying to make love. We both thought it was pretty funny.

But that was it. Aside from that weekend, Dottie and I spent as much of my remaining three weeks in Los Angeles as we could in what turned out to be a kind of erotic, romantic dream time. We even managed to get away for a week to Frazier Park, a wilderness area in the mountains north of Los Angeles. We spent hours inside our cozy A-frame cabin making love, talking, making love, talking. We took breaks and bundled ourselves up in hats, scarves, heavy coats, and boots and walked through the woods and snow, arm and arm, as deer and foxes appeared and disappeared among the trees. It was like a romantic Hollywood movie. Truly wonderful.

By the end of that week in Frazier Park, I knew we had to be together. So one night just before I left to return to New York, I told Dottie that I was only going back to settle my affairs in the city. Then I planned on coming back to LA to live with her. Just like that. She smiled and hugged me.

"OK," she whispered in my ear. She pulled back and grinned. "I guess I'll have to tell John."

Los Angeles Redux

IT TOOK DOTTIE about a month to get her affairs together before she could move in to the town house I had rented on Highpoint Street in Los Angeles with my friend, Jan Holden. The three of us living together made the place affordable, but not really livable. Besides, I still wanted to own. To have my own place seemed even more important at that time because shortly after Dottie and I began to live together, my mother died.

Her death was very sudden, and, in my mind, unnecessary. By then, my Uncle Phil and Aunt Edna had passed away, and my Aunt Myrtle, whose husband Phil had died, had moved into the house to live with my mother. Later their brother Jamie joined them after his wife Grace died. So the place became a family rest home. Everything was as fine as could be expected until October of 1975. I called one Thursday to check up on my mother as I regularly did. Even before my Aunt Myrtle answered the phone, I had a bad feeling. She told me that my mother was too sick with a cold to come to the phone. I knew my mom had a tendency to have her colds go to bronchitis, so I suggested my aunt call a doctor to look at my mother. She said she would.

I called the next day, Friday, only to discover that my mother was still very ill, and my aunt hadn't done anything. Well, she had, but not enough. It seems their family doctor, Dr. Delessio, was out of town and wouldn't be able to come to the house until Monday. (These were still the days of doctors' house visits.) It hadn't occurred to anyone in that house to call another doctor. I was furious, but I had to be satisfied with Monday. I was too far away and without the resources to do anything myself. On Monday morning, Dr. Delessio examined my mother and immediately sent her to the hospital. She died that evening. She was seventy-nine years old.

I knew that all of my aunts and uncle had treated my mother badly for years, belittling or ignoring her, but my aunt not taking my mother's condition seriously when mom was helpless was the last straw for me. Aunt Myrtle had been my favorite relative, but I felt she had killed my mother. I never felt same way about her again and rarely saw her after my mother passed away.

AFTER ABOUT THREE or four months of us living in that apartment, Dottie, who by then had gotten her real estate license (and had gone back to her maiden name, Wine), found an adorable, 690 square feet bungalow on Van Ness Avenue in Hollywood for me to buy. I say me because I never shared finances with any of my partners, even Dottie with whom I was so in love. I had to have that independence. The house was small but had a great patio and was perfect for southern California indoor and outdoor living. And it was inexpensive at $45,000. I had borrowed $500 from my NOW friend Gloria Steinem and another $2,000 from my old Long Island friend Esther to help get me across the country and give me some cushion. I used what was left from that and the little I had just started saving from conducting CR groups again to scrounge together enough for a down payment. Dottie and I moved into our first home together.

On the Road

WITH DOTTIE'S SUPPORT, I picked myself up after my mother's death, reconnected with my LA friends, and plunged back into the movement, determined to somehow make a living working for the cause. At that point, with women from a broad range of circumstances eager to learn about the women's movement and participate in their own liberation, demand for CR was exploding. I was happy to accommodate. Facilitating CR groups became my main income source. I began conducting consciousness raising groups all over California from small towns to big, in living rooms and churches and newly established women's centers at $2 per person per session. It was great. I could see women's lives changing right before my eyes. Aha moments all over the place.

After I had been at this a few months, internal feminist politics poked up its ugly head again. Even though I had codified feminist consciousness raising years earlier, establishing the topics and guidelines that most groups used, I discovered that LA NOW thought CR was theirs. One evening just as I was about to start a session in Fresno, I was handed a cease and desist letter from LA NOW that prohibited me from giving workshops under their name. Basically, that meant I would have to stop doing CR groups.

I thought, "What! Are they out of their minds? I'm the creator of this. It's mine. And I haven't been doing this in their god damn name for a while anyway!"

Adding insult to injury, they had put out a CR manual to replace mine that was antithetical to what I thought of as central to the process. In the LA NOW version, the group was instructed to address a specific question, have everyone take a turn with a predetermined amount of time to answer, and then go on to the next question. My approach was more organic. Sure I had people taking turns, but there were no rigid time limits. I had suggested topics, but they were stepping stones to letting the discussion go where the women wanted it to go. My approach was empowering, theirs was rule bound. So, I ignored NOW's cease and desist letter and handbook and continued conducting CR groups. I never heard from them about it again.

Soon, I had another opportunity to make my living working in the movement. In 1976, I began getting invited to perform *The Many Faces of*

Woman at mainstream and movement venues all over the country. How could I say no? I could make a contribution to the feminist cultural movement and make some money. An added attraction was that Dottie, with her flexible real estate work, could come with me as my accompanist on the piano. At first, I didn't have a manager, but soon demand was so great that I hired Jan Holden, my old roommate, to organize my first six-week national tour. After the popularity of that first tour, I was picked up by a professional agent, Annette Simonini from Williams Management in LA, who organized another nine-week national tour.

Dottie and I travelled as far west as Honolulu, Hawaii, and as far north as Fairbanks, Alaska. Mostly our best audiences were at women's clubs, women's centers, churches, community centers, and on college and university campuses, but I was also booked into well-known mainstream clubs such as The Comedy Store and The Troubadour in LA and A Star is Born in New York City. I even entertained the women at the large engineering firm, TRW.

These tours were grueling. We had a performance almost every day, sometimes two. Our time wasn't our own, before or after shows. Often the members of the many NOW chapters that sponsored the shows would want to talk, share meals, and show us around before shows and party after. I was often too exhausted for that, but since we usually stayed in people's homes, there was always some post-show conversation and expectation for more in the morning. The one time we did manage to be alone became a demanding adventure in another way. After our show in Fairbanks, where, by the way, all the women looked like lesbians to me in their plaid jackets, flannel shirts, and jeans, our sponsors dropped us off in a wilderness cabin. Somehow, they had gotten the idea that I wanted a backwoods experience. The cabin had sunk so much into the permafrost that even short me had to duck to get in the door. There were a few bare light bulbs, a potbellied stove that we had to figure out how to use to get heat, and running water, but no toilet. For that, we would have to go out to the outhouse. We were instructed that to use it at night, we needed to first make noise to scare away the bears. That was not for me. I peed in a cup. The next night, we moved to a condo.

But, it was all worthwhile. We were bringing our feminist message to people all over. In fact, as the fame, or I should say notoriety, of the show spread, I often ended up doing interviews with the local press or on radio shows when we got to town.

I liked to think of the show itself as a comic consciousness raising routine designed to show the ludicrousness of conventional societal views of women's lives and bodies. I wanted women to stop being ashamed of their physical selves, stop listening to convention, and take control. Along with the tampon and menstruation routines, I took on masturbation, gynecologists, contraception, pregnancy and child birth, and the objectification of women's bodies. Interestingly, it took a woman in the audience asking during the improv section for me to do a woman seducing another woman for me to add a lesbian element to the show. Old shames and secrecy die hard. After that, there was always at least one lesbian skit.

One routine that's an example of my method of critiquing society's views of women was what I called a feminist strip tease. While Dottie played and I sang "Be a Clown," the only song I actually sang in the show, I would emerge on the stage heavily made up in a long flowing black lace negligee. Slowly, mock-seductively, I would remove one false eyelash and then another before I proceeded to use my arm to wipe off the thick layer of red lipstick I had applied to my mouth. I continued that with the rest of my makeup, from eye liner to blush.

Next, I ceremoniously removed my wig and tossed it into the crowd. Then, I threw off the negligee to reveal myself in a very Victoria's Secret style, tightly laced black corset that made no secret of my cleavage. But I wasn't finished. I unhooked the corset one unhurried hook at a time, and deliberately and tantalizingly removed that, too, to expose my body with its rolls and bulges in all its realistic glory covered only in a tight black leotard. It may not sound it now, but this kind of mocking of traditional attitudes toward and uses of women's bodies and appearance was pretty radical. After shows, women of all shapes and sizes would pass by and yell to me, "I'm getting a leotard."

As you can imagine, this and my other routines were not the usual fodder for a comedy routine, at least from a non-misogynistic point of view. Women would come backstage after shows to tell me what a relief it was to be able to laugh at how they had always been ashamed of their big, or small, breasts, or at the pain of bad menstrual cramps, or their body hair or their pregnancy waddle. One time at a college on Long Island, a woman came up to me with her two daughters after my second show of the day. The girls looked around eleven and fifteen and, as their mother did, had dresses on. The mother told me that she had come to my earlier show and had had to come back with her daughters to see the later one. She wanted them know they had choices in their lives.

Every once in a while a man would come up to talk to me. I remember two that were particularly interesting. After one show, while I was standing backstage, a very tall, very stocky man wearing a black overcoat came heading for me, moving very fast, his eyes fastened on me.

As he got closer, he put his hands out toward me and I thought, "My god, he's going to hit me." I yelled, "What are you doing?"

I stood with my chest thrust out, my arms akimbo, and my legs spread. Short as I am, I like to think I can be physically formidable when I have to be.

He just grabbed me in a hug and started to cry. "You've just showed me my mother," he sobbed.

Another time, a guy came backstage, also crying. He put his head on my shoulder said, "Now I know why my wife divorced me." More consciousness raising.

It was a great time.

Becoming Gay

AS THE END of 1976 was rolling around, Dottie and I had finished two cross country tours with *Many Faces*, and I had even made a comedy record called "Women's Lip" that featured a few of my sketches. It was time to do something else. My most immediate challenge was to find a more consistent, reliable way of making money. I had saved some money from my shows and was bringing in a little from CR groups I had begun to facilitate again. Sales of the politically themed t-shirts I designed and sold not just for my show but also for other causes I supported also helped. But they weren't enough and I was tired of scrounging. That's when I was offered a job as an administrator at the pioneering Gay Community Services Center on Highland Avenue in LA. Yes, gay—no lesbian in its name. (It's now the Los Angeles LGBT Center and is the largest of its kind in the world.) At the time it opened in 1969, the only other gay center was in Albany, New York, which had started around the same time.

It made sense to grab this job, right? Full time, a movement organization. What was there to object to? Well, it was not so simple. Keep in mind that women, lesbian or straight, had been my thing. That's who I identified with and who made up what I thought of as my community. So taking a job at a gay center where I would have to work with and be sympathetic toward gay men would mean a significant mind set change for me, and in the attitudes of my feminist friends toward me. Making it worse in the eyes of some of the local lesbian activists was that many of the women involved in the Gay Community Center had just concluded a nasty strike against the Center because of its unfair policies toward lesbians. But I was so out of the loop of gay and lesbian politics that I had been totally unaware of the strike and the bad feelings that it had left among many.

ACTUALLY, THE SEED for my shift in identification had been planted in me a few years earlier, in 1973. One January Sunday morning, I woke to my clock radio news reporting "a fire of suspicious origin" that had destroyed the Metropolitan Community Church on Union Avenue. This was no ordinary house of worship. It was the first gay church ever, having opened its doors in 1968 under its pastor, Rev. Troy Perry. Just to make it clear, I wasn't a member of that congregation. I wasn't interested in a patriarchal religion, even in a church that claimed to challenge many of the traditional prejudices. Not for me. At least not then. But when I heard that church members were going to hold a service in the street outside of their burned-out sanctuary, I was moved enough to go down there to at least offer the support of my presence.

I stood across the street from the still smoldering building with the other supporters, lookie loos, TV cameras, reporters, and neighbors as church members, covered in soot and sweat, dragged whatever they could salvage out into the street for a service. A piano and the pulpit had already been placed on a pickup truck. The gay and lesbian church members then gravely filled the ash covered chairs to begin the service. Wow, I thought. Surrounded by the media, they would soon be outed on screens and in newspapers all over LA and probably beyond. It was one thing to be out to each other and maybe those close to us, but this was being out on a whole other level. Most of these men and women were not public figures or activists, but here they were risking their lives, reputations, livelihoods, homes, and families. I was suddenly overwhelmed with the courage of these people, my people, I realized. Emotionally and psychologically, this was the beginning of my transition to the gay movement.

IN THE END, it was a no brainer. I took the job. It was time. Gay liberation was on the move. The first gay pride marches had been held in New York and Los Angeles in 1970. The American Psychiatric Association removed homosexuality from its list of psychiatric disorders in 1973. The first out homosexuals had been elected to pubic office in the United States, both lesbians: Kathy Kozachenko elected in 1974 to the Ann Arbor, Michigan city council and, in 1975, Elaine Noble to the Massachusetts House of Representatives. By the mid-seventies, laws declaring sodomy a crime had been repealed in a number of states, including Colorado, Oregon, Hawaii, and Ohio. A number of locales around the country had actually passed laws that gave gay people some basic civil rights. I wanted to contribute.

My title at the Gay Center was head of the Women's Department. Yes, women's department. "Lesbian" seemed to be a word the gay men who dominated the organization were allergic to. I was in charge of planning programs for lesbians, but I found that my other task, holding workshops and discussions within the Los Angeles county social services departments and other city and state agencies, took up most of my time. My job was to educate government workers out of their misconceptions about and biases against gays and lesbians so that we wouldn't have to endure the physical, verbal, and emotional abuse that all too often came our way when dealing with public officials. In other words, I was doing consciousness raising again, but with straight, mostly male government staffers.

Backlash – Briggs

ALL OF THAT progress in terms of gay and lesbian rights was good, but I knew that there would be a backlash. All my experience and my political intuition told me that anti-gay forces weren't going sit back and let new laws stand or let others be approved. In fact, since around 1975, I had been warning my friends and colleagues not to get too giddy. But they didn't want to hear what they saw as my message of doom and gloom. They wanted to believe that the advances would continue and homophobia would fade away.

They were wrong. In 1977, a coalition of anti-gay forces, fronted by Anita Bryant, a former beauty queen and popular singer, ran a successful campaign to repeal a recently enacted gay rights ordinance in Dade County, Florida. I was very disappointed in Bryant. In the fifties and sixties, I had had a crush on her because of her beautiful voice and face. And now here she was leading the forces of hate.

Spurred by their victory in Florida and spearheaded by Bryant's organization "Save Our Children," anti-gay forces took on gay rights throughout the country, getting pro-gay ordinances repealed as they went. In fact, Bryant became such a symbol of the anti-gay rights campaigns that, taking a page from Cesar Chavez and Dolores Huerta's United Farmworkers grape boycott, the community initiated a boycott of Florida oranges and other citrus fruits, since, along with being a leading gay basher, Bryant was the celebrity spokesperson for the Florida Citrus Growers. Fruits refusing to eat fruit became one of the mottoes of the outraged gay and lesbian communities and their supporters. I even designed a t-shirt for the campaign that read "Anita Bryant sucks oranges." I, and many others, were really pissed.

I KNEW THAT California, that bastion of left wing values and home state of San Francisco, known then as a mecca for gay men, would eventually be a target of Bryant and her ilk. The attack came in 1978 in the form of California Proposition 6, the so-called Briggs Initiative. If passed, the proposition would have banned gay and lesbian teachers from employment in any California public school. Not only that, any teacher who made any positive mention of gays or lesbians in the classroom could also be fired. Obviously, we couldn't let this pass.

To fight the proposition in southern California, I immediately joined forces with Morris Kight, a highly respected longtime activist in the LA gay and lesbian community, to found the Coalition for Human Rights. Shortly after our group got started, a state-wide effort to defeat the initiative called, "Briggs Initiative/No on Proposition 6," was organized with headquarters in San Francisco. Peter Scott and David Mixner, both well-known gay political operatives and professional political campaign consultants headquartered in LA, were hired to run the battle to defeat Briggs. A straight man, Mike Levitt, was then hired as the southern California manager of the campaign. Since I had already spearheaded efforts in our area, I was asked to serve as the Southern California Deputy Director. I took a leave of absence from the LA Gay Center to fully immerse myself in the world of gay and lesbian politics.

While this, like taking the job at the Center, made a lot of sense to me, it didn't to everyone. Lesbian separatists, who had a powerful presence in lesbian circles at the time, were convinced that men would never give up their privilege and women would never be free within the patriarchal system. So women had to live lives apart from men as much as possible. Before my job at the Gay Center, many of the separatists had thought I was one of them. Not unreasonable, really. My causes were women's causes which meant working with women. And since I was a lesbian, living with them. I pretty much only made forays into the straight world for work and for business when necessary. This separation from men hadn't been intentional, but I can see how it might have looked in those heated times.

I think I got a pass from the separatists when I worked in the Women's Department at the Gay Center because of that job title. But joining the male led No on Proposition Six fight was going too far. A number of these separatists turned on me, accusing me of leading them to think I was one of them and then going off and working with men. What could I say? I wasn't abandoning the separatists since I was never one of them in the first place. Besides, Briggs was too potentially devastating to us all to ignore or back off from.

Then there were the gay men working on the campaign. Just as many lesbians were leery of working with men, many gay men were not very eager to work with women, lesbian or straight. It occurred to me then that a good number of gay men lived their own separatist lives, being with other men and avoiding women as much as possible. They weren't eager to let women into their club, even against Briggs.

Problems started in the campaign right away. All the major leaders of the statewide organization were men, as were most of the staff at the LA No on Six office on Wilshire Blvd. where I was headquartered. The guys compounded the problem by making every effort to ignore or be rude to the few lesbians and other women who were there, even lesbians in some highly responsible positions like mine. They made schedules without consulting any of the women. They would set up committees and never asked lesbians or women to join them. They also often failed to notify us of important meetings. Then, if by chance we found out about and managed to attend one of these discussions, we were either talked over or ignored.

I wasn't surprised by this. I had always seen much of gay culture as anti-female, even when gay men pretended it wasn't. Take the custom many gay men had of using femaleness to demean each other, and even themselves. When a guy greeted another with, "Hey, Mary" and flounced, I knew it was a put down. So, too, was responding to a friend's grumpiness with the taunt, "What, are you on the rag?" Then there is drag. Yes, when it is done well, it can be very entertaining. But unlike many who claim that drag presents positive imitations of women, I see it as often having a nasty anti-female edge, exaggerating stereotypes to the point of insulting mockery.

A good example is the men who marched down Santa Monica Blvd. in West Hollywood in the pride parade during one of those mid-seventies years. I was sitting in the bleachers with Dolores who had come to town to visit, both of us enjoying surveying the various gay and lesbian groups which marched by with their signs, chants, and smiles. Then along came about twenty men, almost all with beards and mustaches, dressed in their version of airline stewardesses' uniforms: dainty hats covering outlandish wigs, white blouses buttoned tightly over balloon breasts, and very short skirts. They wobbled past in high heels to great cheers and laughter from the male spectators in the crowd. All I could think was that these were the very images of women Dolores and I and many other women had fought so hard to get rid of. We were pretty disturbed and disappointed, but not surprised.

The women who were involved in No on Six took on the challenge of men's attitudes in different ways. I, for example, knew early on that I had to find a way to deal with not just the men ignoring me, but also with the sexism and put downs of women that was part of their everyday behavior and vocabulary. I didn't want to be angry or yell at them all of the time. That wouldn't be very helpful. I understood, too, that sometimes some guys had no idea how offensive their behavior was. I also knew that other times, other men, knew exactly how provocative and nasty they were being. Either way, I wasn't going to let them get to me, and I wasn't going to let them off the hook. My strategy was to diplomatically point out the anti-women aspect of their comments and gestures, especially when they were particularly overt or obnoxious. There were a lot of, "Do you know that's offensive?" prodding from me and efforts at explaining why. But no outraged screaming. I'm not sure if they got what I was saying a lot of the time, but at least they were more careful around me.

One of the other lesbian activists involved in the anti-Briggs campaign, Gayle Wilson, a well-known and very successful realtor in the area, took another approach. She got tired of the men's behavior real fast. She was especially miffed when she realized that the men felt the women couldn't raise money.

"OK," she declared, "we'll raise our own money and show you."

She set about organizing a women-only fundraising luncheon at the Beverly Hilton. She was well-connected enough to get Midge Constanza, a senior member of Jimmy Carter's presidential staff, to deliver the keynote. And the women came. The luncheon raised $45,000, a very impressive sum in those days. Wilson's was the first big fundraiser for the anti-Briggs campaign and successful enough for the gay men to open the door at least a little for the women.

Truth be told, Gayle's results were something of an anomaly. I had learned in fundraising for the women's movement that, in general, women were not the biggest of donors. I had always thought this was simply because women didn't have very much money, especially compared to men. But I soon understood that men's wealth relative to women's didn't tell the whole story. Less wealthy gay men contributed more money than lesbians in general, and lesbians who did have money and were donors often gave less than their male counterparts. I suspected that at least one of the reasons for this was that women had been excluded from the workings of the political world for so long that they didn't understand how much money it took to grease the wheels of change.

Until women learned in campaigns like Brigg and other battles that were to come to donate more, the whole community would heavily depend financially on men. Fortunately, a good number of gay men, some of them very wealthy, were finding their way to contribute generously to such causes, to a great extent because of the fundraising efforts of the campaigns for gay rights and pride and a push for openness that were sprouting up all over. However, most of these men weren't exactly devoted to gay men *and* lesbians. Only if their battles overlapped with lesbian interests did their money go to women's causes. Still, there is no denying a lot of money came in from the men. I was appreciative of their wealth and generosity and happy to use their money.

THE STRATEGY OF the state wide anti-Briggs campaign was to divide up the work and responsibilities. Peter Scott, David Mixner, Mike Levitt, and others took care of the state-wide public relations and lobbying efforts. My task was to run the southern California grass roots campaign. That was fine with me. Grass roots had always been my thing. To me, the people out on the streets knocking on doors, making phone calls, distributing leaflets, personally lobbying legislators, as well as rallying and marching were the true and visible power. They supplied the momentum. Without them, there would be no movement. Part of that effort this time was to get individual gays and lesbians to come out of the closet and campaign openly on their own behalf. This was an approach pushed by the very influential and dynamic Harvey Milk who had based much of his successful 1977 campaign for a seat on the San Francisco Board of Supervisors on this strategy. Milk was the first openly gay person to be elected to a public office in the California, and I greatly admired him. He believed that being out had energized gays and lesbians and had a positive influence on everyone who knew them. It had worked for him, and he and other leaders were convinced it would work to defeat Briggs.

My job was to get people to come out and then teach them how to actually campaign. We knew it wasn't going to be easy. Notwithstanding Milk's victory, it continued to take a lot of courage for people to come out. There were few protections and still a lot of prejudice. The consequences were clear in the case of Sally Fiske, a prominent reporter from Channel 13 who came out on the air as a lesbian in opposition to the Briggs Initiative. She was immediately fired. Bad luck for her but good luck for us because she then joined the Briggs campaign in the publicity department and became a fervent and highly respected activist in the community.

My team and I decided our best approach was to encourage key community leaders to come out if they hadn't already and get them to volunteer for our trainings. These folks were then to take charge in their own areas and train others who would in turn train others and so on. We started working with small groups of activists all around southern California, from neighborhoods in greater Los Angeles to small towns in the desert. Sometimes they came to us. Sometimes we went out to them. We explained the elements of a campaign, from ways to encourage volunteers to come out and work to the nuts and bolts of finding office space, managing staff and money, and teaching the volunteers how to engage with the people on whose doors they knocked.

It was challenging, exhausting, and inspirational. And it worked. Since this was really the first big state-wide ballot measure California's gay men and lesbians were forced to engage with, we had had no idea if there would be active support in the gay and lesbian community, never mind in straight society. So, the number and commitment of our volunteers was thrilling. The people we trained in turn recruited others to work for the cause, and before we knew it, we had a tremendous grass roots campaign going that brought thousands of gay men and lesbians out and into politics for the first time.

But it wasn't just the grass roots operation that was doing well. The statewide public relations campaign brought other civil rights organizations and big names in state government and in Hollywood on board. The Log Cabin Republicans, a gay and lesbian group formed to respond to the Briggs Initiative, also used their influence to move politicians in the state. As the No on Six campaign progressed, even the Republican Governor Ronald Reagan could see that public sentiment was turning against the intolerance of Briggs. After a meeting with Mixner, Scott, and Milk, Reagan came out in opposition to the initiative. That was the biggest coup of the campaign.

In a tremendous victory for our community, and the state, the Briggs Initiative was soundly defeated. It was also clear after the campaign that we had won more than an election. Gays and lesbians had gained more credibility, power, and straight community support than they ever had before. More important to our future, I thought, was that, in an ironic twist, the proposition that was designed to punish and make gays and lesbians invisible had expanded exponentially the number of gays and lesbians involved in activism in California. They learned that activism can be rewarding and fun, especially, but not only, if you win. Thank you Briggs.

On election night, we celebrated at a great party at the Hollywood Palladium with thousands of us drunk on what we had achieved together, including me. So when I had a chance to get up on stage that night to say a few words as one of the major organizers, I was flying. As usual, I was depending on the inspiration of the moment to find words. I looked out at all our No On Six staff and volunteers, thrilled that not only had gay men and lesbians managed to work together, but that I had formed close bonds with a couple of the men on the staff, friendships I knew I would not have had without the Briggs battle. That was particularly astounding to me. "Look at all the men you've worked with," I thought. So that's what I talked about, how elated I was that gay men and lesbians had grown to trust each other enough so that we could be friends and work together in a strong coalition on issues affecting us all. I was all for working with men, or something like that, I exclaimed.

I guess I hit a chord. My victory speech was met with a huge ovation and much yelling and stamping of feet. A chant began: I-vy I-vy with boisterous calls for me to be the Mayor of LA. It was a very heady moment.

Of course, not everyone thought I was great. Even with the victorious campaign, my publicly professed affection for men got me into more trouble than I had already been in with the lesbian separatists and other women in the movement. The separatists didn't appreciate my comments about the joys of working with men at the victory party. Some felt I wasn't simply slighting women, which was bad enough, but that I was turning against them in favor of men. It didn't help that I was misquoted in *The Southern California Women for Understanding Newsletter* of November-December 1978 as declaring, "I loved working with those men. Let me tell you I will never again be a separatist."

I had indeed praised men and had declared myself looking forward to working with them again. But love is not a word I would use for them. My love was and always would be primarily for women. Still, no matter what I said, no matter how important the cause, my public declaration of affection for men put me over on the side of the enemy. After that speech, many separatists wouldn't work with me again. Just as I had been tossed out of New York NOW for moving toward lesbian feminism, I was being tossed out of radical lesbian feminism for embracing the causes of gay men as equally important as those of lesbians.

At the same time, even though they sympathized with the battle against Briggs, a number of feminist activists thought I had become too publicly known as part of the gay and lesbian liberation movement. The old Friedan fear of too much association of women's rights with lesbians, while somewhat moderated, had refused to die. These women also felt that I had switched sides, this time from women's liberation to gay liberation, and, like some of the lesbian separatists, refused to work with me.

Both of these political breaches were painful for me, but in a way, both groups were right about me. While I was still committed to women, my focus had shifted to lesbians, and since I had learned from Briggs that working in coalition with gay men was the most effective way to fight homophobia, that was the way I was going to go.

Even if I had had any doubts about prioritizing lesbian and gay concerns after Briggs, which I didn't, they would have been crushed by the shocking assassination of Harvey Milk just a few weeks after the election. We had been friends. I had even had breakfast with him shortly after the election. His murder, along with that of San Francisco Mayor George Moscone, by a fellow supervisor, Dan White, shook us all deeply. My community was galvanized once again, but this time in sorrow and rage. That horrible act only strengthened my commitment to the lesbian and gay community. So no more women only, lesbian or straight. The last time that I worked with straight women on a women's rather than gay or lesbian issue during that era was as a member of the Los Angeles City Commission on Violence Against Women which I had been appointed to in the late seventies. By the early eighties, I had moved on. Sort of.

On the Radio

AFTER THE DEFEAT of Briggs, since I had been a leader in the campaign, I found myself being interviewed by the media fairly regularly. On one of these occasions, as I was leaving after an interview at KHJ, a liberal LA radio station, I passed by the station manager's office. On the spur of the moment, I stopped and asked him if he would consider letting me do a radio show featuring gays and lesbians.

"Hmmm," was basically his reply. "I'll think about it."

I didn't blame him for his hesitation. The idea of such a show was pretty new and radical. A few days later, though, he gave me the go ahead for two slots on Sundays, one in the morning and one in the evening. Thus, was born "It's a Gay Life," (yes, even I gave in to the word "gay" covering us all). In 1977, at fifty-one years old, I had a weekly radio show and was about to be out over the airwaves.

This wasn't a call-in show. I only interviewed people who had credentials and/or were knowledgeable in the areas we were discussing. Partially this was because I didn't want to give homophobes the opportunity to spout their venom and lies, but more importantly I wanted real information to get out there. Consciousness raising again. In fact, we often ended up discussing issues that had been topics in consciousness raising groups. I was committed to gay and lesbian liberation, but I still understood gender discrimination as the central impediment to freedom, even for gay men. Their being considered unmanly or too much like women is what caused much of the bias against them. Get rid of gender oppression, I believed, and the world would be a much better place for everyone. The best way to combat it was to take it on. So I interviewed women who had been raped and those who had had abortions. I interviewed lesbians about the closet and about being mothers. I discussed radical lesbianism and patriarchal oppression.

Probably the most graphic, and radical for their time, were the shows that featured transsexuality. Since Christine Jorgenson had gained fame in the early fifties as the first American to reveal she had had male-to-female sex reassignment surgery, there had been little attention paid to the issue. That is until the transition of Renée Richards, a professional tennis player, hit the news big time just around the time of my show.

Renée, who in 1975 had transitioned from male to female, was prohibited from playing in the Women's US Open tennis tournament in 1976 because she refused to take the chromosomal test that had been established for women players by the tennis authorities. This test was clearly started just because of her. There had been no such requirement until Richards transitioned and indicated her intention of playing in women's tournaments. (Note that men did not have to take such tests.) Richards took her case to the New York Supreme Court and, probably to just about everyone's surprise, won her suit. The tests were found to be discriminatory. A big win for the transgender cause. (Just in case you're curious, she did play in the Women's Open in August of 1977, losing in singles in the first round but making it to the finals in doubles. She continued to play professionally until 1981.) So when Renée burst into the news, I decided it was time to try to educate the general public about what sex reassignment meant.

Over a couple of weeks, my fully transitioned transgender guests and I discussed their experiences, including, in as vivid detail as radio permitted, descriptions of the actual gender change surgery they underwent. One week we discussed a man transitioning to a woman and the next week vice versa. If I was ever going to hear anything from the Federal Communications Commission (FCC) about my programs, I thought it would be about those sessions since the topic was pretty radical and the descriptions very graphic. But there was not a word.

The show went along fine for about a year or so. Then I had the comedian Robin Tyler on. I had met Robin and her comedy partner Patty Harrison in 1969 when they were first performing comedy. Robin had been in the closet for years in her comedy, but by 1977 or so, she had become openly lesbian in her work and life. But the lesbianism wasn't the problem for the FCC. If it had been, I would have been shut down way earlier. Instead, what troubled the regulators was that Robin used the phrase "tits and ass" in the course of our interview. How shocking! At least that's how the federal authorities saw it. Neither of us had even noticed it. We had just gone on with the show.

About four days after that program, I got called into the station manager's office. "We got a letter from the FCC. They're really upset."

"About what?"

"One of your interviewees said the words 'tits and ass.'"

I said, "And . . ."

"Well, you can't do that on the air."

"Why?"

"Because they're considered obscene."

Oh my God, I thought. You have got to be kidding. "Oh, for . . ." was all I could say, I was so exasperated and angry.

I couldn't believe I was going to be censored or be asked to censor myself or my guests over stuff like this. I had been through too much, women had been through too much, lesbians and gays had been through too much for us to put up with ridiculous rules now. At that moment, too, I realized how exhausted I was. I never had time to relax or for Dottie. Something had to go. It was going to be the show.

"I'm outta here," I told the manager and that was that.

Post-Briggs

AFTER BRIGGS, I needed a job or some other source of income. I thought of going back to the Center, but the nine-to-fiveness of that job didn't thrill me. It wouldn't allow me the freedom I wanted to do my activist work. I had a little money coming in from my t-shirt business, but that wasn't going to be nearly enough. I mentioned my problem to Gayle Wilson, the realtor who had raised so much money from women for the No on Six campaign. Her response changed my financial life.

"Don't go back to the Center," she advised me. "Get your real estate license and come work with me."

Not a bad idea, I thought. I remembered enjoying working as a realtor on Long Island early in my marriage and that it had given me time with my kids when I needed it. I also saw that Dottie had a lot of flexibility with her time. At the same time, I knew that this line of work wouldn't sit well with the Marxist feminists and others. They would say I was selling out to the capitalist system. But I truly believed that guiding people through the volatile housing market of southern California could help them secure their futures and achieve their American Dream of home ownership. I still believe that. So I went for it. In the spring of 1979, I got my realtor's license. I joined Gayle's firm, then one of the most successful in LA, and began to make a good living at something I really enjoyed doing. It sure beat working for nonprofits in terms of income.

Once my livelihood was settled, my next task was to put my new found Briggs notoriety to good use in the community. I had had my radio show, but, otherwise, I wasn't sure of my direction. I was both encouraged and discouraged by the post-Briggs state of affairs. Even though we had won in California, the hatred of gays that was expressed during the campaign from our opposition, coupled with the shattering assassination of Harvey Milk, had put me in something of a sad and angry funk. On top of that, in other parts of the country, many pro-gay and lesbian bills and ballot measures had devastatingly gone down to defeat and others that had already been passed had been revoked or rescinded. Save our Children had made inroads. On the other hand, I was heartened that we had been so successful in the electoral process. That gave me a glimpse of the way forward.

The battles we, gays and lesbians, had been conducting for recognition and rights as full citizens and human beings had been carried from living rooms, bars, community centers, and the streets into the legislative system. If I wanted to contribute to the movement and continue to be effective, I knew I had to get on this new wave. We might actually be able to get laws, and mainstream society's views of gay people, changed.

So I leapt more fully into mainstream political life. Jerry Brown, the liberal who followed Ronald Reagan as governor of California, helped with this. After the successful anti-Briggs campaign brought gays and lesbians into the limelight, Brown took the still radical step of appointing gays and lesbian to various state boards and commissions. I was one of the first of his appointees. I am pretty sure I became the first open lesbian selected for any state commission when, in 1981, I became a member of the California Commission on Aging. I wasn't exactly aged, though. Just fifty-five years old. But I wasn't young. Maybe that helped in the PR department. I might have been a homosexual, but I wasn't one of these young, wild eyed, highly sexual radicals.

Unfortunately, my first foray onto a government commission wasn't pretty. While voters might have cast ballots against bias by voting against Briggs, that didn't mean they didn't still harbor prejudice in their hearts. For many people, gays and lesbians were still at best curiosities and at worst pariahs. That was as true for people on the commission as for anyone else. In addition, because the presence of an out lesbian on a state commission was still very controversial, I was swarmed by reporters and photographers at the first meeting of the commission. I could see that the other members might well be pissed at this invasion of their previously low-profile group. Still, I didn't expect to be shunned the way I was. At meetings, only one woman was willing to sit next to me and talk to me. No one else listened to me or even addressed me.

Besides this aggravation, I was frustrated that travelling all over the state for the commission meetings took me away from Dottie, from my more specifically gay and lesbian projects, and from my real estate work for what I saw as a waste of time. I stuck it out for a year before I called it quits. I think the Commission was very happy to have me gone, and I was glad to go.

The Coming of AIDS

IN THE SEVENTIES, after Briggs, I was active in a number of other gay and lesbian civil rights efforts, but most of these activities faded in importance starting in 1981. A dark storm was on the horizon.

The first real lightning strike for me was the illness and death of one of my good friends, Ken Schnorr. By this time, I had a number of gay male friends. Some were political connections. A number were from my real estate work. One of these men was Eric Scott, another agent, whom I met shortly after Briggs. We've remained very close friends. Another was Will Capps who, with his partner Larry, were real estate clients. Will and I stayed close even after he broke up with Larry and Larry moved away. Perhaps what is most remarkable about these relationships is not so much that these guys were guys, but that Eric, Will, and Larry have stayed alive long enough for me to have extended relationships with them. Which brings me back to Ken.

Ken and I became friends around 1979. I had recently joined the Stonewall Democratic Club, a progressive political organization for gays and lesbians founded in Los Angeles in 1975. The LA chapter was the first in what became a national political organization that encouraged and supported gays and lesbians who ran for public office. There weren't that many doing so. Even in California and even after the Briggs victory, gays and lesbians running for or holding electoral office were rare birds. People were still afraid to come out in such a public way, or leery that if they did come out, they would lose. So why even try?

By the time I joined, the organization had decided to add a focus on convincing straight candidates to support gay and lesbian causes, promising endorsements and get out the vote efforts when they did. We had the resources to back up our promises: expertise, experience, a crowd of newly minted activists from Briggs impatient for action, and a donor base that was open to supporting candidates who were willing to fight for gay and lesbian rights. We also had a community of voters eager to support those who supported us. All that could mean a lot of votes. Soon, we had candidates coming to us to ask for our support rather than the other way around.

Ken was also a member of Stonewall. One day in 1979 after a Stonewall meeting, I ended up hanging around talking gay politics with a very short young man with an adorable perky face. After a while, his eyes widened, and he said with some amazement, "You're Ivy Bottini!"

"Yes," I responded, surprised by his sudden look of shock since I was well known in the community by then.

He explained, "I used to come over to see Laura."

Laura, I thought to myself. Who's Laura? I was thinking of all the political Lauras I knew. Then he reminded me that when my daughter Laura was about fourteen and I was still married and living on Wantagh Avenue in Wantagh, Long Island, he was one of Laura's friends. Oh my God. To me he had just been one of a number of indistinguishable boys who would come by to hang around and talk with Laura, go out to the soda fountain with her, or do whatever kids do at that age. Years had obviously passed. He had come out as gay and moved to Los Angeles and here he was. What a blast from the past. From then on, despite our age difference, we became good friends.

BY 1981, TWO years or so after we had reconnected, Ken had become president of the LA Stonewall Club. He was cute, bright, and full of energy and ambition and seemingly doing well. He had opened a landscaping company early that year and by December the business was thriving. But something wasn't right. For much of 1981, he had been ill off and on. He would have thrush in his mouth. He would have fevers. He would have diarrhea. No one knew what was wrong. All his doctors said they were just infections and would prescribe antibiotics. He would get better for a while, keep going, and get sick again.

Then, one day in December, he fell ill as he was driving home after he had signed a contract to do a big landscaping job that would have solidified his future. He pulled over and collapsed unconscious in his car. He was discovered by someone passing by and was rushed to the hospital. The next day I got a phone call from his mom. She told me that Ken was in the hospital.

Worried, I asked, "Why? What happened?"

"I don't know. He's very sick. Nobody really knows what happened. He's full of black and blue marks. I'm sure they're from the staff treating him badly here at the hospital because he's gay." She paused. I could hear her crying softly. "I don't know what to do."

I asked to talk to Ken, so she handed him the phone. I tried to have a conversation, but it wasn't working. He would say something, but it didn't relate to what I was saying. It took me a while to realize that he had lost his hearing, and he didn't know it. By the time I got off the phone, I knew in my gut that we were in for a lot of trouble in the gay male world. I sometimes just get these feelings. I think it stems from that ability I mentioned earlier of my being able to put puzzle pieces together to get a vision of an entire political action or situation. I pick up fragments and create a whole before I'm even aware that that's what I'm doing. In this case, I put Ken's situation together with the information I gleaned from a couple of articles published in the *LA Times* and the *New York Times* in June and July of 1981 reporting a mysterious disease that was hitting gay men, a so-called "gay cancer." I had a terrible sense of foreboding.

I picked up the phone and called the Center for Disease Control (CDC) in Atlanta. I thought of the CDC only because I remembered it had played a major part in warning about and then vaccinating against polio, the scourge of the years when my kids were growing up. It was the only agency I could think of that might have some information. I actually got someone there to talk to me. I told her about what had happened to Ken, including the black and blue marks. The person I spoke to wasn't very forthcoming, but I could tell something was going on because of her awkwardness and hesitancy. I knew she was holding something back. I hung up and thought again, something awful is going to hit. I called Ken's doctor, Joel Weisman (who eventually opened Pacific Medical Group, one of the very first to deal with HIV and AIDS) and pushed him for information. He, too, was resistant about saying anything definitive to me.

A week after his collapse and hospitalization, Ken was gone. It was January, 1982. He was among the first known AIDS cases in Los Angeles. No one called it AIDS yet, but we knew enough to be scared, especially as stories of more and more men having the same symptoms as Ken quickly spread. Since we had no idea how these infections were transmitted, we were afraid of the dead as much as we were the living. When the members of the Stonewall Democratic Club executive committee and I went to pay our respects to Ken at the funeral home, we hesitated when we saw that there was an open casket that we were expected to approach. Even this distant contact with the body of someone who had died of this strange illness felt like a threat to us. We all managed to gather our courage and do our duty, but it wasn't easy.

Ken's funeral turned out to be the first of many, many that were to come. Within a month, it seemed like cases of what some researchers were calling GRID (Gay Related Immune Deficiency) were everywhere. That's when Joel Weisman decided to confide in me. Desperate for information so that my activist self could begin to do something to help, I hadn't stopped nagging him.

Finally, one afternoon he called and said, "Let me take you to meet somebody."

I joined him at UCLA where he took me to a lab deep in the basement of one of the research buildings. There he introduced me to Dr. Michael Gottlieb, who would later co-author the first CDC article about HIV/AIDS with Joel. Gottlieb eventually became one of the pioneers in the discovery of HIV and the fight against AIDS.

Gottlieb was pretty forthright about what they didn't know at that point. "We're trying to find out what it is. It's all very unusual. What your friend was experiencing with the black and blue marks is Kaposi sarcoma. We've pretty much only seen it before in older Jewish and Italian men. We've never seen it anywhere else."

Nowhere else! He was clearly worried.

Henry Waxman, our local congressperson, was one of the first public officials who became concerned about the epidemic in a positive way. He clearly knew something serious was going on. Early in 1982, he came down to the Gay Center, which was still on Highland Avenue, and held a press conference about what was becoming a national news story. Waxman confirmed to the crowd what I and others already suspected, that while other groups were afflicted by this disease, more and more cases were being reported among gay men. He warned that we had to be prepared. This illness wasn't just going to go away. Later that year, in April of 1982, he convened the first Congressional hearing on the disease, sending out an alarm to the country and calling for positive action. This call fell on deaf ears, as did all such calls for almost the next ten years as the epidemic raged on.

IN THESE EARLY days, all that was known for sure was that this disease spread rapidly, was horrible to experience or watch, and virtually everyone who got it died from it, more often sooner than later. Soon hundreds, thousands, of gay men were afflicted. Alarming rumors and conflicting information spread about its transmission and treatment. It was clear that the community needed to have more reliable, up-to-date information.

The Gay Men's Health Crisis was founded in NYC in January of 1982 as a telephone hotline to do some of this, but we had nothing like it in Los Angeles. So, I set to work. Around March or April of 1982, I put together what came to be called AIDS Network LA. I began looking for people who came in contact with a lot of other people. I invited community organizers, business owners, clergy, and others to meet. I explained my idea of all of us gathering as accurate and complete information about the epidemic as we could and getting it out to as many people as possible as quickly as possible. We got going.

Once a week or so, about fifteen of us would rush in, sit in the lobby of the Gay Center for twenty minutes, maybe half hour an hour, compare stories and rumors, and share news and information we had gathered so we could get some sort of a picture of what was really going on. What did you hear? What did you hear? The Valley? What's going on? Then we would all hurry back to whatever organizations or businesses we were affiliated with to spread the word.

I wanted to do more. By mid-1982, things were getting worse. More and more often I was hearing so and so is sick, and so and so is in the hospital, and so and so died. I decided that a town hall type meeting would help get the community together and see where we all were. Dr. Weisman, Ken's doctor, agreed to be the official medical voice. He trusted us, he told me, not to have an anti-gay agenda. I was stunned to think that people might. Shouldn't they just care that people were dying? Again, naïve.

Legally, Fiesta Hall in Plummer Park in West Hollywood holds about a hundred and fifty people. We had about three hundred and fifty men sitting and standing wherever they could squeeze in. Dottie and I were the only women I could see. The size and intensity of this crowd was a good indication of how concerned gay men were about the devastation all around them. You could hear their fear and anxiety in their low murmuring and see it in their wide eyes and clenched fists. People had started to be afraid of leaving their homes or going to places where a lot of people gathered in case the disease was spread in the air or by touch. Businesses in gay areas began to suffer.

The disease itself and not knowing how it was transmitted was terrifying everyone. But I thought they were wrong to worry about air and touch. I was convinced that it was passed sexually. It was the only thing that made sense. I looked at how Ken and other gay men in the area conducted their lives. I knew, for instance, that many of the guys called The Probe, one of the local bars in West Hollywood, "church" since they would go there on what was basically very early Sunday mornings after leaving the other bars very late on Saturday nights. That was only one of the establishments that were filled with men drinking, dancing, taking drugs, "bathing," and having sex. Nobody used condoms. What were those?

I started the meeting speaking briefly to make it clear that the point of the gathering was to hear accurate information about what was going on instead of relying on ignorance, fear, and rumors, which was all that most of us had at that point. That was the only way we could move forward. Then Joel spoke. He told the group that he believed that this disease, whatever it was, was passed sexually and warned people that they needed to be careful about their sex lives and not sleep around so much. Not everyone wanted to hear or believe this.

While gay men were extremely distressed by the disease, many, especially at the beginning of the epidemic, felt that they had just gotten some freedom to live full, open, sexual lives within the past few years. They weren't about to give that up. This became an on-going argument as a number of gay men, as well as business owners, resisted limits on sex in gay bars, clubs, and bathhouses that others proposed as a way to prevent the spread of the disease. I just wanted to save lives. If that meant closing the bathhouses, then let them close. I guess for a lesbian that was pretty easy to say.

By the end of that year, 1982, the situation was critical. Enough was known then about the disease to have relabeled it as AIDS (Acquired Immune Deficiency Syndrome) which took a bit of the onus off of gay men in medical terms. But in reality, it was often generally perceived as a disease of gay men and drug addicts. The death rate in those two groups was soaring, but there had been little government response to the epidemic. More gay men and some lesbians realized that if anything was going to be done, the community had to do it. Following the lead of New York's hotline, in October 1982, Max Drew, Matt Redman, Erv Munro, and Nancy Cole Sawaya set up a hotline literally in a closet at the LA Gay Center. To raise money to support and expand their service, the group held a fundraiser around Christmas that year. The fledgling organization raised $7000 in one night, an indication of the community's craving for reliable information and services, and the willingness of gay men, mostly, to step in when the government failed.

This was the beginning of APLA, AIDS Project Los Angeles, which grew to be one of the largest and most effective AIDS organizations in the country during the worst of the epidemic as well as in its later, waning years. With the money they raised that Christmas, the founding group began plans to expand their mission. The first official APLA board meeting was held in January, 1983. Diane Abbitt, a well know lesbian activist, and Joel Weisman were elected the first board co-chairs.

About a month later, Steve Schulte, then the executive director of the Gay Center, encouraged me to get involved in this new organization with him. "Come on, come on. Let's do this together."

So I signed up. In short order, the organization moved from the Center to a converted motel on Cole Street, increasingly taking over rooms as the need and contributions multiplied. But, of course, as happens in many of these situations, a rift about the priorities of the organization developed. It seemed to Steve and me that the organization, while certainly serving gay men, was focusing too much of its message and educational efforts on the straight community in the hopes that they would come around and do the right thing regarding funding, treatment, and services. Steve and I wanted to concentrate more on gay men. But don't get me wrong. It wasn't a big rift. We all had the same goal of fighting the disease and helping those who had it. Still, it was enough of a split for Steve and me to resign from the board to work on our own.

Since APLA and other organizations that were emerging were taking over collecting, validating, and disseminating information, those of us from the AIDS Network turned our attention to another aspect of the epidemic that was causing much pain to the men who were afflicted. Out of prejudice or fear of contagion based on misinformation, many people would not do business with or touch the men who were sick. This was particularly serious when it came to the medical profession. Some doctors would not treat HIV patients, and many home health care aides refused to work for people with HIV. Once it became known around 1983 that the virus was transmitted through blood and other bodily fluids, getting dentists to treat AIDS patients was also difficult.

Housing was another big problem. Some landlords were evicting people with AIDS out of unjustified fear of contamination. These landlords would then often refuse to rent to gay men in general, even those who were not ill. There were no laws prohibiting these actions. So the AIDS Network became a kind of clearinghouse of information about professionals, organizations, and landlords who would treat or do business with gay men with or without HIV. But I didn't want to get bogged down in the bureaucracy of that effort. I didn't think that played to my strengths, one of which was educating people so that they would do the right thing.

I decided to target service providers, reaching them by taking advantage of the networks I had developed over the years in service organizations and real estate. I also reached out to people in the civic sector who had been involved in my educational seminars from the days when I had worked at the Gay Center. I became a crusader, going anywhere, talking to any one, trying to catch the ear of anyone who had influence or who themselves could catch an important ear. I educated them about the truth about AIDS transmission, and then how ignorance and discrimination deprived gay men and people with HIV the simple services they needed to get on with their lives as well as they could.

Another project I took on had to do with the police. Not surprisingly, violence against gay men greatly increased during the epidemic. It's not as though this hadn't been a problem before, but it took on a special viciousness in those years. It wasn't generally as public and dramatic as Harvey Milk's assassination, but the possibility of violent homophobic abuse haunted every gay man, and, to a lesser extent, butch-looking women. In Los Angeles, physical and verbal street harassment was especially widespread in areas around Pershing Square, a well-known pick up area in downtown LA, and in West Hollywood, the center of gay life in LA and the home to a lot of bars and other gay hangouts. But really, the problem extended all over the city.

Unfortunately, in general the police were no help. Too often when they were called to assist gay men who were being harassed, bullied, and attacked on the streets, they didn't respond at all. Perhaps worse, when they did appear, they were almost as bad as the homophobic thugs they had been called in to stop. The police did their own degrading, restraining, and beating of the gay men who had already been victimized. It was a very bad situation. Something had to be done. At that time, in 1984, I had just become president of the Stonewall Democratic Club where we were trying to get people who were knowledgeable about and sympathetic to folks with AIDS and supportive in other gay and lesbian issues elected.

We discussed the Club using its clout to pressure politicians to pressure the police, but in the end, Steve Schulte and I went for a more direct approach. Together, we pestered police officials until they agreed to meet with us. We did what I had done back in my old Women's Department job at the Center, tried to disabuse these government workers of stereotypes of gays and lesbians to get them to recognize and rid them of their own homophobic attitudes and actions. And then to get the rank and file to change, too. It was exhausting, but in this case it yielded results. After a series of meetings, we and the police put together the Los Angeles Lesbian & Gay Police Advisory Board, one of the first panels of its kind to officially address violence against gay people.

This was just one of the tasks I, and thousands of others, ended up having to take on during those horrible years. We took them on because we had to. Throughout the epidemic, in one of the more shameful episodes in American civic life, governmental institutions were doing very little to help although thousands were dying, not just gay men, as if that would have justified this refusal to act. Ronald Reagan might have come out against the Briggs Initiative as governor of California, but as President from 1981 to 1989, among the worst years of the plague, he was a disaster. Until the very end of his second term, he wouldn't even say the word AIDS, never mind do anything about it. But he was not alone in either ignoring the epidemic or calling it somehow justified as a judgment of God.

Even with all the educating and coming out we had done to defeat the Briggs Initiative a few years earlier, the bias against gay men was still powerful, so powerful that for many years the gay stigma of the disease masked consideration of others who were HIV positive. Even when it became clear that the virus was passed blood to blood through sharing needles and blood transfusions in addition to certain sexual activities, AIDS was, and still is, thought of as a gay disease.

So the gay and lesbian community, and their friends, stepped up. It seemed hundreds of groups emerged to assist people with HIV and agitate to get the government and researchers to respond to the virus in a meaningful way. Given how movements are so often splintered, it was remarkable we all managed to work together. Sure there were inter- and intra-group disagreements and dissension. We argued about public health measures to be taken to stem the spread of the disease as well as the best ways to protest. We argued about funding and what kinds of services different constituencies should get and got. But we formed alliances, organized fundraisers and services for people who were ill, and then volunteered to provide these services.

We lobbied politicians, staged dies-ins, marched, and wrote letters, putting the lessons of Briggs to good use. Certainly there were a number of straight people who took up the cause, but it was really gay people, mostly gay men with a substantial number of lesbians, who refused to accept that those with HIV should hide, lie down, and die. Not all the gay and lesbian organizations of the eighties were directly related to AIDS, but all were affected by the epidemic. They had to stay vigilant. The whole culture and community was being threatened. Armed with tremendous anger and anguish at the illness and death, we became a community in a way we had never been before.

Ironically, the epidemic also brought thousands of people out of the closet. Many were forced out by the disease itself since, with the diagnosis, the secret of someone's sexuality was often revealed. As a result, friends, families, and colleagues were forced to acknowledge that they personally knew someone who was gay. That was very powerful in changing people's attitudes. It was one thing to condemn strangers, but it was another to reject family members, good friends, and colleagues. And if the person forced out of the closet by an HIV diagnosis was famous, it had even more impact.

Take Rock Hudson, the epitome of handsome, straight, movie star manliness in the 1950s and 60s. When he was diagnosed with AIDS and became visibly ill in 1985, his formerly closeted homosexual life was revealed. His story and gaunt features were splashed all over tabloids and the mainstream popular press. "How could this be?" many familiar only with the most stereotypical images of gay men asked themselves. "This manly man is a pansy? He has AIDS? What does this mean, then, about our ideas of who gay men are? Does this mean other masculine men we admire are also gay?" This wasn't very good for Rock Hudson, but it was good for us. For many straight people, stereotypes began to crumble.

At the same time as some men were being forced out, many gay men willingly and defiantly came out, fed up with the horrible homophobia and condemnation of gay people that had been let loose in society as a result of the AIDS epidemic. Enough was enough. The more gay men were condemned and characterized as oversexed, immoral, and irresponsible enemies of society who deserved to be punished, something heard a lot, the more gay men and their lesbian allies came out. Coming out, then, became a political as well as personal act. To me, for anyone to be in the closet at that time was almost unforgiveable.

In fact, one of my favorite paintings took coming out and the closet as an inspiration. I was, whenever I could, still doing art. Sometimes it was the t-shirts I designed and other times graphics for the movement, but painting was still in my heart. When I could paint, I was doing brightly colored acrylics. In this one, I branched out into collage. The painting was made in part out of wooden letters of type I had bought for $20 from the woman who had owned the farm where the Blue Door Gallery was. I dragged that type around for years, figuring I would one day find a good use for it.

The painting that emerged from them is called "The Closet." I filled the background of a 20x30 vertical canvas with the colors of the rainbow flag, which had had its debut as symbol of the gay and lesbian movement in 1978 at the San Francisco gay pride march. Over the flag, I painted a closet with the large word "CLOSET" spelled out in those wooden letters. On the bottom section of the canvas was a jumble of letters, representing the fear and confusion of a person in the closet. I wanted to show that being in the closet is a kind of betrayal of yourself and of the gay and lesbian community. For me, it remains one of my most powerful paintings.

One of Ivy's head shots, 1980.
Courtesy of ONE Archives at the USC Libraries

Personal Issues

THE AIDS EPIDEMIC was consuming not just my time and energy, but also my emotions. Dottie and I began to have issues. By 1983, we had been together for eight years and we were in trouble.

Starting in the late seventies when I was active in the anti-Briggs campaign, Dottie had started to work seriously with the southern California based Whitman-Brooks Foundation, an organization that set up meetings and conferences on coming out and provided leadership training for gay and lesbian activists. When she first started there, I was very happy to see her take more of a role in the movement. In fact, I had kind of pushed her into it. When Dottie and I first were together, I didn't expect her to be engaged as deeply as I was, but I did urge her to get more involved than she had been as a member of her local NOW chapter. She often told me she saw me as her mentor and she seemed to appreciate my urging her on, at least at first.

Gradually, she put herself out more and became comfortable meeting new people in political situations. In fact, after a while, she could work a room better than I could. I didn't enjoy the small talk that was often required to get people involved, but she did it beautifully. She also became a very good public speaker. Over time, she grew more independent and took up more of her own causes rather than getting involved in the same organizations or campaigns that I was working with. I got it. She didn't want to be seen as tagging along after me. Besides, I was always going from one project to another—beginning and ending, beginning and ending. Dottie liked to find a cause and make a long-term commitment. Whitman-Brooks was one of those causes.

I liked that Dottie had found her place in the movement. I was also relieved that she had something worthwhile that would take up her time and energy since so much of my time and emotion over our years together had been given not to her but to Briggs and then to AIDS and other campaigns. But by 1983, when men were getting sick and dying all around us, both of us were heavily involved with our own crusades, under a lot of pressure, and often exhausted and distracted. Dottie was on the board of Whitman-Brooks, and I was fully engaged in my own projects, not to mention both of us trying to make a living. Things were not fine. We were still in love but we were failing each other. How could we be there for each other when we were rarely home and rarely alone when we were there?

I should explain. Much to my surprise, I had received a small inheritance from my mother when she died. I have no idea how she had saved money, but she had. I also managed to put it aside, but around 1980, I had used it for a down payment on a two-story craftsman house in Silver Lake, a not yet trendy neighborhood just northwest of downtown Los Angeles. With five bedrooms spread over the two floors, lots of room for guests and meetings, and even a place for me to paint, it was a far cry from the tiny place we had been living in. In no time, even though Dottie and I were the only ones living in the house, it became a center of activism. The house was often noisy with lesbian activists coming and going for strategizing sessions, poster making, letter writing, phone calling, and theoretical discussions and arguments. And, yes, partying, too. That was fine with us. We were happy to have the community use our space. Then, in 1982, Lorraine Abruzzo, a friend of Dottie's from Whitman-Brooks, asked to rent a room from us for a short time. We figured why not. We had plenty of bedrooms. Lorraine ended up staying for thirteen years. She was just the start.

In 1983, the year after Lorraine moved in, the real estate market was languishing, and I wasn't making much from the freelance graphic design work I had started to do to bring in a little extra money. Dottie wasn't doing well financially either. I decided to rent rooms in the house to help make ends meet. Dottie and I had moved our bedroom downstairs for privacy when Lorraine moved in, so there was no problem with renting out the entire second floor. I installed a microwave oven and refrigerator and provided a small table and a few chairs in one room and got out the word to people I knew and trusted that rooms were available to lesbians they could vouch for. No men. Men, even relatives, weren't even allowed to visit any of the rented rooms, though I have heard rumors that brothers and other male relative were sometimes smuggled in. I had a lot of male friends by this time, but I had my limits. After all, this was my home.

We had up to four renters at a time, plus Lorraine. This could have been a nice little lesbian community, with Dottie and me mentoring the mostly young renters, but it didn't work out that way. We couldn't even take care of each other. We were rarely home at all, never mind home at the same time. And if we were there together, there always seemed to be other people around. In a way, that might have helped us last longer, because when we were with each other, I found that I was more and more often annoyed. I began to think that what Dottie saw as discussing things, whether personal or political, I saw as her lecturing and being argumentative. Her tendency to want to take care of me, which I once liked, began to feel like smothering. The way she ate, the way she walked, the way she interacted with others, all began to get on my nerves. I didn't know if my exasperation with her was reasonable, but there it was.

In retrospect, I see that it was a two-way street. If Dottie was aggravating me and not giving me what I needed, I know I could be irritating and not giving her what she needed either.

As it had been since I got involved in liberation movements, my political work came first. If the phone rang when Dottie and I were together and the call was about one of my battles, I would be off and running, even mid-conversation and no matter what Dottie and I had planned to do together. Often, I was so distracted by political work that even when we were together, my mind wasn't there. That kind of dismissal was bad enough, but it was made worse when we would go to some event and everyone would crowd around wanting to talk to me and ignore her even as she became active and known in her own right. I know that really disturbed her. There was really nothing I could do about the way others treated her, but I should have been better at home. Instead, if I thought about it at all, I figured that we were both doing the work we wanted to do, and since I assumed her work was as important and fulfilling to her as mine was to me, it was good enough. It didn't occur to me that she might need more from me. I was just doing my thing.

What I do know is that with the pressures of the AIDS crisis and our own personal issues, we both needed more than we knew how to ask or to give.

IN LATE SPRING or early summer of 1983, Dottie and I hit a crisis point. One night, she came home from a meeting at Whitman Brooks and I knew, I just knew that she had been with another woman. She had a different energy. I could feel it. I confronted her in the kitchen where she had gone to get a snack. She immediately admitted that I was right, she had been unfaithful, but rather than being ashamed or even defensive, she looked sheepish, like she had just gotten caught with her hand in the cookie jar. I was terribly hurt. This having affairs when in a relationship is something I don't get. I can look and like and flirt with the best of them, but I know the line that shouldn't be crossed. Obviously, others, including Dottie, didn't have that same line.

As deeply wounded as I was, I didn't want to lose Dottie. In spite of all that had been going wrong, I still felt tremendously connected to her. Apparently, she didn't want to lose me either. When I demanded that she call her friend, Anita, immediately and tell her it was over between them or it was over between us, she hesitated at first, but she made the call and pledged to end the liaison. I had my doubts. I suspected that it couldn't be that simple, especially since they worked together, but I still loved her. I chose to believe her.

Both of us wanted to get our relationship back on track, so we went to therapy together. We talked about our irritations with each other and how we could give each other what each needed. We tried to learn to find a balance between our political work and our relationship. Most important for me, I learned to trust her again. Without that, there would have been no relationship. So we stayed together and continued our work.

Other Family Issues

IN THE MEANTIME, in the midst of all the traumas of the AIDS situation and Dottie, there were family demands. All the time I was in California, I spoke to my daughters regularly and saw them when I could afford the time and money. That usually meant one or two visits to the east coast a year. But that didn't always work out the way I wanted it to. I couldn't attend either of their spring 1983 weddings.

By that time, I had seen both of them through their share of relationship problems. Laura, always headstrong, had chosen not to go to college after high school. Instead, she had moved to upstate New York with her boyfriend, Jeff. When that didn't work out, she moved back closer to the city. She was now going to give it a go with Norman. Lisa, much more quiet and placid in general, was marrying her college boyfriend, Ed. The problem was that both my daughters were getting married within two weeks of each other. The real estate business had been slow for a couple of years, so I had virtually no extra cash. I had even taken on an additional job working on call for an ad agency in West LA designing advertisements.

As luck would have it, the company called me with an assignment that would conflict with the two weeks I would have needed if I were to go back east and stay for both weddings. I couldn't afford to give up the work, and I couldn't afford flying back and forth twice. Dottie didn't have enough money to help, and I didn't want to borrow money from any of my friends. I wasn't sure when or if I could pay them back. It didn't seem right for me to choose one wedding over the other, so I didn't go to either. I'm not sure I did the right thing, but it seemed the only option at the time.

At least Dottie and I were able to get to Houston, Texas, where Lisa was living with her husband, on the day Lisa brought Jason, my only grandchild, home from the hospital in 1985. I was able to stay a few weeks and help her through those sometimes trying first days of motherhood. Luckily for me, though, and unfortunately for Lisa, I didn't have to make the trip to Houston again. When my kids were living near each other, I could see them both during one visit. But, I couldn't afford a trip to Texas and a trip to New York. I was spared the conflict of having to choose between daughters and visits because not long after Jason was born Lisa and her family had a financial crisis, as seems to happen in my family. As it also seems to happen in my family, they moved in with my aunt and uncle in Lynbrook. This wasn't great, but at least Lisa was able to help take care of her Great Uncle Jamie, who was then ill, living in the house, and confined to a wheelchair. Jamie, quite well off and with no children of his own, had paid for Lisa's college education, something neither Eddie nor I had the resources to help her with. We were all greatly appreciative. So Lisa was doing what she could to pay him back.

Since Laura was living with her husband Norman in Long Island City at the time, I could visit them both on one trip. For many years, I would stay in Long Island City with Laura and Norman for a couple of weeks in the summer and also make sure to visit Lisa and Jason wherever they might be in the area. That hadn't included Ed. He had turned out be a batterer, and Lisa had managed to leave him and move upstate to Armonk with Jason. Armonk was a little distant for me from Laura, but when Lisa later moved to Connecticut and took up with Charlie, it was easier. I started staying with them for about a month around Christmas, taking time to visit Laura during my stay. Sometimes we would all meet in the city and have dinner together. A few visits supplemented by frequent phone calls was the frustratingly little contact I had with my daughters and grandchild, but that's all any of us could afford. It was tough.

No On LaRouche

WHILE ALL OF this was happening, I was becoming more and more involved with the AIDS epidemic. How could I not? Thousands of gay men were dying and the government refused to step in and help. Then, just when we thought things couldn't get any worse, they did. A backlash against gay people standing up for themselves and demanding their rights from an indifferent establishment was on its way. It appeared in California in 1986, four years after Ken's death, in the guise of Proposition 64. Prop 64 would have put AIDS on the communicable disease list along with diseases such as smallpox, tuberculosis, and plague. With AIDS on the list, people with the illness could be pushed out of their jobs and homes en masse without recourse and possibly quarantined. Sure, the first two were already happening way too often, but quarantining a portion of the country's population! Whose idea could this possibly be? Were we going to go the way of Hitler and his concertation camps for a variety of undesirables or our own country's shameful treatment of Japanese Americans after Pearl Harbor?

Apparently, that's what the pudgy, always frowning cult leader Lyndon LaRouche wanted. Prop 64 was his brainchild. Prior to this, LaRouche and his small but dedicated group of followers had become notorious for the many conspiracy theories and far out positions they espoused and spread in their own publications and often at booths on college campuses. These included the accusation that Queen Elizabeth of England was a major drug smuggler and that the Rockefellers, the Rothschilds, and others of their kind (whatever that meant) were in a conspiracy to take down the United States government. Homosexuals had been another of LaRouche's targets. For LaRouche, gays, like these others, intended to destroy America. Their weapon would be the destruction of America's moral fiber. His rhetoric made it clear that he would have liked to have all gay people killed, but he knew he couldn't do that. Instead, he used the AIDS epidemic as an opportunity to try to get rid of gay men.

What made LaRouche's argument more distressing was his taking advantage of the rhetoric of the times that divided people with AIDS into two camps, "innocent" victims and those who deserved to get the disease. The innocent ones were epitomized by Ryan White, whose story exploded in the national media in 1984. Ryan was a thirteen year old hemophiliac who had contracted AIDS through an infected blood transfusion. This was before people understood the blood to blood transmission of the virus and began testing blood to prevent this kind of thing from happening. By 1984, when the White story hit, it was well known that AIDS was not transmitted by simple contact. Nonetheless, Ryan was expelled from his school because some parents were terrified that he would infect the other children simply by being near them. Heaven forbid, he might touch them or breathe on them! That this was ridiculous didn't matter to the many who sided with the school in the ensuing national debate.

Hysteria and sometimes seemingly willful ignorance about the disease was unfortunately very common. This isn't to say that there weren't many people who contended that Ryan should be able to stay in school, arguing against the irrational and panic-inducing misinformation about transmission. Either way, one thing was for sure, whether people agreed with Ryan's expulsion or not, they were all sympathetic to him. The needle sharers and gay men who contracted the disease got none of that compassion from the general public. Ryan was the innocent victim and the others were the guilty carriers of the disease.

Not only that, in a devastating blow, the U.S. Supreme Court validated Georgia's anti-sodomy laws in their 1986 decision in the Bowers v. Hardwick case. So, not only was homosexuality immoral, it was OK for states to say it was illegal. Gay people were criminals.

I knew, then, that with Prop 64 we were fighting for our lives. The homophobes had to be stopped. It was time for our side to organize again, so I began mobilizing grass roots ground troops just as I had with the Briggs Initiative. And, as with Briggs, at the same time as my efforts were getting off the ground in southern California, a well-funded statewide organization to oppose the initiative was being put together with its headquarters in San Francisco. So, again, I got a phone call from David Mixner, the same political consultant with whom, along with his partner Peter Scott who had since died of AIDS, I had worked with in the campaign against Briggs. David, again central to the statewide effort to defeat an anti-gay proposition, invited me and the people I was working with to join his organization and share the space the statewide organization was renting for the southern California campaign. A short time later, I was asked to co-chair the southern California grassroots campaign, and I accepted. In effect, I ended up being the only chair since my co-chair left for the headquarters in San Francisco early on, and, after meeting him just once, I never saw him again.

I have to say that even though many of us had been through the Briggs battle together, it was tougher going within the organization this time. This didn't have to do with the old conflict between men and women. That was still an issue, but this time the problem had more to do with the "suits," that is the big money, big PR people, not having as much respect for the "streets," the grassroots, as they had before. One issue was a strategy dispute. I felt a "No on LaRouche" themed campaign would work best. People would remember a name better than a number. Mixner and the state crowd didn't agree and led with "No on 64." I was supposed to fall in line, but I didn't. I already had a No on LaRouche grassroots campaign up and running when they got organized. I knew they were perturbed and I sometimes wonder if Mixner had invited me in to share offices just so the campaign could keep an eye on me.

The lack of understanding of the concerns of the grassroots workers was also an issue. This showed itself in a conflict Mixner and I had about security at the third-floor campaign headquarters on Wilshire Blvd. While a lot of the grass roots work took place outside of the office, we were often at the headquarters for tasks such as meeting and planning, making phone calls, stuffing envelopes, and preparing and distributing information packets. Often, because many of the volunteers worked during the day, they would come at odd hours, including late at night. That was OK. We were open. The problem was security.

When the campaign first started, whenever anyone wanted to enter the building, he/she would have to ring the bell on the first floor and someone would have run down from the third to let them in. There was no buzzer from our floor. That was obviously a hassle, so David decided just to leave the building door unlocked. That was fine during the day or early evening when there was a lot of staff around inside and a lot of people on the streets, but it could get dangerous later at night when there were few people in the office. There was a serious amount of antagonism toward our campaign floating around and a lot of crazies who knew where we had our headquarters. That meant when it was mostly my people who were coming and going, anyone could just come walking into the building.

I agreed with David that locking the building door was just too inefficient, so I asked for a security guard for the evening hours. Repeatedly. I was told over and over it would be taken care of, and repeatedly nothing happened. I don't think Mixner took the problem seriously because nighttime security wasn't as much of an issue for his staff. Maybe it was because they weren't on the streets and didn't see the hate and anger in the eyes of many close up as often as my volunteers did. Maybe it was because I was a woman and more sensitive to safety concerns than the male Mixner. I don't know. Finally, I told Mixner that if we didn't get a guard at night, I couldn't compromise the safety of my volunteer workers and would have to take all my people away. I am sure he thought, "Yeah, sure," so again there was no progress. Then, true to my word, a few days after my threat, I pulled my troops. Before you knew it, we had a guard at that door.

The main tasks of my volunteers was to go house to house educating people about the issues, registering people to vote, and, later, getting them to the polls. We knocked on doors as far north as Santa Barbara and as far south as San Diego. We also held rallies and events throughout the LA area. And, again, we came out of the closet. We had to show the world that we weren't a dangerous, immoral menace to society that needed to be cordoned off. I give credit to the media campaign for their many ads that featured gay men and lesbians being out and talking about their lives. These ads, and our door to door campaigning, gave us faces, humanized us, to a frightened general public. We were their colleagues, family members, and friends, and many of us were sick and dying. This was a powerful force. I was a great believer in this openness as part of the strategy to victory. I still am. Prop 64 was defeated.

Ivy selling T-shirts at Christopher Street West Festival, c. 1985.
Tell Me David

Ivy (center) with Jean O'Leary (left) and Jeanne Cordova (right), c. 1985.
Courtesy of ONE Archives at the USC Libraries

Ivy speaking at a No on LaRouche (No on Proposition 64) rally, 1986.

Ivy speaking at a NOW reproductive rights event, c. 1988.

Dottie and Ivy at a Whitman-Brooks event, c. 1990.

Activism Continues

THE PROP 64 threat may have been stopped in California, but prejudice against gay people was still strong. Homophobia and discrimination were still raging as a result of old prejudices inflamed by the epidemic. In the meantime, little progress had been made to treat or cure AIDS. For six years, the government had refused to act in any meaningful way as thousand died and thousands more became infected. We were getting increasingly frustrated and angry. So a second National March for Lesbian and Gay Rights in Washington, DC was called for October 11, 1987. The first had been in 1979 when seventy-nine thousand brave souls came to DC. This time three hundred to five hundred thousand gays and lesbians and their supporters turned out, making it the largest of all gay and lesbian rights demonstrations to that point. Unfortunately, I was not one of them. I couldn't afford to go.

This meant that not only did I miss the march, I also missed paying homage to all those memorialized in Cleve Jones' NAMES Project AIDS Memorial Quilt which was displayed in its entirety for the first time. Just seeing photos of the thousands of three feet by six feet patches created by friends and families of people who had died of AIDS quilted together and covering much of the national mall flooded me with sorrow, frustration, and rage. I can't imagine what it must have felt like to walk the aisles between the sections and be reminded of all those we had lost.

While I couldn't get to the march, I heeded the urging of the organizers and speakers to continue to put American society on alert that we would no longer be invisible and pushed around without fighting back. I wanted to find a dramatic way to harness the anger and inspiration the marchers brought back from DC and the energy that had been released by the victory in the LaRouche campaign. I was impressed with the confrontational style of ACT UP (AIDS Coalition to Unleash Power), a New York based organization that had been formed in 1987 in frustration at what the organizers saw as the too moderate approach of mainstream AIDS organizations. They brought a very in-your-face approach to the fight. They had already wrought havoc at the New York Stock Exchange and the FDA, shutting them both down in raucous, loud, very angry, very attention getting demonstrations. Their furious, rowdy protest at the Supreme Court over the Hardwick case had punctuated their presence at the march a few days after the main event.

As a graphic designer, I also appreciated their adoption of the print Avram Finkelstein had just produced, an inverted triangle, Hitler's symbol for gays in concentration camps, painted pink with what became ACT UP's slogan, Silence=Death, inscribed on its face. Very smart. I liked the creativity and the drama of ACT UP's protests but wasn't sure of their ultimate positive effect. I wanted drama but of a different kind. So, after the march, a group of about eight of us started what was basically a guerrilla theater group that we called March On.

We travelled to cities all over California to stage die-ins. We would find a park, hopefully where a lot of people could see us, and begin our silent ceremony. Some of us would lie on the ground while others outlined our bodies in chalk. We would then write the name of someone who had died of AIDS in each chalk outline. To make sure onlookers knew what we were doing, at the same time as the chalking was going on, someone from our group would hand out leaflets that explained our actions to the crowd that would inevitably gather. We would invite others to "die-in," too, and many, straight and gay, young and old, all ethnicities, joined us in laying down their own bodies for us to chalk. Each would then somberly, sometimes in tears, write the name of someone he or she knew who died of AIDS in their outline. It was always very, very moving.

We also made it our business to target politicians to pressure them to actually do something to help. So, in 1988, we appeared at the sites of the state conventions for the California Republican and Democratic parties. At these gatherings, we made sure not only to have our dying fields visible to the convention goers, but also see that each of them got one of our leaflets as they came and went from their convention halls and meetings, sometimes forcing our leaflets into their hands. At least it seemed forced at the Republican convention. Those convention goers were often nasty, muttering phrases like "Get away from us," or "You're filthy. You deserve to die," when we approached them. Democratic conventioneers were more gracious, expressing understanding or sympathy for the attention we were bringing to the disease and the people dying of it. That was an improvement but also frustrating. Being nice didn't matter if no one did anything, and no one did. Forget the sympathy. We wanted action.

For me, the most profound of the die-ins occurred at the 1988 March on Sacramento for Lesbian and Gay Rights. This whole event was fraught for me, even before the day of the action itself. One of my jobs as a major organizer was to be responsible for all the expenses we accrued from busses, sound systems, staging, security, and clean-up. By the weekend of the demonstration, the bill had already come to around $19,000. This included about $2500 a friend had put out for t-shirts that I had designed and planned to sell. It might not sound like a lot now, but it was a good deal then. Still, I was pretty confident that all these bills would be taken care of by donations from passing the hat and the sale of the t-shirts. That had always worked before. But when I woke up on the day of the march, it was raining. Hard. Yes, in California. I panicked. Morris Kight, another of the organizers, was staying down the corridor in the same Sacramento motel I was in.

I ran to his room, my blue work shirt flapping untucked over my jeans. As soon as he opened the door, I began to wail that it was all going to fall apart, no one would come, and I wouldn't be able to pay off our debts. Always a kindly gentleman, he took me under his arm and said, "Now, now little sister. Everything will be OK. Let's get you an umbrella." I calmed a bit. As we walked down to the motel office for an umbrella for me, it suddenly seemed so absurd to me, to be going for an umbrella to solve this problem. I looked up at him, smiled, and we both burst out laughing. Kight, the sage and longtime organizer and friend, certainly knew how to defuse a situation.

I felt better until we arrived at the parking lot that I had reserved for the busses that we were expecting for the one p.m. rally. It was empty. Not only that, the lot had turned into a mud pool from the rain. My barely dissolved panic returned, worse. Now I was worried not only that no one would come and we would lose all that money, but also that those who might come would have to wade through mud just to get out of their busses. There was nothing to be done, though. All we could do was wait under our umbrellas. We kept reassuring each other that the busses and people would come. Around ten a.m., after we had stood waiting for about forty-five very long minutes, busses began to emerge out of the rain and mist. Bus after bus after bus of protestors from all over the state ready to demonstrate. All these folks coming out in the rain felt like a miracle to me.

By the time of the march and rally, it had stopped raining and the sun was out. The sidewalks had dried. Thousands had gathered and were rallying as team members from March On began chalking bodies, this time on the plaza and sidewalks surrounding the capitol building. I was running around taking care of event details, so I hadn't been able to see how many people were participating. By late afternoon, I was exhausted, but my work was not done. I found myself trudging up the long, broad, marble steps of the capitol building to speak to Susan Kuhner, one of the other organizers of the march.

I paused near the top and turned around. There covering the vast cement surfaces that surrounded the capitol building were thousands of chalk body outlines, each inscribed with the name of someone who had died of AIDS. I lost it. Suddenly overwhelmed by the enormity of the loss our community had suffered, I started to cry. I sobbed and sobbed right there alone on the capitol steps. After a few minutes, Susan came down and hugged me while we blubbered together. It was one of the few times I actually broke down in public over all the deaths from AIDS and government's indifference to the epidemic. I just hoped our actions would make a change.

By the way, we sold the t-shirts and collected enough money to pay off all of the bills.

Breaking Up

AS 1988 CAME around, I was getting exhausted. At least my tenure as President of the Stonewall Democratic Club would be ending, so I would get some relief. But I wasn't confident that would make much of a difference. There was always so much that needed to be done. I don't know when I had time to sleep. For sure, I had little time for Dottie. It was as though I only had room for one passion at a time, and when push came to shove, I chose the cause over personal relationships. Turns out that while I was spending pretty much all of my time in campaigns to help others, many of whom I had never met and would never meet, I was losing my relationship with Dottie.

The breaking point with us came in 1988. I knew that tensions were developing again. As before, we were not spending much time with each other. In addition, I was still getting more attention in activist circles than Dottie was. I knew this was hard on her. But I told myself that our issues were a function of the pressure of the times. When things returned to normal, we would return to normal. We had gotten through this before and we would again.

So, I was totally stunned when I picked up the phone extension in the kitchen at home one day, not knowing Dottie was on the line, and overheard heard her tell Anita, the same seductress from Whitman-Brooks she had had an affair with before, "I'll dream of you if you dream of me."

They were involved again! I couldn't believe it. I thought we had gotten over the bad times and everything was fine. As soon as I heard Dottie hang up, I rushed into the living room where she had been on the phone.

No preliminaries, I demanded, "How long has this been going on?"

She knew exactly what I was talking about. She calmly replied, "Four months."

Four months! This was way worse than before. I was beyond outrage. I knew that somewhere in my heart I wanted to forgive her but I couldn't. Not a second time. This was it.

I started to scream at her. I wasn't really thinking, but when I get angry, I yell, not just at Dottie but at anyone I am upset with. I also knew that Dottie had never figured out how to handle that anger except to walk away. Whether it was that or she was just ready to leave, when I started yelling, she turned from me, went in the bedroom, packed a few things, and walked out. I stood immobilized. I had managed not to follow her into the bedroom, but when I saw her leave the house, I went after her.

"One thing I have to ask you," I pleaded. "Please don't stay at her house tonight."

She didn't reply. She just got in her car and left. I couldn't leave it at that. I drove by her girlfriend's house (yes, I was that obsessed) and there was Dottie's car. That was the final indignity. She was done caring about what I wanted. I knew our relationship was over. I was crushed.

I began to fall apart. For the first few weeks after Dottie left, I tried to stay and work at the Silver Lake house that was then empty of not just Dottie but all of our renters. And many of those who had used our house as a meeting space had moved into the offices of the various organizations that had sprung up everywhere to fight AIDS. I isolated myself. I wouldn't go out unless I absolutely had to for work or groceries. When worried friends, like Jeanne Cordova or Jean O'Leary dragged me out, it wasn't fun. Those two tried to distract me by taking me to movies, but even that didn't work. I was too emotionally off to pay attention.

My depression got worse. After a while, my mind was so cloudy and I was so gloomy and distracted that I was having trouble coping with anything that required much thought or calculation. I couldn't even manage to pay my bills. I knew I needed help, but I also knew I wanted to go to someone who would understand the degree of devastation and sense of loss I felt from Dottie's betrayal. I thought of Donald Ferguson, a friend of Dottie's from Whitman-Brooks whom I had gotten to know pretty well. He would be perfect. Not only did he know both Dottie and me, I knew he would be on my side in the break up because he had also suffered from the pain of Dottie's duplicity.

They had been intimate friends, he had told me. At least he had thought they were. They used to go out together and have what Donald thought were deeply honest conversations about the most private aspects of their lives, but it turned out that Dottie had kept her affair secret from him for months, too. He only found out about it after the night she left me. Like me, he had been fooled by her. Once I realized that he had not been covering for Dottie about the affair but had been betrayed by her, too, we bonded even more. He was happy to help me in my despair. He took over managing my bills and other personal paperwork.

I was in a very dark place. I hurt all over and was very anxious, depressed, and exhausted. I wanted to crawl out of my skin. I felt very alone. Not just about Dottie. I had lost so many people close to me from AIDS. I had to be with people. Then, within only a few weeks of the breakup, the Silver Lake house began to haunt me. It held too many memories of my good, and hard, years with Dottie. I couldn't stay there. So I began wandering, moving from friend to friend, or even acquaintance to acquaintance, wherever I could grab a couch or a bed. I returned to the Silver Lake house only for short periods in the mornings and evenings to take care of my two cats and dog. I would rush in, give them food and water, clean the kitty litter, and take the dog for a short walk. That was it. I could barely stand being in the place.

The friends and the women I stayed with could sometimes get me out to go to a bar where I would try to drink away my sorrows. That didn't help. Neither did work even though I would drag myself into the real estate office. I had to. I had no other source of income. That didn't mean I functioned well there, especially since, on top of my general state of despair, I was exhausted. I wasn't getting much sleep. One day, I arrived at the office clearly hung over and depressed. I was barely able to lift my head to work. A gay male associate there who had been watching me fall apart over the previous month or so took me aside.

"You need help," he told me. I certainly couldn't argue with that. "I know two women you should talk to."

I was just desperate enough to go along with whatever he suggested. I even stayed when he took me to a twelve-step program meeting in Los Feliz to introduce me to the two young law students. I didn't identify with much of what the speakers at the meeting said about alcoholism specifically, but I saw some parallels in my relationship to Dottie. I recognized that just as they were addicted to alcohol, I was addicted to her. I felt couldn't live without her, but also knew that my need for her was destroying me. Separating from her was like going cold turkey to get off of a drug.

Understanding that helped, but mostly what was comforting to me was that these two law students took me in and let me sleep on the couch in their living room for a few weeks. Before that, I had been vagabonding from house to house just about every night. Once I discovered that they had been members of Los Angeles NOW, even though I hadn't known them, I felt more comfortable with them. They were very kind. They even let me sit between them in their king size bed on the few Sunday mornings I was there. We drank coffee, chatted, and read the newspaper. This was the most stability I had had since the breakup. But I couldn't stay there forever. I moved on.

This wandering and misery went on for a couple of months. Then one day, I gave up. I was on my way to my therapist when I just couldn't go on. I drove back to where I was staying—another friend's place—and called Donald. I asked him to pick me up and take me to the psychiatric ward at Century City Hospital. He obliged, no questions asked. I guess he could tell I was pretty deeply into the dark.

As soon as I checked myself in, I felt safer and more secure. It was the best thing that I could have done for myself. With a nice clean room and a quiet roommate, I didn't have to worry about where I was going to stay every night. The fear and anxiety that had plagued me, the dark depression, the necessity to carry on, to take care of myself and business, to interact with people, all were eased. I could relax. I spent my time writing, talking with others in group therapy, and working with my own, very good therapist once a week. I even managed the energy and emotion to flirt and had a small crush on one of the other women. That was a ray of light. It made me realize that depressed and anxious as I was, as down as I was, there could be life after Dottie.

Unfortunately, after a month, my insurance ran out, so I had to leave. Real life again. Where could I go? I might have been feeling better, but I was still not ready to go home. That's when Jeanne Cordova stepped in and invited me to come and live with her and her partner Lynn Ballen in their house in Beachwood Canyon for a while.

By this time, Jeanne and I had been friends and partners in activism for about fifteen years. The image of her I have of when I first saw her is still emblazoned in my mind. It was shortly after Dottie and I had gotten together. We were having dinner at the Women's Saloon and Parlor, a feminist restaurant opened in Los Angeles in 1974 by Colleen McKay, when I noticed a stunningly beautiful butch dancing on the small dance floor. She was gorgeous. She had a handsome face framed by short, very dark, wavy, shiny hair, and lovely breasts, exposed for all to see because the white shirt she had tucked into her jeans was open to her navel. Once I discovered that this beauty was Jeanne Cordova, 1971 founder of *The Lesbian Tide* and still its editor and a local activist, I was even more determined to get to know her. As far as I was concerned, we just had to work together. And we had. By this time, we had put in many years of activism and friendship. Now I really needed her.

Lynn was kind enough to clear out her study for me so I, and they, too, could have some privacy. That one room was really all that I needed. In spite of my hospital stay, I was still not ready to be with people very much. I went to work at the real estate office, but I couldn't interact with my movement friends and colleagues. I just couldn't. I was too embarrassed about having such a hard time getting on top of my situation and having ended up in the nut house. I felt like a woman who was too weak to manage her own life when my old colleagues and friends were getting things done. I was a fake and would be an interloper. That was a problem at Jeanne and Lynn's because activists were always coming and going for various meetings, discussions, and actions. I stayed in my room as much as possible.

Even though both Lynn and Jeanne were tolerant of me isolating myself and gracious about my presence, I still felt like I was imposing, which I was. After all, this was their house and there I was, just a lump. I couldn't just stay on and on. Besides, I knew I had to get on with my life. So one night, after I had been with Jeanne and Lynn for about two weeks, I packed my bags and called Donald and asked him to pick me up and take me back to the Silver Lake house. I didn't tell Jeanne or Lynn about my plans. That made my actual leaving awkward. That evening, the dining room that I had to cross to get to the front door was filled with people I knew. They were there for some kind of organizing meeting. I hadn't seen most of them for a while, but, instead of stopping, I just plowed on through. I didn't say a word to anyone or make any eye contact. Eyes forward and out the door. Rude? Absolutely. But that was the space I was in at the time. Later I found out from Jeanne that Lynn was pretty peeved at me for fleeing that way. She had felt abused. I didn't blame her. She had moved out of her own study for me, and I had simply left with no thanks or good bye. Not my best moment.

BACK IN THE Silver Lake house, I had to deal with Dottie again. It took her three months to move all of her stuff out, but I rarely saw her during that period. I insisted she not come to the house when I was going to be there. I was still horribly hurt and furious at her. And still in love with her in spite of her duplicity. I couldn't stop caring about her. I was afraid if I saw her in person, I might beg her to come back to me. I knew that wasn't a good idea.

Moving On – Back to Performing

AS THE EIGHTIES ended, I was exhausted. I was well into my sixties and was worn out from my personal ordeal and burned out by the trauma of the AIDS epidemic. The only comfort I took was in the progress being made in combatting AIDS and recognizing the needs of people with HIV. The increasingly angry protests against the immoral lack of official action regarding AIDS and people with AIDS; the media attention that the Rock Hudson and Ryan White cases received; and the growing number of people coming out, were finally beginning to create cracks in public and government resistance to action. In 1990, The Ryan White Comprehensive AIDS Resources Emergency (CARE) Act was passed providing some funding for services for people with HIV and support for research. More positive and sympathetic attention to the epidemic came in 1991 when the popular basketball star Magic Johnson revealed that he had HIV. Finally, when Bill Clinton became president in 1993, the federal government began to engage more fully in providing services and finding a cure. The tide was turning.

Even before this, though, all was not doom and gloom. The community still had its parties and celebrations. One I remember especially fondly was the time I rode down Santa Monica Boulevard in the Christopher Street West gay pride parade with my six-year old grandson Jason and daughter Lisa who were visiting from the east coast. I had been selected as 1991 Woman of the Year by the City of West Hollywood, so I got to ride in my friend Don's gorgeous, late fifties, bright red Cadillac convertible. It had a sumptuous white leather interior and those really large fins. I had added "and her daughter Lisa and her grandson Jason" to the placards on the sides of the car that announced my name and award. We sat on the top of the back seat and waved at the crowds along the parade route with Jason doing the fingers together, half turn queen wave. The crowd chanted, "Ivy, Ivy," then "Lisa, Lisa," and "Jason, Jason." Needless to say, Jason was elated. I was, too.

I felt, good, too, about my own participation in the recent battles. For the first time, I had been the type of leader I had wanted to be. Yes, I had taken charge all my life, from the gang of neighborhood kids and my sports teams on, and had been recognized for my leadership with much praise and many honors in both the women's and gay and lesbian liberation movements. I greatly appreciated and was moved by them. But it wasn't until the AIDS crisis that I thought of myself as a true leader. Within the AIDS movement, starting with AIDS Network LA, I had created programs rather than carrying out the ideas and programs of others. I had been a pioneer. This, for me, was the mark of a true leader.

Still, I needed a break. My art helped somewhat. Starting in 1991, to get out some of the emotions of the AIDS epidemic and my own personal problems, I began working with the bold colors and strokes of permanent markers on paper after years of working with acrylics on board. That wasn't enough. I turned to one of my earlier passions, theatre.

It was a good time to do that. Celebration Theatre in LA, which opened its doors in 1982 as part of that wave of newly created and out gay and lesbian culture, was going to present Kelly Masterson's *Against the Rising Sea*, which had premiered in New York City in 1989. It had been a while since the breakthrough lesbian play, *Last Summer at Blue Fish Cove* by Jane Chambers, had hit the boards. Premiering in New York in 1980, it played to gratified, sold out audiences. It was clear why. For once in a piece of art, the lesbian main characters weren't ostracized, constantly in emotional pain, and didn't commit suicide or die in any other way because of their deviance.

Blue Fish was about lesbians as people, their everyday lives and usual traumas and dramas, not about lesbianism as a problem. It finally arrived at the LA Women's Saloon in 1981. That's where I, and, it seemed every other lesbian in LA and the surrounding area, saw it. But the success of *Blue Fish* hadn't translated into tons of good plays written by and featuring gay men or lesbians, especially lesbians. Even at Celebration Theatre, there were far more productions about gay men than lesbians. The boys simply had more money and influence when it came to sponsoring gay-centric theatre

Finally, we had another lesbian offering in Masterson's lesbians-as-people play. I decided to audition. I had always enjoyed performing and hoped maybe this would help pull me out of my still dark funk. Maybe I would even meet someone to date. As I said before, I didn't do well living alone.

Against the Rising Sea centered on two lesbian couples, an older one and a younger one, who meet in front of the Provincetown, Massachusetts, beach home of the older couple. I was one of the older lesbians, a salty butch sea captain type living with my more sedate, maternal, long term partner. Yes, pretty butch/femme. The younger couple was also a contrasting pair, a stiff corporate type and a free spirit who always liked to watch the whales that could sometimes be seen from the beach. In the play, the beach house is for sale. The conflict in the play centered around the desire of the corporate type to buy the property and turn it into a business, sacrificing its beautiful view of the sea and whales, versus the free spirit who wanted to preserve the natural beauty and harmony the house represented. Profit versus people, business versus nature. Not the horrors of being lesbian. Adding to the mix was the backstory to the older couple: they had survived the inhumanity of a German concentration camp together. To top it off, my character had a benign crush on the free spirit. Yes, there was a lot going on in the play, but again, it was not about the horrors of homosexual life.

Loads of folks in the community showed up to see it. We were still starved to see representations of ourselves on stage, even if we weren't all presented as nice. As long as the disagreeable aspects came from something other than a character's lesbianism, that was progress. The production also got the attention of the mainstream theatre establishment. It won the LA Dramalogue Award for best scenery and I won best performance of the season. It had been a great experience. It reminded me how much I liked to perform, especially in live theatre where I could feel the immediate reactions of the audience.

After that experience, even when I went back to prioritizing political work, I kept up my performing. A few years later, in 1994, I performed with Patty Duke, a well-known TV and screen actress at the time, in a two-women show by lesbian activist Jan Holden, called *Conversations With and Without Another*. I also had small parts on a number of television shows, including the well-known *All in the Family*. I was particularly gratified when Marian Jones and Mary Casey decided to name the new non-profit theatre they established in West Hollywood in 1998 after me. It's the Ivy Theatre. That was a very proud moment.

ANOTHER THING THAT helped me feel better about my life was that things were looking up financially. My real estate income had again become erratic, so in 1993, I began to supplement my income by working as a salesperson at the *Community Yellow Pages (CYP)*, a directory of services, professionals, and businesses that were usually lesbian or gay owned and operated and eager to serve a gay and lesbian clientele. This was another one of those institutions that had emerged in the eighties to bring the community together.

In a way, I had had a hand in founding the *CYP* back in 1981. The idea for it emerged from a discussion Jeanne Cordova and I had as we were driving up to Fresno for a political event. Briggs had just been defeated, but both of us knew that that wasn't going to be the last battle over civil rights we would have to fight. There would be many campaigns ahead of us, and those campaigns would need money. So we were speculating about how the movement could best proceed. That's what we were always doing, brainstorming for new ways to be involved and fight the good fight.

At one point, Jeanne turned to me and asked, "How about we start a gay telephone book? There's a straight one. We could have our own."

We began to toss the idea around. We could build on the newly awakened pride in gay identity and sense of community that working against Briggs had created. Jeanne and I knew that we would prefer a lesbian or gay owned business or service provider over a straight one and were certain others would, too. All we had to do was know who they were and we would patronize them. Then, when businesses or practitioners saw that members of the community were behind them, maybe when it came time to ask for contributions for a gay or lesbian cause, they would feel more inclined to give. We could even list gay and lesbian community service organizations. Everybody would win.

Jeanne made the fantasy real and the *Community Yellow Pages*, the first such directory of its kind, was born in 1981. Through the difficult AIDS years, the *CYP* was invaluable in letting people know which businesses were friends to the community and would serve people with HIV and which not. As I said earlier, this was not a pretty time. And it was still needed and going strong by the time I joined the staff twelve years later. My experience selling real estate and my connections from all the years I worked in the community were a boon when it came to convincing individuals and businesses to list in the directory. That job helped provide me with some economic stability over the fifteen years or so I ended up working there off and on. But I wasn't the best salesperson. That would be my good friend and rival, Randy Espensheid. Over the years, we would compare our sales at the end of the day or week to see who had done the best. He usually won. The last time we did it, I had sold $40,000 in one day and I thought I was pretty good. But he sold $52,000. He had me down cold.

What was interesting about Randy was that while he had the outgoing personality necessary for sales, he stayed in the closet for a long time, even when others were coming out. He was a good example of how far gay people still had to go to be comfortable with themselves and out in those days, even at a gay and lesbian work place like *CYP*. In fact, I thought he was straight for quite a while. The first time I saw him, he was leaning over a partition that divided CYP's main work room. He was gabbing to another worker about his hot blonde fiancée, clearly a woman. I wondered why this straight guy was at *CYP*. I figured that was his business and let it pass. I also never heard another word about the fiancée, or anything else about Randy's love life as we became friends. At lunch during the day or martinis after work, I talked about my romantic entanglements and he listened and then we would talk about work. It took a number of months before he casually slipped some remark into the conversation about a guy or a date or an evening at a bar. That was his way of coming out to me. Very sad, I thought, that he was so reticent about his own gayness even with other gays and lesbians. I know he wasn't unique.

Dottie Again

I HAD DATED a lot of people since I had broken up with Dottie but no one had grabbed me. It wasn't that I didn't want to be in a relationship. I did, sometimes almost desperately. In fact, I had a pattern. I'd start in on a new relationship almost immediately after breaking up from the previous one. When, not unexpectedly, these rebound relationships didn't work, I would start another as soon as I could. In the meantime, between relationships, I would run around from friend to friend, often staying over rather than being home alone, just as I had right after I broke up with Dottie. Not healthy. Sometimes I suspected that the reason I didn't want to be alone was because I wasn't sure I would like what I discovered in myself if I looked closely. By 1995, at almost seventy years old, I began to wonder more, "Was I not a nice person? Was I going about this life business all wrong? Had I failed others? Myself?" But I repressed those thoughts and filled up my time.

Even with all the trying, I couldn't get anything meaningful going in my romantic life. Seven years after my break up with Dottie and I was in an emotional funk. I needed comfort, community, and something to anchor my life. Something larger. I knew I had to look in different places than I had before. I wasn't a believer in a patriarchal god, but I did have a sense of a transcendent force in the universe. So in 1995, I turned to my local Metropolitan Community Church (MCC), one of the many gay and lesbian denominations by this point, where Nancy Wilson was the pastor. As was my pattern, when I got involved in something, I got very involved. Not only did I begin to attend services regularly, I also served on the church board for four or five years.

Joining MCC worked to get me back on track emotionally. Or maybe I was just ready to open myself to new ways of thinking about relationships. Whatever it was, when Reverend Wilson gave a sermon about the importance of forgiveness one Sunday, I listened. I thought about Dottie and how I had held onto my anger and hurt over her betrayal and our breakup over all these years. Dottie had contacted me now and again, but I was just too hurt to respond. Suddenly, that Sunday, it came to me that nursing that pain was really stupid. It was holding me back and down, not doing anyone any good. Besides, it wasn't very nice to ignore anyone's efforts at reconciliation.

So, when Dottie called me in August around my birthday to invite me over for dinner at her place, I was determined to do the right thing. Instead of an instant angry refusal, I agreed to come. After we confirmed the details, just as we were about to hang up, she added, "If you want to, bring an overnight bag. You know, in case you want to stay over."

I was too stunned to reply. She said good bye and I followed. At that time, I was staying with Jane Wagner, a well-known child psychologist and activist in the area, and her partner Joan.

They both knew the struggle I had gone through getting over Dottie, so when I told them about the overnight bag comment, Jane said anxiously, "You're not going to do that, are you?"

I replied with a vehement no, knowing all the while that I probably would, and I did. When it came to Dottie, I just couldn't help myself.

The evening at Dottie's was strained as we labored to get over our mutual hurt, but I found myself exhilarated having her near me. As fate and my pre-formed decision would have it, I stayed over. I reasoned that something casual wouldn't hurt. But as we were cuddling in bed, I heard the words fall out of my mouth: "I love you so much."

Dottie just stared at me, mouth dropped open. I think we were both stunned. Maybe I expected a positive response since she was the one who had asked me over and mentioned the overnight bag. But no. We just looked at each other and the moment passed. Nothing was clearly resolved about how we felt, but we began our dance again anyway. I should have known better.

I knew that Dottie had just broken up with her girlfriend of about three years, and I assumed that it was over. It sure seemed it. So, once we started going together again, we talked about living together. We decided to hold off on that. Besides, she had bought a condo in Lomita just a few years before, in 1993, and she wasn't going to move. Instead, I put in a second phone line for activist and other business and set up a corner in her living room for my art supplies and painting for the times I would be at her place. Other times, she would come to mine. I thought everything was going fine.

About a year into this routine, one evening when I was at her place, Dottie got a phone call. When she hung up, she announced, "I've got to go over to my old girlfriend's place because there are some things we have to talk about." A couple of hours later, she came back and dropped a bomb. She had to give that relationship another chance. She was still in love with this other woman. I packed my overnight bag and left.

About a year and a half went by. Sometime around 1997, they broke up again, and again I was available when Dottie contacted me. I can't remember the details of our reunion, but before I knew it, we were a couple again. I guess neither of us could really get the other out of our system. This time there was no talk of us moving in together. We knew better. For one thing, we both understood that we had a long way to go for the kind of trust that involved. For another, we understood that we both needed space and freedom to pursue our own activities in a way we hadn't managed before.

Just as I was known in the LA area for my work, Dottie had established herself in the lesbian and gay community in the South Bay, an area south of Los Angeles. She had started an LGBT center in the Torrance-Manhattan Beach area in the early 1990s and was still very involved. She had no desire to leave that and her condo behind, and I didn't want her to. And I wasn't going to move to the South Bay, not just because it was far from the center of my LA activities, but because I had finally, in my seventies, exorcised some of my demons and actually wanted to live by myself. That had meant I had had to move from the Silver Lake house.

By 1997, the Silver Lake place had once again filled with tenants, women, and politics. I was finally comfortable living there again. But, as soon as I had started my back and forth with Dottie a few years earlier, it began to haunt me again. The place was just too reminiscent of the rough years there when things had gone so wrong between Dottie and me. Whether we were together or not, I wanted to put that behind me. Besides, I knew it wouldn't hurt to have some place that didn't cost so much to maintain. The constant scrambling for money was getting to me.

So I sold the Silver Lake house in 1997 and bought a small, second floor, one bedroom condo on Crescent Heights and Fountain in West Hollywood. This place was so tiny that it could barely accommodate me, never mind my art supplies. Art had been a constant positive force throughout my life, and I wasn't going to give it up. For one thing, I still needed my tools to continue designing t-shirts for the movement. They were still bringing in a little extra cash. But just as important, and probably more, it's through my art that I have been able to express my moods, emotions, and even political ideas without hurting anyone or myself. So no sacrificing the art supplies. Even with everything crowded in, the Crescent Heights place worked. It calmed me down. For the first time that I could remember, I was comfortable living alone. In fact, I loved it. I wasn't going to give that up, not even for Dottie.

Dottie and I started our newest phase. During the week, Dottie had her activist life and I had mine. On weekends, Dottie drove up to my place in West Hollywood where we would devote the days to each other and non-political LA activities, going to movies, driving to the beach, going out to eat. We had great hopes that this would work.

Turn of the Century

AS MUCH AS I had loved the Crescent Heights apartment, after a while its clutter and crowdedness got to me. With Dottie on weekends, me, and all the painting materials stuffed in there, I had no room to actually paint. Besides, my knees were beginning to feel the strain of the apartment's stairs. So, one morning in October of 1999, I woke up and told myself, "I have to buy a new condo." I had bought that house in Levittown many years before the same way. I got it into my mind one day and set off to make it happen. I was still in real estate, so I easily put together a list of the condos that I might be interested in. The first one, on Kings Road in West Hollywood right off Santa Monica Blvd, had just gone on the market.

When I arrived to take a look, the listing broker was just putting out the For Sale flags. I was her first possible buyer. We took the elevator up to the second floor of the four-story building and walked a long hall to an impressive, double door entry. As soon as I walked in, I knew the place was for me. The living room was a good size and brightly lit. It had a balcony that looked out into a screen of trees, as did the large dining room picture window, a great feature in an urban area. It also had two spacious bedrooms, two baths, and plenty of room and light for a studio. It was perfect. I immediately ran down to my car, wrote a contract, brought it back to the realtor, and was in escrow by that evening.

EVEN FAMILY AFFAIRS seemed to be taking a positive turn, at least in terms of having my children nearby. My daughter Laura had been at loose ends for a while in New York. She had separated from her second husband and had not been able to get herself going again.

"I need a change," she told me. "How about I come out to Los Angeles and live with you?"

Without thinking through what this would really mean, I told her I thought that would be great. I could have at least one of my daughters close by. That was enough incentive for me to give up my alone time. I had already spent way too much time away from my kids. So in 2001, Laura moved into the extra bedroom in my West Hollywood condo.

We did fine for a while, but after our honeymoon period, we just weren't getting along. Maybe after having lived alone in my condo for two years, I wasn't ready for a roommate, or maybe she wasn't. Or maybe it was just a mother-daughter thing. Whatever it was, I didn't like some of the things she was doing, and she didn't like some of the things I was doing. For about a year and a half we held on until, no matter how much both of us had hoped living together would work out, we accepted that we would be better off if we each had our own places. Once Laura moved into an apartment nearby, our relationship evened out. We were near but not on top of each other. We got along much better.

It was good to have my daughter around then, too, because in 2003, Eddie died. He had been living in rural Pennsylvania with his second wife of ten years. When we got a call that he had contracted a very serious staph infection after having surgery for a stomach aneurysm, both my daughters went to him immediately. I wrestled with what I should do. In the end, I decided it wasn't right for me to be there. I hadn't seen Eddie for years, and I didn't want to make the situation awkward for anybody, especially his second wife. I especially didn't want to put any pressure on Eddie. He died a few days after his surgery. I know I did the right thing by staying away, but I regret that I never got to say good bye to him. I still felt a great deal of love for him. I also never got over my guilt for leaving him even though I know it was the only thing I could have done. He was a good man and I was sad to hear about his passing.

Senior Housing

MOVING TO THE Kings Road condo more firmly entrenched me in activism in West Hollywood. As the century was turning and I was reaching my mid-seventies, it became my ground for further battles. The gay and lesbian rights movement had made progress, but there was still plenty to do, and I was ready to do it. I knew the city and understood it was a great place to pioneer policies. With a large and involved gay population, it was more open than many to rules and regulations that served and protected its gay and lesbian residents. And because LA was the media capital of the world, and West Hollywood arguably one of the most influential centers of gay life, there was a good chance that any actions we took in West Hollywood could have a nationwide impact. I plunged in.

In 1999, I was appointed to the Lesbian and Gay Advisory Board for the City of West Hollywood and served as its chair from 2000 to 2010. I only left the Board when I resigned in mid-2015. I also was active on city committees and commissions dealing with problems in the community that were just beginning to get attention, issues like battering within relationships and an increase in methamphetamine addictions. But I also hadn't forgotten my old NOW roots. I ended the twentieth century chairing the National Organization for Women's annual national conference, called Pioneer Reunion, in Beverly Hills in 1999. The new century was looking good.

THEN A NEW challenge emerged that involved me once again in a major campaign. One evening sometime around 2000, the year before Laura moved in with me, John Fournier, the head of senior services at the Village, one of the facilities of the LA Gay and Lesbian Center, called.

"Ivy," he asked urgently, "do you have any idea where there might be a bedroom or a room somebody might rent for tonight? Cheap. Available now."

I thought for a while but was stumped. "I haven't a clue. Why are you asking?"

"Well, an elderly gay man was thrown out of his house by his partner. He has nothing and no place to go."

I was shocked. "That's awful. I wish I knew a place, but I don't. Sorry I can't help."

"Well, if you think of something."

All I could do was repeat, "That's awful."

John agreed. "Yeah, he's very upset; they've been fighting, his partner has been hitting him, and now he's been thrown out."

I couldn't stop thinking about this man and his problem. It's not that the general issue had not been on my mind. Affordable housing for our gay and lesbian seniors in West Hollywood had been a topic of discussion when I was part of the lesbian and gay coalition forming the Alliance for Diverse Community Aging Services in the City of West Hollywood. But it wasn't until this call that the reality of the situation hit home. I knew that if this one person was having severe housing issues, others would also be. So, as I usual, I decided to get organized.

A few days after John's call, I called him back. "John, you have a room in the Village, the black box theater. That would be great for a meeting about this elder housing issue. I can invite some people and we can start talking. How about it?"

"Fine," he replied. He sounded relieved. I'm sure he was happy to have someone else deal with the situation.

I immediately started inviting all the directors of gay and lesbian organizations, heads of foundations, and money people that I could think of who might possibly be interested in this issue and maybe even take it on. Since I was pretty well connected, I managed to get representatives from at least twenty-five organizations spanning all sorts of racial, ethnic, religious, and class identities to show up for the first meeting. Not surprisingly, most of us were older, gay or lesbian, and concerned about others like us but less fortunate. Interestingly, I was reminded that this wasn't the first attempt at getting such an enterprise going. Just as we started the meeting, one of the men took a worn-looking piece of paper out of his pocket and unfolded it.

He said, "Look at this."

It was a twenty-year old list of people who, under the name Project Rainbow, had attended meetings to talk about building housing for gay old folks. And my name was on the list. Twenty years earlier! I had no memory of it.

"Well," I said, "It's about time we did something."

With John Fournier supplying us with coffee and Danish, our group met once a week for many months to brainstorm about what could done. Obviously, we needed money to get us going. We weren't the fastest coalition off the ground, but we worked steadily. We had one token young guy in our group, Brian Nemark. He had been inspired to join us by the housing problems of his straight grandfather. With his help, in 2003, we got a $98,000 startup grant, our first substantial money, from the Department of Aging in California, whose head, perhaps not incidentally, was a lesbian. We hired Brian to be the executive director and front man of our group at $36,000/year. The Village gave him space for an office. Using our grant money, Brian provided the statistical analysis that officially validated our cause, proving to the state that yes, many of our seniors did indeed have a hard time finding affordable housing. With this stamp of approval from the state we could apply for city, state, and federal funds, and for the permits we would require. But we also knew we had to get more community support or we would go nowhere.

Brian got to work looking for people with money, connections, and the energy and commitment to join the campaign. The real turning point in that regard came when he managed to get Ron Gelb, a wealthy gay doctor friend of his, interested. Ron, an experienced fundraiser for many gay causes, had a beautiful home in Laurel Canyon. He offered to host a party, and, with the help of his well-off and well-connected realtor, lawyer, and doctor friends and the contacts the rest of us on the original committee brought in, we managed to gather and recruit quite a crowd of wealthy and influential people.

One of the most important of the contacts I brought to that meeting was Ruth Tittle, the lesbian owner and president of Capitol Drugs, a drug store chain in the Los Angeles area that specialized in the alternative medicines and treatments that many people with HIV took advantage of. I had met Ruth at Metropolitan Community Church, which I was still attending as this housing endeavor was getting off the ground. Ruth ended up being one of the most committed board members involved in the project from the beginning, contributing immense amounts of time, intelligence, energy, and money. With the support and commitment of many from this party and others in the community, we were ready to go. In 2003, Ron Gelb, Brian, and I signed the incorporation papers turning our group into an official non-profit named Gay and Lesbian Elder Housing.

Then luck and years of having forged connections with local government gave us a big push. Because of the ambitious nature of this project, all the politicians in the city knew of our efforts to get this housing off the ground. One afternoon, just after the board had settled on a multi-apartment plan, Ruth and I were at her office when we got a call from one of Eric Garcetti's deputies. Eric was then on the LA City Council. Over the years, he had been an ally to the gay and lesbian community, and we had worked on a lot of issues together. I knew we could trust him. His aide told us that a car was coming over right away to bring us to the Council meeting. That was unusual enough for us to imagine there was something pretty important going on. We hopped in the car and went.

As we seated ourselves in the spectator section of the chambers, we caught Eric's eye. He smiled. He stood up, turned to the council, and made a motion to give our organization a grant for $1.6 million as well as permits for a plot of land and blueprints for a building. Turns out, we were the beneficiaries of another organization's money woes. The musicians' union had previously drawn up plans for senior housing for their members in Los Angeles and had gotten this million dollar plus grant from the city to proceed. They had completed their plans and received all the permits for their building, but they hadn't been able to raise the rest of the money they needed. They were forced to abandon their project. Their grant, plans, and permits came to us. Good for us, unfortunate for the musicians.

Eric's motion passed unanimously with the whole Council present. It looked like all the time and energy I and others had put into educating and working with local and city officials over the years on gay and lesbian issues had paid off. There was some fairness in the world.

That $1.6 million was nice, but by then we knew we needed a lot more, $26 million to be precise, to build the 104 affordable units in a multi-apartment dwelling we wanted. Over the next few years, the board raised a tremendous amount of money, some from grants, some from private donors. The community really came through. But we needed more. With the help of Mercedes Marquez, a local lesbian activist whose firm worked on setting up urban communities, we partnered with a developer who specialized in low income housing. We were off and running.

We broke ground in 2005. Shortly after that, I left the board. I had served for about a year. I was still deeply committed to the mission, but that was my way. Rather than spending a lot of time on boards, I would start something, help it get going and settled, and then move on. I had no doubt this project was in good hands and in good shape. And it was. In April of 2007, Triangle Square, the first such complex in the nation, opened in Hollywood.

Vision Problems

WHILE GETTING TRIANGLE Square opened was a great victory, the year 2007 also marked a negative milestone for me. It introduced me to one of the greatest challenges in my life. I was diagnosed with macular degeneration and was going blind.

This vision problem came on slowly. In the late nineties, after I had broken up with Dottie but was still living in Silver Lake, I had been diagnosed with cataracts in both eyes. Not a big deal, I thought. A typical older person thing. Another little adventure for me. That's how I have always tried to think about things like this. I might get scared, or angry, but then I tell myself I have to make whatever challenges come my way into opportunities to learn something new. I had two cataract procedures a month apart. At my request to my ophthalmologist, I was awake during the procedures. At that point, I was more curious than afraid and found the procedures fascinating. I was able to recover from each surgery on my own at home.

The macular degeneration was and is another story altogether. With it, I have no vision in the center of my eyes, but I do have some peripheral vision. I see colors, though they are variable, but day light glares and nighttime darkens beyond the usual dark. My world also has no sharp edges. I can't recognize people's faces unless they are about eight inches from my own. It helps if people identify themselves verbally to me. I cannot read unless I am very close or have a magnifying glass, and then only if I focus on one letter at a time. This is much too difficult to make it practical. So I am cut off from reading or sending any electronic or other correspondence. I watch a large screen TV and can go to movies but am unable to recognize actors' faces. My spatial senses are off so that I often reach for something that is farther away than I perceive it to be and end up with my hand waving in the air. I also sometimes pour coffee over the top of my cup. I manage around the house by familiarity and other places by constantly scanning with my eyes to catch things and people with my peripheral vision.

Not being able to drive has been a particularly bad blow. That came on unexpectedly and abruptly early in the degeneration process. One day shortly after my diagnosis, I had just pulled out of the underground parking garage in my building and suddenly, out of nowhere it seemed to me, there was a car right in front of me. I had no idea where it had come from. All I could think at first was how lucky I was there had been no accident. More frightening was the thought that it could have been a person I didn't see. I turned the car around and parked it back in the garage. That was the end of my driving. I never got behind the wheel again. It was too scary.

I had already started walking with a cane because of balance problems complicated by my vision problems, so the end of driving was a really serious blow. It left me dependent on people in a way I didn't like at all. Not only did I need someone to drive me to events or meetings, I also needed someone to pick me up to take care of shopping and errands and to visit friends, even just go out to lunch at Joey's, my favorite West Hollywood lunch spot that is just a block away. In a way, not being able to drive has been harder for me than not being able to see. But it's a close call.

In the months and years after the macular degeneration started in 2007, my increasing blindness and isolation were getting me down. With Dottie only around on weekends to catch me up on things, I knew that I was missing a lot that was going on in the community. I didn't hear about things because I couldn't read email, and even if I did learn about an event, I couldn't get there unless I got someone to take me. I would get angry, too, because it felt like nobody picked up the phone to just chat. It was as though they had forgotten how to communicate that way and were instead glued to their screens. Which I couldn't use.

I told folks, "You know, it's like, it's a phone, it works. I have one right by me. Would you pick it up? It's got numbers. You just do the numbers and talk to me."

But there was nothing I could do about it. I was able to have some treatment in 2012 that stopped the degeneration in one eye by sealing leaking blood vessels, but that didn't stop my essential vison problem. Basically, nothing could stop the deterioration. I was and still am legally blind. I have had to accept that.

Movement Changes

IN AND AROUND 2010, my vision was not the only thing getting me down. At eighty-four years old, I was beginning to feel I was losing myself not just because of the blindness, but also, ironically, because of the recognition I was getting at the time, the prizes, plaques, and other honors, including being featured in the 2009 film *On These Shoulders We Stand* as one of the ten most important LGBT activists from the early LGBT rights movement. That same year, I had a one woman show at the LA LGBT Center's Advocate art gallery at the Village. I also even had a tree planted in my name in the Matthew Shepard Memorial Triangle at Crescent Heights and Santa Monica Blvd. in West Hollywood. In 2001 the City Council of West Hollywood, prompted by council member Sal Guarriello, an ally to the gay community for years, and his deputy Donna Saur, recognized my efforts to fight the AIDS epidemic and provide service for those with HIV.

I was pleased and especially honored because my California live oak was to be situated across from the blooming magnolia that had been planted to honor my friend, Morris Kight, the LA based pioneer for gay and lesbian rights. But I was more gratified because I saw myself as a representative of all the women who had worked for the cause and who had not been as recognized as they should have been. OK, OK, my tree has died and been replaced a few times, finally with a blooming magnolia like Morris's. Even this has not exactly thrived, staying short and tired looking, just like me. But we are still alive and kicking.

The problem with this public recognition was that it brought with it another kind of recognition that disturbed me at that stage in my life. Strangers would come up to me on the street, in supermarkets, at meetings, wherever, saying thank you, thank you, without having any idea who I really was besides this famous activist. I was beginning to wonder myself who I was.

But looking around at my gay and lesbian friends, I realized there was more to my identity problems than that. I wasn't the only one having an identity crisis. Many in the gay and lesbian community were trying to find ourselves in the shift of the movement from the kind of grassroots and ad hoc organizational activism of us old time lesbian feminists and gay men to the domination of large organizations like the Human Rights Campaign (HRC) with its large budget and larger influence. Mixner might not have understood us in the dispute about security during the LaRouche campaign but this was a whole other thing. It seemed that instead of people gathering in the streets or working neighborhoods to fight for our causes, they were writing checks and leaving the control to bureaucrats, PR people, and lobbyists. Worse in my mind was the desire of many gays and lesbians to blend in instead of taking pride in our differences and culture. It seemed to be becoming more important that "they" accept us than that we maintain our own identity. The most popular crusade of the day, gay marriage, was a perfect example of how this tendency to move away from the grass roots and gay and lesbian identity could backfire.

I was never a big fan of gay marriage. I thought it needlessly assimilationist, just as the campaign for gays and lesbians in the military had been. I wondered why anyone would want to be in the military anyway. And why would anyone want to participate in an arrangement like marriage, filled as it was with controlling and possessive words from shoulds to oughts to mines? Besides, I didn't like this being grateful that they, mainstream society, were showing their tolerance of us by letting us into their institutions. It doesn't indicate respect or acknowledgement of a person's full humanity. It's not enough. Worse, by participating in patriarchal traditions, we can end up accepting systems that are fundamentally oppressive to women, lesbians, gays, and trans people, not to mention any number of ethnic, racial, and religious minorities. Finally, by accepting the terms of the patriarchal society, we stand the chance of losing ourselves. This is what assimilation is about.

All that being said, I also got that marriage had to do with the recognition of gay and lesbian relationships as legitimate and that many people wanted that kind of validation. I accepted that times and views change and that both gays in the military and gay marriage had the potential to move society in general toward less harassment and wider opportunities. And in the end, if someone wanted to join the military or get married, who was I to stop them? That's what choice is all about.

By the time Proposition 8, which would ban gay and lesbian marriages in California, hit in 2008, the marriage fight had been going on in the state for a while. When the Mayor of San Francisco, Gavin Newsom, decided in 2004 that prohibitions against gay and lesbian marriages were illegal, sentiment in California seemed to be turning toward supporting such unions. Photos of jubilant couples lined up to get married or kissing after their ceremonies went a long way toward humanizing what had been demonized. After that, there were ups and downs in the campaign, but many felt victory was won when, in early 2008, the California Supreme Court declared that banning these marriages violated the state Constitution. Then came Proposition 8 to fight the Court's decision, and the misguided, homophobic response of our side against it. Equality California, the organization in charge, one of those large, corporate type groups, favored assimilationist messages and media over identity and grassroots.

Their campaign featured a lot of TV commercials and billboards with straight people declaring that gays and lesbians were OK, rather than having gays and lesbians speak for themselves. Sometimes the message, delivered by people who were clearly supposed to be seen as straight, was an abstract one about rights and freedom in general without even a mention of the G or L word. One of the better TV ads featured an older, white straight couple bemoaning the fact that their gay daughter and others like her could not get married. At least that one used the term "gay." That was the best they could do. No wonder our side was defeated and gays and lesbians lost the right to get married in California. I'm still pissed off that they wasted my donation with these ads. Apologizing for yourself to the rest of the world doesn't work. Out of the closet, into the streets, and onto TV screens and billboards works. Us being visible, vocal, and unashamed is what changes people's minds.

Around the end of 2010, after this campaign and the challenges it and others presented to gay and lesbian identity, as well as my own sense of loss of myself, I felt the need to lay claim to just being in my art. At first, I painted a large black "I AM" on a white background. That's what I felt I needed, a stark reassertion of myself. But then, considering that so many of us seemed lost, I decided to claim a more positive community identity. I abandoned the black on white I AM and switched to an I AM in the bright, bold colors of the rainbow flag on the white background. It struck a nerve. It became the design emblazoned on the 2011 LA Dyke March t-shirts. Trying to keep myself and others upbeat, I continued painting in those broad strokes and bright colors. For one thing, they were all I could see. For another, they suited my political mood: broad strokes for broad social change. With dark strokes here and there. I was trying to be an optimist, but I was also a realist.

Flyer for sales
of prints of Ivy's
paintings, c. 2010.

Ivy at her easel, 2011.

Ivy and her paintings in the
t-shirt she designed for the
Dyke March, 2011.

LIFE WAS LOOKING better by then, but these identity issues were still on my mind when I was told I was going to receive the 2013 Melissa Etheridge Award, presented to a community activist by Los Angeles area lesbians. The awards ceremony came during the Dyke March that took place the Friday night before the main LA Pride parade and festival. I decided to use the opportunity to "tell it like it is." Since I wanted to talk about what it meant to be a lesbian, speaking up then seemed particularly appropriate. After all, the Friday night lesbian event had been devised years earlier to keep lesbians from getting lost in the larger gay male dominated community.

While the event was still called the Dyke March, I knew many of the younger women who came out for it didn't call themselves lesbians or dykes anymore. For them, both terms were too old fashioned, harkening back too much to what many saw as androgynous, sexless, humorless feminists. Instead, they liked to call themselves queer or gender fluid. In my talk, I acknowledged that theirs was a different world than mine. But I also warned them that using these terms often ended up erasing the terms gay and lesbian and all that they meant. In particular, I was concerned about losing lesbian, a word that had been used to describe women as uppity, too aggressive, and not knowing their place. I told these young women those labels were the very reason they should hold on to it.

"After all," I asked, "what does it mean to be lesbian? It means making your own choices in a patriarchal society, affirming to the world that you can be who and what you want to be. It means asserting independence from roles and expectations assigned to women in our society. It means loving women and not needing the status, support, or protection that men are supposed to provide in society. It's a declaration of independence. If a woman proudly proclaims who she is, then she has all the power. She is free. So being a lesbian and claiming it are among the most powerful statements a woman can make. Even if women don't think they are playing along with the erasure of lesbianism and all it stands for by using the term queer, they are wrong. They are rejecting the idea of strong women that the term lesbian represents and that all these other terms don't."

That was my message. I hope these younger women understood. Always consciousness raising. We'll see what happens.

Ivy (left) at the *Community Yellow Pages* with (left to right) unidentified, Lynn Ballen, Jeanne Cordova, c. 1993. *Courtesy of ONE Archives at the USC Libraries*

"The Supreme Court," (left to right): Robert Arthur, Ivy Bottini, Quentin Crisp, Morris Kight, and Patricia Nell Warren taken at home of Victor Burner. *Patricia Nell Warren Papers. Courtesy of ONE Archives at the USC Libraries*

Ivy (left) with (left to right)
Kate Millett, Barbara Love
and Ti-Grace Atkinson
at a Veteran Feminists
of America event, 1994.
*Courtesy of ONE Archives at
the USC Libraries*

Ivy with Malcolm Boyd. *Courtesy of ONE Archives at the USC Libraries*

Ivy (left) with Morris Kight (center) and Sheila Kuehl (right).
Courtesy of ONE Archives at the USC Libraries

Marion Jones (left) and Mary Casey (right), founders of the Ivy Theater, with Ivy (center) c. 1998. *Courtesy of ONE Archives at the USC Libraries*

Morris Kight and Ivy as Grand Marshals of the Christopher Street West Parade in West Hollywood, c. 2001. *Courtesy of ONE Archives at the USC Libraries*

Family Troubles

DURING THE SUMMER of 2012, my daughter Lisa found herself at loose ends just as Laura had a decade before. After problems with her marriage, she had been living by herself in a large house in a semi-rural part of Danbury, Connecticut. She was unhappy and directionless. Jason was living in Hawaii with his girlfriend of five years, so wasn't around to give her support. I felt very bad for her. I thought that maybe a change was what she needed, so still with that extra bedroom, I invited her to live with me. Pretty naïve of me, especially given what had happened when Laura had moved in with me. The only time I had actually had someone living with me since Laura had been the few months in 2005 when I had a bad fall in the shower and Dottie moved in to take care of me while I was recuperating. Even with my vision issues and some unsteadiness on my feet, I had been managing on my own with Dottie still coming up on weekends. Still, Lisa was my daughter, and I was excited that with her at my place and Laura down the road, I would have both of my daughters nearby. Lisa moved in in August of 2012 with her Chihuahua, miniature poodle, and calico cat, all joining me and my two cats. Luckily all the pets got along.

Dottie was not thrilled. She had gone through my trials with Laura living with me, which had been hard enough. But she also recognized that Lisa was more needy and demanding than Laura had been at that point, and that I was more willing to bend over backward for her than I had been for Laura. Dottie warned me that with Lisa living with me, our relationship would have to change. She understood that from then on my attention would be split. Weekends wouldn't be ours alone. I dismissed her concerns. I didn't see why we couldn't all get along. But it soon became clear that Dottie was right. I ended up paying more attention to Lisa than to Dottie. I was just so happy Lisa was there and we could get to know each other as adults, not like all the years when she had lived back east and I was in California and we only saw each other a few times a year for short periods of time at most. And if I could help her emotionally, I would.

But without me knowing it, Lisa had already had a major turn in her life. The daughter who had been married twice and had had many boyfriends had fallen in love with Beth, a woman she had met at a wedding about eight months earlier, and Beth had fallen in love with her. Lisa informed me of this on the phone just before she set out for California. She was still going to move to LA, though, because, simply put, she had little money and few prospects back east. Living with me would be cheap and maybe she could get a new job and make a new start. That was fine with me. I didn't mind being used in that way. In fact, that she had discovered that she loved women brought me to feel closer to her. I showered her with my time and attention.

Dottie became increasingly irritated at the situation. I don't really blame her. She was getting less and less of my time and energy. My focus at home was almost always on Lisa who was still having a hard time finding good employment. And missing Beth, who she couldn't afford to see so only spoke to on the phone. The tension in the condo over my attention to Lisa created a very heavy atmosphere when we were all around. There was no yelling or anything like that, just a lot of edgy silence. Finally, Dottie couldn't take the uncomfortable atmosphere and being neglected. In the middle of one weekend, she got up and went home.

I was upset, but, in a way, relieved. The stress of being pulled between two people I loved had been getting to me. At that point, I felt I had to choose my daughter. I sat Lisa down and dictated a long email to send to Dottie explaining that as much as I loved her, we had to break up. It was unfortunate that this had to go through Lisa, but given my vision issues, what else could I do? Call in a Notary Public? I felt very bad about the whole thing, but I didn't see any alternative.

That was that for my intimate relationship with Dottie. She tried to keep in touch with me over the next year, but I wasn't very responsive. I guess I felt too guilty. Finally, I got out of myself a little and was able to talk to her more. We became good friends again. In a way, how could we not? We had been together as a couple for almost thirty of the thirty-five or forty years we have known each other. Aside from my kids, Dottie has been the most significant relationship in my life.

Another Campaign

AMIDST ALL THE disruptions and challenges in my personal life, my activist life revived. It had to. It was my life line. Especially with my physical limitations, my isolation, and my frustrations with the movement, I had to find a cause to dedicate myself to. The issue that emerged brought me back to my women's rights' roots: statutes of limitations in rape cases. While prosecuting rape cases had always been difficult, this aspect of the problem hadn't been given much attention until a series of women accused the well-known, well-liked, highly respected, comedian and actor, Bill Cosby, of drugging and raping them. Interestingly, these accusations came out into the larger world only after another comedian called Cosby a rapist in a routine in late October 2014. Obviously, others had known, or had at least heard rumors about Cosby's behavior. More women came forward with their stories of Cosby drugging and assaulting them. Lots of shock. Lots of publicity.

It turned out that Cosby could not be prosecuted for these acts of violence and abuse in most of the states where the violations took place because the statute of limitations on rape cases had run out. In the end, of all the women who had gathered the courage and support necessary to make their complaints, only one woman was actually able to bring charges and sue Cosby. Given the trauma surrounding rape in the first place and the difficulty women have in being public about such experiences in the second, I thought this outrageous, another set of laws favoring and protecting men over women. I was enraged and galvanized. My political instincts also told me that this was the perfect storm of public outrage and publicity that could help get the California law, which had a ten year statute of limitations on such cases, changed to no time limit.

By this time, I had trained people to call and let me know about events and had amassed a support network of women who enabled me to stay involved, making sure I got information I needed, got to meetings, and could make phone calls myself. In this case with the assistance of Lynn Ballen, I called as many women activists in the area that I knew for a meeting. West Hollywood Council member Lindsey Horvath got us the use of the community room in the West Hollywood Library at no cost.

About thirty women showed up, many I had known for years, like the president of LA NOW, Terry O'Neill; and the vice-president, Karen Eyres; the well-known attorney Gloria Allred; the comedian, activist, and promoter Robin Tyler; and the friends who often helped me out in many ways and transported me, Margaret Smith and Sue Sexton. Some of the women I had never met, including Caroline Heldman, a professor of politics at Occidental College and a co-founder of End Rape on Campus (EROC). Two young women, Lili and Victoria, arrived willing to go public about having been raped. The meeting was filled with high emotion and determination. In no time at all, we had formed an action committee. Because I was so impressed with her, I asked Caroline to join me as a co-chair. We were off and running. I advised and participated as much as I could with a cadre of friends and supporters who were willing to take me to and from meetings and demonstrations, read documents to me, and type up what I wanted to say.

We were unstoppable. Over the next several months, our group held rallies and speak outs, wrote letters to newspapers and politicians, sent a group up to Sacramento to lobby state legislators, and had well-publicized demonstrations at Bill Cosby's star on Hollywood Blvd. Our efforts and those of other groups and individuals throughout the state bore fruit. In the summer of 2016, State Senator Connie M. Leyva (D-Chino) introduced a bill to abolish statutes of limitations on rape and sexual assault in California. SB 813 Justice for Victims Act was passed unanimously by both the Senate and the Assembly. In September of 2016, Governor Jerry Brown signed the bill and it became law. Another victory for feminist activists working together.

Kicking off the 2016
Dyke March with t-shirts
designed by Ivy, Wehoville.

Ivy (right) with Lili Bernard at
radio KPFK Feminist Magazine
interview regarding End Rape
Statute of Limitations.

Ivy (right) with Karen Eyres
performing at Hollywood NOW
The Vagina Monologues, 2017.

Ivy (left) with Judith Branzburg, c. 2017.

Ivy on her 91st birthday, 2017.

Life Goes On

WHILE I WAS consumed with that campaign and my other West Hollywood involvements, my personal life, particularly my living situation, was in flux. By the fall of 2014, Lisa had lived with me for about two years. Things were OK, but not great. Then her girlfriend Beth moved to Los Angeles and Lisa moved out.

Over the previous two years, Lisa and Beth had continued their romance mostly through long phone calls. Since neither had much money, they had only managed to see each other twice during that time, once when Lisa went back east and once when Beth made the trip out west. That's when I met her. She seemed nice, and Lisa was happy with her, so I was happy. I wanted their relationship to work. So when I heard that Beth was moving to LA, I was eager to help, but I knew they couldn't stay with me. The two of them and their pets and me and mine in my condo would be too much. Besides, I imagined they would want some privacy. So even though it meant that Lisa would move out, I took some of the money I had managed to save and bought them a small, one bedroom condo in nearby Hollywood. It was great. I had both my daughters nearby, and I had my condo to myself again.

Then more family came. In 2015, my grandson Jason left Hawaii with his fiancée Heather to come to LA to start a new life. Since neither had jobs or resources of their own, they moved in with Lisa and Beth. It took only about four months of the four of them, plus the animals, being crowded together in the one bedroom, one bathroom apartment for them to realize that that arrangement wasn't going to work. Besides, even with them all sharing, money was short. Neither Lisa nor Beth had found the work she wanted. Making things worse, both Lisa and Beth began having health problems, the kind that drained and debilitated but didn't kill you. It was all getting too much for them. So they decided to move in with me in my larger condo. At least that's how I saw it. They, on the other hand, thought they were doing me a favor. OK, OK, they may have had some reason to think that it would be good for me to have someone around.

I was approaching ninety, so, even though I was generally in good health aside from my blindness and limping around, I was no spring chicken. And I had taken a few falls around the house in recent months. I hadn't been hurt, but Lisa and Beth decided it was best for me that they move back in with me. Jason and Heather would stay in the condo. Apparently, I didn't have much say in the matter.

Lisa, Beth, and their pets living with me didn't last long. For one thing, Lisa and Beth continued to struggle financially, which got both of them down. For another, we didn't exactly all get along, especially Beth and me. You might say our personalities were too big. I wasn't totally surprised then when, in late 2015, after Lisa and Beth had been with me for about a year, Lisa announced that she and Beth would be moving to Sebring, Florida, where Beth's family lived. They thought they had better chances of finding suitable work there and were looking forward to a less urban environment.

They invited me to come with them. Even with our tensions, I was tempted. I was eighty-nine years old, legally blind, and not sure any more how well I could manage living on my own. Besides, the idea of my daughter living across the continent again was heartbreaking. I had gotten used to having both daughters nearby. In the end, I decided to stay in West Hollywood. I know moving was the right thing for Lisa and staying the right thing for me. My life is here. My politics are here. It's where I can be most effective. There was more work to be done.

And I got lucky. Once I admitted to myself that it would not be a good idea for me to be on my own because of my physical limitations, I began thinking about having a roommate. Just at that time, I heard about the plight of an acquaintance, Dan Morin, a gay man in his seventies. I had met Dan through recent meetings concerning overdevelopment in West Hollywood. He was very familiar with the problem. At the time we met, Dan had just become a victim of the infamous Ellis Act, a California law that allows landlords to evict tenants if the landlord is going to "go out of business," that is not rent apartments in the property any more. Often this means a condo conversion of the building, which was what Dan's landlord claimed was his plan. So Dan was being forced to move out of the West Hollywood apartment he had called home for almost forty years. With limited income, he had little chance of finding a place to live anywhere in or around his old area. He needed a reasonably priced place, hopefully in West Hollywood, and I needed someone to live with me. So Dan moved in with me in March of 2016. It was a match made in heaven. He was a godsend.

Not only did he fill my vacant room, he became a wonderful companion and helpmeet in my activist life. Dressed in smartly cut suits with matching ties, hats, and handkerchiefs, living up to his Dapper Dan nickname, he has accompanied me to everything from award dinners to activist meetings to protests to social events. Icing on the cake, he has a wonderful sense of humor. And even though he is the neat Felix to my messy Oscar, we are great roommates and companions. He, along with my longtime friends, helpers, and sister activists, have kept me out and about.

Final Thoughts

SINCE I EMBRACED political activism in the mid-1960s, political engagement has been my calling and the axis around which all else in my adult life—my family, my romantic partners, my friendships, and my art—has revolved. Recognizing when there is an injustice and taking action to correct it, particularly to better the lives of women and members of the gay and lesbian community, has been the vision that has guided my life. It is also what saved my life. The women's and gay and lesbian liberation movements may have shattered one version of myself—the rule following, conventional, miserable one—but they enabled me to create another, more authentic one. They awakened parts of me that had previously lain dormant, revealed skills and a commitment to activism I had no idea were in me, and finally allowed me the space in which to be myself and to express my love for women. I say that even though I realize that along the way, I have often made a mess of relationships with people close to me by choosing to give so much of my time and energy to improve the lives of people I will never meet. This has sobered me but not dissuaded me from my purpose. Because that's who I am. Even now, while I may have lost my physical vision, I have not lost my political vision and will to change the world.

SO I WAS happy to accept the NOW apology as their recognition that feminism and women's liberation are all about making a world in which people can define themselves and live up to their full potential. As stated in the NOW proclamation, "No individual should ever be asked to closet themselves, . . . activism inspires generations of lesbian and women activists to be true to who they are, no matter who or what is pressuring them to live in the proverbial closet."

And that is, in the end, my point. I want us all to help create a world in which people are not accepting of, tyrannized by, or limited by the definitions others have of them. I want people to come away from my story understanding that they can be activists, too. While there are many times when they might think that's just how it is, as I often did early on in my life, that's not always true. They can create their own destinies. That's what we activists did. In those early days of our liberation movements, we envisioned a world that didn't yet exist and then dug deep and challenged ourselves and others to make it real. No idea is beyond imagining, comprehension, or reach. We don't all need to be leaders. Everyone in a movement is valuable. But we do have to move. We all can.

As my college art teacher instructed us, "Know where you want to go, get out of your own way, and go." Accept the pain, accept the joy, always move forward.

Ivy's Acknowledgments

Until I started talking to Al Schnupp and Ellyn Lerner about the play they wanted to write about my life about seven years ago, it didn't occur to me that my story would be of interest to or inspire others. Reflecting on the lessons I learned through my almost ninety years at that point, that being alive and life are two different things and that any life fully lived will contain both pain and passion, I thought my story might make a difference. So began this project. I'm very grateful to all of the following for making it real:

Al and Ellyn for getting me going.

Judith Branzburg, my very patient as-told-to, for her four years of listening to my stories, shaping them into something that makes sense, and reading drafts over and over again, always believing in the importance of my life and the memoir.

Amy Ryan for her kind, years' long assistance looking things up online, reading drafts to me, and what must have seemed like endless proofreading.

Dan Morin for his support throughout this project.

Dottie Wine for our continuing years of friendship.

More generally, the many women who have touched my life and hopefully whose lives I have touched in a positive way.

And finally, Bedazzled Ink for bringing to life what hopefully will be one of their biggest hits.

Judith's Acknowledgments

Any project such as this is a product of many hands and minds. I am tremendously grateful to the following for their generous contributions and support:

Ivy Bottini—without the inspiration of her life, and her great stories, humor, and patience, there would be no book.

Al Schnupp and Ellyn Lerner for offering me the transcripts of their interviews with Ivy so I could get started.

To the members of Lezerati, my writing group—Lynn Ballen, Jane Ward, Claudia Rodriguez, Robin Podolsky, Ellen Krout-Hasegawa, Alicia Vogl Saenz, Talia Bettcher and Jeanne Cordova (RIP)—for helping me find a voice and encouraging me to keep going.

To the members of my reading group—Jan Sutherland, Jane Hallinger, Pat Rose, Pat Savoie, Mike Riherd, Chris McCabe, Bill Farmer—and other Pasadena City College colleagues, Jill O'Hora and Teri Keeler, for their close readings of the entire manuscript and their invaluable feedback.

To Susan Merzbach, also for reading and critiquing the entire manuscript, and for her warm support in this and all my endeavors over the years.

To Brian Kennedy and Martha Ertman for the advice and encouragement that helped get me through the challenging last stages of getting the manuscript out and over the finish line.

To Loni Shibuyama, Librarian at ONE Archives at the USC Libraries, for her assistance in sorting and scanning photos for the book.

To Dan Morin for making Amy and me welcome during all our intrusions into his life and space.

To all my friends who showed an interest in and enthusiasm for this project over the years. Your patience and encouragement were worth more than you know.

Finally, to my partner Amy Ryan, not just for checking and validating information, selecting and scanning photos, reading sections of the manuscript aloud to Ivy, and the hours and hours she spent reading and rereading various drafts, but also for her astute advice, inexhaustible patience, constant inspiration and support, and invaluable love.

Judith V. Branzburg, Ph.D., is an emeritus professor of English at Pasadena City College (PCC) in Pasadena, California. For over twenty years at PCC, she taught nonfiction writing, women's studies, gay and lesbian studies, and American literature. She has published essays in publications ranging from the *Lesbian Review of Books* and *Contemporary Lesbian Writers of the U.S* to *Radical Teacher* and *Callaloo: A Black Southern Journal for Arts and Letters*. She has also published a novel, *The Paris Adventures of Judith and Amy* and has worked as a free-lance editor.